Beyond the Field

SPORT AND SOCIETY

Series Editors
Aram Goudsouzian
Jaime Schultz

Founding Editors
Benjamin G. Rader
Randy Roberts

For a list of books in the series, please see our website at www.press.uillinois.edu.

Beyond the Field

How Soccer Built Community in the United States

BRIAN D. BUNK

UNIVERSITY OF ILLINOIS PRESS
Urbana, Chicago, and Springfield

Manufactured in the United States of America
1 2 3 4 5 C P 5 4 3 2 1
∞ This book is printed on acid-free paper.

Publication supported by a grant from the
Winton U. Solberg US History Subvention Fund.

Library of Congress Cataloging-in-Publication Data

Names: Bunk, Brian D., 1968– author.
Title: Beyond the field : how soccer built community in the United States / Brian D. Bunk.
Description: Urbana : University of Illinois Press, [2025] | Series: Sport and society | Includes bibliographical references and index.
Identifiers: LCCN 2024058419 (print) | LCCN 2024058420 (ebook) | ISBN 9780252046681 (cloth) | ISBN 9780252088780 (paperback) | ISBN 9780252048265 (ebook)
Subjects: LCSH: Soccer—Social aspects—United States. | Immigrants—United States—Social life and customs.
Classification: LCC GV943.9.S64 B86 2025 (print) | LCC GV943.9.S64 (ebook) | DDC 306.4/83—dc23/eng/20250304
LC record available at https://lccn.loc.gov/2024058419
LC ebook record available at https://lccn.loc.gov/2024058420

To Zoe, from her dad

Contents

Acknowledgments

Many of the people I write about in this book labored in dangerous and sometimes deadly conditions. It is with an enormous sense of humility that I try to tell something of their experiences at both work and play. I am able do this because of my position as a senior lecturer in history at the University of Massachusetts Amherst. Although much of the research and writing was done during the COVID-19 pandemic and its aftermath, my experiences in that extraordinary period never reached the same level of peril they faced almost every day. I am also privileged to be a member of a union, an opportunity most of them never had. The Massachusetts Society of Professors ensured that I continued to collect a paycheck during those challenging years and that I had leave time to work on the book. Faculty and staff in the UMass history department supported and encouraged the project. Archivists and librarians at the Rhode Island Historical Society, the Smithsonian Institution, and the Vermont Historical Society helped in obtaining research materials. Folks from the Hagley Museum and Library, Hockey Hall of Fame, John R. Borchert Map Library at the University of Minnesota, Minnesota Historical Society, San Francisco Public Library, and Vizcaya Museum and Garden Archives provided some images for the book.

Without the help of my friend and collaborator Ed Farnsworth, this book would never have been written. He was the first to discover accounts of the Watson brothers and of A. W. Stewart's financial shenanigans. We wrote an essay together that covers some of the same ground as the Pawtucket chapter in this book, "Gentlemen of Color: Oliver and Fred Watson and New England Black Soccer," in *Race and Resistance in Boston. A Contested Sports History,* edited by Douglas Stark and Robert Cvornyek and published by the University of Nebraska Press. I also drew heavily on Ed's essays about Fall River, Pawtucket, and other areas. He graciously read an early version of the manuscript and offered many helpful suggestions.

Tom McCabe reviewed drafts of various chapters and his thoughtful comments helped improve the book. Brian Quarstad gave suggestions and corrections on the chapters on Twin Cities soccer and Jimmy Matthews. His tenacious research helped uncover new information, including photos of the James Matthews Memorial Shield, college soccer player Wen Ping Pan, and the death of Alec Smith. Scott Hollander helped navigate the early soccer scene in Buffalo. My colleagues in the Society for American Soccer History proved once again to be a supportive and welcoming community. It has been a joy to work with all of them but especially Zach Bigalke, James Brown, Dan Creel, Christian Hesle, David Kilpatrick, George Kioussis, Gabe Logan, Kurt Rausch, Arrow Salkeld, Patrick Sullivan, and Kevin Tallec Marston. The work of previous historians of US soccer, including Roger Allaway, Colin Jose, and Mel Smith, remains an inspiration.

Thanks go to all the folks at the University of Illinois Press for their help and encouragement. I am grateful that Daniel Nasset saw potential in this somewhat unconventional approach to the subject. The knowledgeable, anonymous reviewers offered detailed comments, critiques, and suggestions. Mariah Schaefer helped shepherd the project over the finish line. I am sure the copyeditors will do a great job, just as they did on my previous book, *From Football to Soccer: The Early History of the Beautiful Game in the United States*. Hopefully, thanking them here will partially make up for the fact that I failed to do so in that book.

I thank my family Laura, Zoe, and Buster for always supporting me and my work. Laura is the love of my life, Zoe is a good egg, and Buster is, as always, himself.

Beyond the Field

Introduction

Beyond the Field: How Soccer Built Community in the United States is a series of essays tracing the sporting history of cities across the United States. Each location developed in its own way, but taken together they represent a vision of the United States, or at least what this nation aspires to be: people of diverse backgrounds uniting around the ideas of companionship, fair play, and equal opportunity. Even though soccer is often considered a foreign game here, this book demonstrates the important role the sport has played in the nation's history when viewed at a community level. Soccer was integrated into the lives of those who came to this land from elsewhere and those who were born here. Most had roots in Europe, but people of African, Chinese, Hawaiian, and Filipino descent also helped build the game. Scots were important figures in developing soccer communities in Detroit and Miami, while the Welsh played a key role in the area around Scranton, Pennsylvania. Oliver and Fred Watson of Pawtucket, Rhode Island, are the earliest known African American soccer players, and another Black athlete lined up for a team in Buffalo. In Hawai'i, young men of Chinese descent won championships, and for a time famed surfer Duke Kahanamoku roamed the midfield for his school side. Some players and fans had wealth and lived comfortably, while others knew scarcity and days of aching toil. Many soccer players in San Francisco sat behind desks and pushed paper around, while in Barre, Vermont, they cut and polished granite. Regardless of background or status, the game brought them together and allowed them to forge links with others.

The histories reveal the importance of community in good times and in bad, after both triumphant victories and dispiriting losses. People bonded over a shared love of the game, but it was more than just that. Teammates and fans stood side by side, both on and off the pitch. The first documented soccer game in Cincinnati raised money to help a family whose father had been killed in a fire. When Fred Watson broke his leg during a game, local squads organized a benefit match and donated all proceeds to the injured player. In these and other communities, soccer aficionados came together to share meals, sing songs, and celebrate milestone events like weddings and funerals. In Denver, San Francisco, and Scranton, many men joined soccer clubs as much for the socializing as they did for the recreation. Players and fans from Vermont, Minnesota, and Colorado toasted their teammates' marriages and mourned their friends' deaths. Soccer gave them a sense of local pride when facing teams from other neighborhoods, cities, and nations. Portland's soccer club developed a fierce rivalry with the nearby town of Astoria, Oregon. An all-star team from San Francisco visited British Columbia, and Canadian sides regularly took on teams in Buffalo and Detroit. Visiting clubs from England trounced the opposition in Cincinnati. Soccer communities in Hawai'i and Miami organized "international" contests featuring local players representing Scotland and England.

The sport created bonds of fellowship and family that helped them navigate the challenging world of industrial America with all its promises and dangers. Things were not always perfect, however, and too often familiar problems arose. Arguments about money and fairness split communities and sometimes caused teams and leagues to break up. In Detroit, a dispute about payments caused one squad to nearly come to blows with each other, and in Cincinnati teams walked off the field over refereeing decisions. Physical violence, whether on the pitch, in the stands, or on the battlefields of Europe, shattered feelings of togetherness and fellowship. Several players from Minneapolis's soccer scene perished in World War I, and a league president in Denver lost a son in the same conflict. Unpredictable events such as poor weather, workplace accidents, labor unrest, and economic recession upset the fragile balance of these mostly working-class communities, causing them to fail. Ice and snow led to canceled seasons in Denver and Pawtucket, a stonecutters' strike in Detroit derailed the local club's title run, and the Panic of 1893 had lasting effects almost everywhere. For the most part, though, players and fans were resilient and almost always returned to the field, the clubhouse, and the saloon. Despite many challenges, soccer gave them a reason to persist and to rebuild a sense of belonging. Even if it was not the same as before, people continued the struggle of creating communities that were linked by something more than just a game. Highlighting these stories helps to remember the mostly forgotten lives of these ordinary Americans.

The essays cover a period of roughly forty years, from the beginnings of organized soccer in the United States in the 1880s to the start of a new era for the sport around 1920. Each chapter tells the stories of clubs and cups, wins and losses, but also of joy and sorrow off the field. The book focuses on smaller, less well-known locations where soccer was played in the United States during this period. This was a deliberate choice. Soccer communities in cities like Fall River, Massachusetts, and St. Louis, Missouri, were so large and complex they merit detailed books of their own. Other locations, such as Chicago, Illinois, and Philadelphia, Pennsylvania, have already been extensively studied. Work on these and other areas is important and ongoing. My goal is to look beyond these vital locations to find the stories that may not otherwise be told. This book is not meant as a comprehensive history or statistical compilation of each location. There are no league tables or lists of cup winners and goal scorers. Instead, the focus is on the people who made soccer what it was, and what it continues to be: a simple game that gives meaning and joy to the people who love it. The overall organization is roughly geographical, dividing the country into three broad vertical zones: East, Central, and West. Each chapter can be read on its own so that the reader may follow their own path through the book.

1

The Watson Brothers: The First African American Soccer Players

Pawtucket, Rhode Island

On July 21, 1900, Charles and Lucy Watson hosted a concert in their home at 80 Meadow Street in Pawtucket, Rhode Island. Charles was born in January 1833 in Lebanon, Connecticut. His parents, Peter Watson and Marietta Brewster, were listed as "freed colored persons" in the 1830 United States Census. By 1863, Charles had settled in Rhode Island and on May 6 he married Lucy Adeline Curless. She came from Burrillville, Rhode Island, a small town about twenty miles northwest of Pawtucket. The couple had five children: Charles, James, Eugene, Oliver, and Frederick, all born in Pawtucket. The last two arrived on the same date, May 29, Oliver in 1872, and Fred in 1875. The couple's middle son Eugene, a saxophonist, directed the concert, and his younger brother Fred sang and played the mandolin. In addition to popular songs of the day, the musicians that evening performed a couple of hymns—"The Heavenly Song" and "The Holy City." It makes sense that a concert involving the Watson family included religious music since they had long been active in various congregations in the area, including the Gaspee Street AME Zion church, later known as the Winter Street church. For many African Americans, the church had long been a source of spiritual and social uplift as well as a primary center of the liberation struggle.

Eugene was also active in a variety of other fields that sought to expand the freedoms of Black communities: civil rights, politics, and journalism. In 1894 he gave an organ recital as part of an anti-lynching meeting in Providence, Rhode Island. The gathering featured speeches by Frederick Douglass and Ida B. Wells, two prominent leaders of the early civil rights movement. At an event in 1896 commemorating the anniversary of the signing of the Emancipation Proclamation, Eugene gave a stirring speech that celebrated African American history and denounced lynching and other acts of violence. Around the same time, he became involved in local politics as an officer of the Colored Republican Club of Pawtucket. He was secretary of the American Protective League, an organization founded in 1898 by newspaperman Joseph W. Henderson. The purpose of the group was to create patriotic communities of African Americans united around self-protection and mutual aid. Its first major endeavor was the purchase of the hamlet of Rome, New Jersey, with the idea of turning it into a model African American town. As a journalist, Eugene was associate editor of the *New England Torchlight* and part of the Douglass Afro-American Press Agency. By 1915 he was managing editor of the *Advance* newspaper in Providence. That same year he was featured in the book *Who's Who of the Colored Race*. Historian D'Weston Haywood argues that men like Eugene and the newspapers they worked for played a "crucial role in shaping black public opinion, signaling racial challenges and uplift, building racial consciousness, and envisaging a better physical space for black people."[1] Overall the Black press helped encourage racial solidarity and promoted a vision of racial equality.

Fred Watson made a public name for himself through his athletic abilities. He and his brother Oliver are the earliest known African American soccer players in US history. For their entire careers, the Watsons played on and against teams made up of white athletes, some of whom were native born like themselves and others who were immigrants. The presence of the Watsons as part of this sporting community indicated their acceptance into this important social and cultural space. At a time when other sports, notably major league baseball, excluded most people of color, soccer had a more welcoming attitude. After some initial skepticism outside of Pawtucket, the Watson brothers joined this group of sportsmen and were celebrated for their abilities on the field. Within their sporting community, the Watson brothers became respected players much like later athletes, including Jack Johnson, Joe Louis, Jesse Owens, and Jackie Robinson, did on a national scale. Although many prominent African Americans felt sports had little to contribute to the struggle for equality, such attitudes began to shift by the 1920s. Influential writers like W. E. B. Du Bois and James Weldon Johnson soon acknowledged the powerful impact that successful athletes had not only on white attitudes but also on the ways that African Americans viewed themselves. The achievements of Fred and Oliver Watson prefigure this change and reveal the ways that sport worked alongside churches and the Black press to uplift and inspire the African American community.

Rhode Islanders took to soccer at an early stage of the sport's development in the US. They participated in some of the first documented efforts to form an administrative body to govern soccer in the country. A delegate from Providence attended the inaugural meeting of the American Football Association (AFA) in Newark, New Jersey, on May 24, 1884. The Pawtucket Free Wanderers organized on Christmas Day 1885 and became the most successful club in the state's early history. The Wanderers quickly emerged as the dominant force in the Rhode Island Football Association (RIFA) when it formed in 1886. They repeatedly took home the RIFA trophy, a tall silver urn with handles valued at $250 (over $8,500 in 2024).[2] Soon, however, they decided to test themselves against the biggest clubs in the northeastern section of the country. They challenged teams from nearby Fall River, Massachusetts, and entered the AFA Challenge Cup, also known as the American Cup, for the first time in 1887. The competition, largely regarded as the national championship, mostly featured sides from New

The 1892–93 Pawtucket Free Wanderers with trophies earned as winners of (from left to right) the American Cup, the New England League, the Rhode Island Football Association Challenge Cup, and an unidentified competition. (Author's collection)

York and New Jersey, along with a smattering of New England teams. It must have been a thrilling time to be a soccer fan in Pawtucket during this period. Important matches regularly attracted crowds of between 3,000 and 5,000 people, each willing to pay fifteen cents to see their heroes compete. The Wanderers joined a newly formed regional competition called the New England League in 1891. They won the championship that year and again the next season. The local soccer community had grown rapidly, and its success was capped in the 1892–93 season, when the hometown Wanderers captured the American Cup. Although we have no information about the Watson brothers' early lives, they probably knew of and perhaps followed with excitement the growth of the game. Oliver was just thirteen and Fred ten when the Wanderers organized, and the club's string of successes occurred as they grew into teenagers and young adults. They could have learned the game in their neighborhood, at school, or through the local YMCA.

The Pawtucket YMCA routinely sponsored athletic events that featured track and field sports as well as a five-a-side soccer tournament. In 1891, a group of young men, including the brothers James and Robert Holburn, formed a regulation soccer club. The pair came to the US from Scotland as children and their father worked as a tailor. The family became deeply involved in the Rhode Island Scottish community, with James Sr. serving on various committees for Pawtucket's Clan Fraser. It was perhaps through these activities that the Holburns came to know another Scottish immigrant family called the Meiklejohns. James and Elizabeth Meiklejohn moved from Glasgow, Scotland, to Rochdale, England, in 1869. The couple's eighth son, Alexander, was born in England on February 3, 1872. The family lived as part of a workers' cooperative called the Rochdale Society of Equitable Persons. The group espoused the values of religious toleration, justice, and democracy, ideas that proved to have a great impact on young Alexander. In the spring of 1880, the family responded to advertisements placed by the J & P Coats textile firm seeking employees for their Conant Thread Company plant in Rhode Island. By 1884, the Meiklejohns had settled in Pawtucket, where James worked at a print works and co-owned a music store with his brother John. Alexander graduated from the city high school in 1889 and enrolled at Brown University in Providence. He eventually earned a PhD in philosophy from Cornell University and went on to have a long and distinguished career as an educator. He served as president of Amherst College from 1912 to 1923 and then led the Experimental College at the University of Wisconsin between 1927 and 1932. After retiring from Wisconsin, he cofounded the School of Social Studies in San Francisco, a group now known as the Meiklejohn Civil Liberty Institute.

In 1963, John F. Kennedy selected Alexander Meiklejohn to receive the Presidential Medal of Freedom, the nation's highest civilian award.

In addition to his academic interests, Meiklejohn was also an athlete. He had learned to play cricket and soccer as a boy in England and at Brown took up the sport of ice polo, a game similar to hockey. In the fall of 1892, he was voted captain of the Pawtucket YMCA soccer club. According to historian Adam Nelson, Meiklejohn stood five feet, eight inches tall and had a "strong, sinewy frame and shrewd, sharp eyes."[3] Such features enabled him to patrol the midfield for a YMCA squad full of pace, endurance, and agility. Perhaps due to their relative youth, the players lacked a certain amount of technical ability. Still, they were talented enough to hold their own against more experienced clubs in the region as they competed in the RIFA and the American Cup. In the 1893–94 season, they began in the New England League but dropped out to contest the Pawtucket Mayor's Cup against city rivals the Free Wanderers and North Ends. In a series that was at times a bit testy, the young YMCA team prevailed over both clubs to take home the trophy. On June 4, 1894, the cup was presented to the squad at a ceremony held in Clan Fraser Hall. The Honorable Mayor Henry E. Tiepke spoke, as did President of the Mayor's Cup Charity Association John Meiklejohn. As captain of the winning side, Alexander Meiklejohn accepted the prize on behalf of his teammates and his remarks underscored the importance of fans: "If you want fellows to play good, square, honest football, give us a good, square, honest crowd to encourage us."[4]

A few months earlier, local newspapers reported that in a game played on April 14, 1894, John Armstrong of Providence Juniors broke his leg. The accident happened as Fred Watson of the Pawtucket YMCA team tried to kick the ball but instead connected with his opponent's leg. The match report is significant because it records the first documented appearance of an African American soccer player. Generally, matches of this type received little attention from the press, and the unfortunate fracture is probably why the story was written. Fred could have been a part of the YMCA reserve team since the fall, when players were generally signed, but never earned a first team appearance during the 1893–94 season. Oliver Watson joined the YMCA reserves in September 1894. It took a few months before he played in the first team on December 22, 1894. The Y arrived in Fall River with a depleted squad, which may explain why he got the chance. Nevertheless, he made the most of his opportunity. The Pawtucket side faced the powerful Olympics team and ended up losing decisively 8–2. Oliver, however, showed some promise by scoring the opening goal for the visitors. The local press noted that he was African American, and the *Fall River Globe* declared that he "caused no end of fun by his funny talk and antics."[5] It is unclear what such a description could mean since Oliver had little motivation to play the fool and may have been trying to impress in the hopes of becoming a regular starter. Perhaps the unknown writer was relying on common racist stereotypes of Black performers, including those linked to minstrel shows. Such events were popular entertainments in cities like Fall River and Pawtucket during this era. On Christmas Day the YMCA played the Free Wanderers and Oliver was once again on the team sheet. The first half was evenly played, but the YMCA managed a slim 2–1 lead at the break. The second half was all YMCA as they scored three unanswered goals to grab the victory 5–1. The *Evening Bulletin* praised Oliver's play, noting that he combined well with his partner on the left side of the attacking line.

Fred and Oliver are not only the earliest known African American soccer players, but they are also among a handful of documented Black players in Great Britain during this period. Robert Walker was the first notable player of African descent in Scotland. Walker's father, Alexander, was Scottish, and his mother, Judith Jarrett, was from Sierra Leone. He was born in Africa but was taken to Scotland as a child. As an eighteen-year-old during the 1875–76 season, he lined up on the right wing for Third Lanark and later had a trial for the Scottish men's national team. Andrew Watson (no known relation to Fred and Oliver) was the first player to represent Scotland in an international match. Watson was born in Georgetown, Guyana, on May 24, 1856, his father Scottish, his mother Guyanese. He took up soccer as a student in London before relocating to Scotland. Described as one of the best defenders of the time, Watson was part of the Scotland side that defeated England 6–1 in London on March 12, 1881. He lined up for a variety of clubs over his career but had his greatest success with Queens Park Rangers, winning the Scottish Cup three times. Ghana-born goalkeeper Arthur Wharton is often called the first Black professional when he lined up for Bootle FC in 1887. Willie Clark and John Walker, both Scottish-born wingers, had careers that overlapped with the Watson brothers.

By the spring of 1895, the YMCA side had earned a berth in the quarter finals of the American Cup against the East Ends of Fall River. Oliver Watson became the first African American player to appear in the competition. Played on a muddy pitch in front of about seven hundred hometown fans, the YMCA squad went into the break down 3–2. The visitors dominated the first thirty minutes of the second half before some nice passing sent Oliver on a breakaway and he slotted the ball home to tie the score. Both teams tried desperately to tally the next goal, but the YMCA soon pulled away, winning comfortably 6–2. The victory set up a semifinal contest against the Free Wanderers. The game took place on April 20, 1895, in front of the largest crowd of the season, numbering around 1,200. Lining up in black and gold, the YMCA team must have been considered the underdogs. The veteran Wanderers had reenforced their squad by bringing in several former players. The teams opened with a nervy first fifteen minutes, as the YMCA midfield did some great defensive work. Nevertheless, the Wanderers increasingly dominated play and the YMCA side was lucky to be only down one at halftime. A tactical shift led to more effective YMCA attacks, but they failed to generate many great scoring chances. Eventually, they leveled the score and even went ahead on a goal by Oliver Watson. The Wanderers quickly equalized, and although the game finished as a draw, the fans apparently got their money's worth. The *Evening Times* declared that "the game will live for a long time in the foot ball history of Pawtucket."[6] The replay of the American Cup semifinal took place on May 4, 1895. Because of a previously scheduled baseball game at the Dexter Street grounds, the contest took place at the YMCA's home pitch. The rematch failed to generate the excitement of the previous game even though it was close throughout. In the end the YMCA players seemed to wilt, and the Wanderers moved on with a 4–2 victory. Less than a month later, they lost the American Cup final to the Newark Caledonians by a score of 4–0.

Although Pawtucket had a number of soccer pitches, all the big games took place at the Dexter Street grounds. Historian Ed Farnsworth has called it "one of the legendary grounds of early American soccer history."[7] A match between the Wanderers and Fall River Rovers in 1889 attracted a crowd of over five thousand, a figure approximately equal to a sixth of the city's total population. It was the first site outside New Jersey to host the final of the American Cup, doing so in 1890 and 1891. Bounded by Dexter, Pine, and Barton Streets, it was adjacent to the sprawling Fales and Jenks Machine Company works and the smaller Pawtucket Manufacturing Company facility. (Currently, the area of the historic soccer field is home to a restaurant, car wash, and laundry.) The field was enclosed in the late 1880s, and by the end of the decade, the Wanderers had made substantial improvements at the site. The enhancements included the construction of a clubhouse, dressing room, and separate bathroom. Upgraded accommodations for spectators, likely raised and covered grandstands or bleachers, were also part of the project. Supporters could buy tickets at one of two windows and entered the grounds via three gates located on different sides of the facility.

Fans made their way to Dexter Street for more than just the soccer games. In August 1886, Henry Mellor was arrested for illegally selling alcohol at 40 Dexter Street, just a short walk from the grounds. (Today the general location is home to an auto parts retailer.) The police confiscated

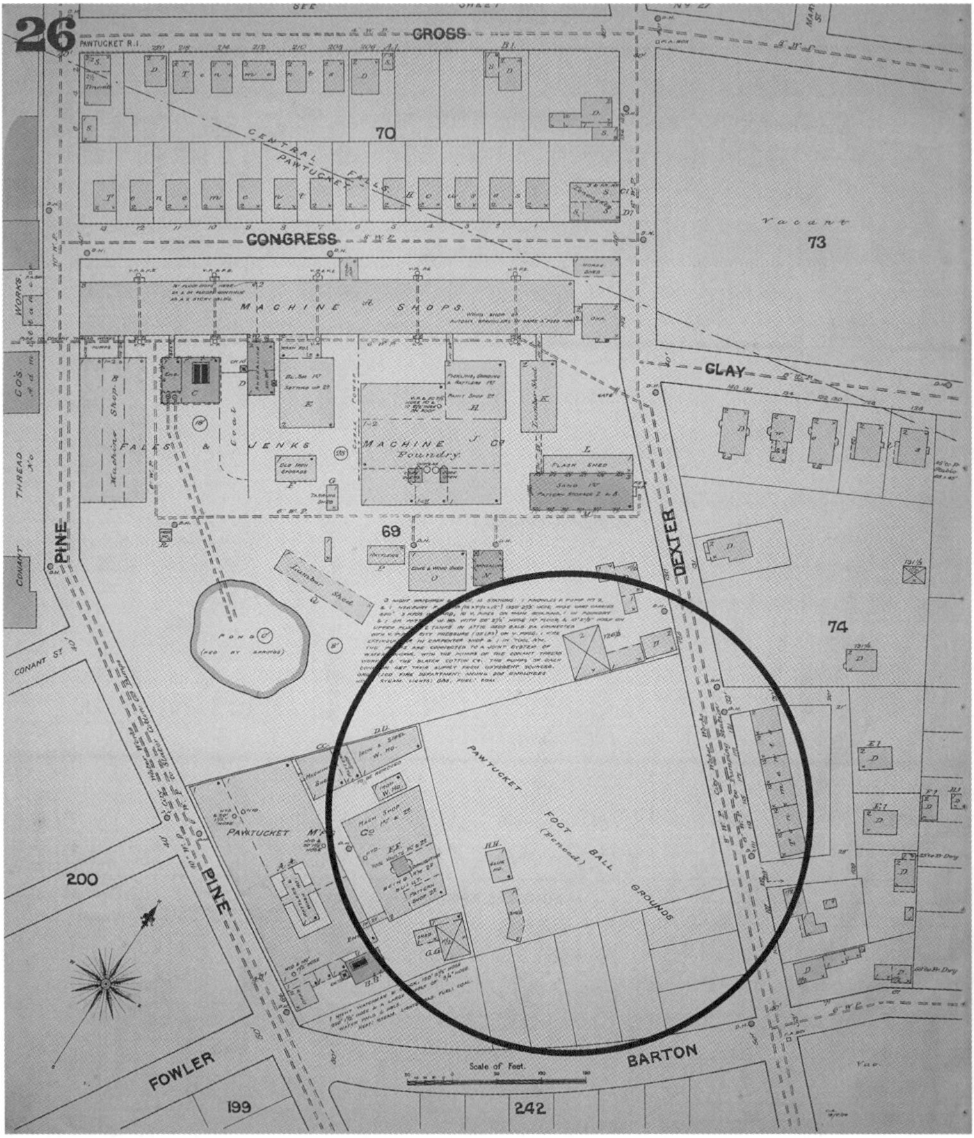

Map showing the location of the Dexter Street grounds in the heart of industrial Pawtucket, 1890. (Source: Library of Congress, Geography and Map Division, Sanborn Maps Collection.)

two barrels and two pails of beer and charged him with intent to sell liquor. In 1888 Bernard Wilkinson applied for a liquor license for the premises. A few months later, in October, the Free Wanderers held their annual meeting at the saloon. At some point the place became known as the Football House. Perhaps not surprisingly given the popularity of soccer, the city had other bars named for the sport, including the Wanderers' Call and the Corner Kick. The exact locations of these last two establishments are unknown. Wilkinson seems to have remained the proprietor for several years before he listed the Football House for sale in March 1891. It is unclear who purchased the tavern, but it was soon run by an Irish immigrant and bakery delivery driver named Martin McMahon. By 1892 the Football House had moved to 62 Dexter Street, and the original structure was eventually replaced by an office building. By 1895 McMahon was out, and a man named Luke Doyle petitioned the city for a pool table license. Soon the Foot Ball House hosted billiards tournaments that attracted players from around the region. Within two years the bar seems to have fallen on hard times and in May 1897 the fixtures were sold at public auction. The sale gives us a glimpse inside: a twenty-foot bar, presumably made of wood, five beer pumps, two pool tables, and four smaller tables, a couple of them topped with marble. Despite the closure of Doyle's pool hall, the area remained a popular spot for having a cold one. In the year the Football House shut its doors, one could still enjoy a robust pub crawl up Dexter Street, visiting at least sixteen saloons over about two miles.

The Watson brothers returned to the YMCA squad for the 1895–96 season. Fred and Oliver played together in the New England League opener on September 28, 1895. It might have been the first time they both turned out for the YMCA's senior side. Unfortunately, the result did not go their way, as the Pawtucket team was batted aside, losing 7–2. The local newspaper noted that Oliver seemed a little rusty but praised Fred for his defensive work despite the lopsided score line. Like the rest of the team, the Watson brothers had potential but needed a bit more experience and confidence. The *Evening Times* wrote that Oliver and another forward "would be more effective if they put a little more life into their play" and that Fred had settled in the back line and was "improving every game he plays."[8] Perhaps Oliver read the paper's criticism and responded positively, scoring a brace in the club's next match, a 6–2 rout of the Fall River East Ends.

In what was the biggest game of the season thus far, the YMCA and the Free Wanderers met in the first round of the American Cup at the Dexter Street grounds on November 9, 1895. The match was so important that Alexander Meiklejohn returned home from graduate school in New York to take part. It was end-to-end action from the start, but the first goal only came after a mistake by Fred Watson. Thinking that the whistle had blown, he picked up the ball. The referee awarded a free kick and the Wanderers converted to open the scoring. The YMCA squad fought back and soon equalized after Meiklejohn headed the ball to Oliver Watson, who put it away. After a chaotic second half, where both teams "displayed a terrible lack of judgement in the matter of scientific football playing," the match ended in a 1–1 draw.[9] After this game, Oliver, who had been a regular in the side, no longer appeared in match reports. Perhaps he was injured, or his form dipped, and he was dropped. Poor weather, combined with a seeming lack of interest by the public, caused the New England League to shut down shortly after the turn of the new year. Few games would be played in the region over the next several seasons, threatening to end the Watson brothers' soccer careers just as they were taking off. It would be almost three years before a Watson next appeared in a match report. Fred was part of the Free Wanderers side that beat the Fall River Floats on October 29, 1898. Calling the Pawtucket side "newly organized," the paper offered Fred a somewhat backhanded compliment: "Watson played a rare good game at fullback. He saved pluckily, is very fast, and kicks with good judgement."[10] Once again snow and ice wreaked havoc with the schedule, leading to postponements and cancellations. Ultimately, the season degenerated into a series of exhibition games.

By the fall of 1899, the Watson brothers had changed teams, now lining up for the Attleboro and Dodgeville (AD) squad. The club was based in Attleboro, Massachusetts, a jewelry-making center less than ten miles from Pawtucket. Although they spent just two seasons with the team, it was probably the most successful period of the brothers' careers. Despite being from Massachusetts, the ADs competed in the Rhode Island Amateur Football League (RIAFL) along with the Pawtucket Rovers, Pawtucket North Ends, Lonsdale Blues, and Thornton. Few match reports have been found but it seems the ADs could play lovely soccer. On November 25, 1899, they defeated Rovers 7–1, showing "better passing, better individual playing, better interference and better spirit."[11] The general lack of press coverage makes it difficult to know the results of the 1899–1900 season or if it had been cut short. The RIAFL resumed play in the fall of 1900 with the ADs, Rovers, Blues, Thornton, Manville, and Atherton sides. Newspaper coverage of the league was again spotty, and match reports often contain little information beyond lineups, scores, and brief summaries. Nevertheless, the ADs emerged as one of the circuit's better sides. Clad in maroon and white, they triumphed 5–1 over the Lonsdale Blues on November 29, 1900, with Oliver Watson notching a hat trick. By the spring they led the league, and a 3–2 victory over the Rovers on April 20, 1901, meant they were champions. Both Watson brothers played regularly during the season, becoming the first African Americans to win a competitive soccer league in the US. The RIAFL trophy and medals for individual players were presented to the squad at a celebration held on May 8.

The following season saw the Watsons move to the Thornton team, but the club withdrew from the RIAFL after only a few months. At that point Oliver seems to have stopped playing, at least temporarily, and Fred joined the Free Wanderers. The team was a member of the New England League, a competition described by the media as fully professional. Reports also noted that the Pawtucket club had signed over a dozen pro players. Unlike today, squad sizes in this era were generally small and twelve players might have constituted the bulk of the side. Although there is no way to know for certain that he was being paid, Fred's presence with the Wanderers suggests that he was the first Black professional soccer player in the United States. After joining the team, he enjoyed a good run of form. Sportswriters praised his defensive work, especially his ability to block shots. Once again, the conditions were at times less than favorable and one match between the Wanderers and the Pocassets of Fall River was played on a field of snow covered with a layer of ice. Kickoff was delayed while officials tossed sand and sawdust on a few of the worst patches. Nevertheless, during the first fifteen minutes "the ball went up and down the field, and the players went up and down on the ice."[12] Once he found his footing, Fred had another strong outing, but the Wanderers ended up on the losing end of a 3–0 score line.

Unfortunately, Fred's season came to a crashing halt when he broke his leg in a match on Christmas Day, 1901. The Wanderers were in Fall River to face the Pan-Americans when, on a contested play, Fred missed the ball and kicked an opposing player on the bottom of his foot. Fred went down instantly and after being removed from the field was taken by ambulance to the hospital. The incident revealed how much he meant to his teammates and other members of the soccer community. Several Wanderers players stayed in town after the match and visited him in the hospital. A Fall River paper called him "one of the most popular players that ever came to the city."[13] Almost immediately, plans were made to have a benefit match with the proceeds going to the injured defender. The break proved more serious than initially reported, and Fred stayed in the hospital until January 15. The benefit match turned out to be a great game between the Wanderers and Pan-Americans on January 25, 1902. Three thousand people turned up at the Dexter Street grounds to see the visitors escape with a narrow 2–1 victory. The game raised a tidy sum for Fred, although some fans reportedly entered without paying. When he was given the money, Fred expressed "his gratitude for the kind remembrance by local followers of the game."[14]

Fred must have been happy to receive the funds, as he might have been out of work for as long as two months. Throughout their lives, the Watson brothers labored in a decidedly blue-collar occupation—they made steel bolts. The money from the benefit may have come close to matching Fred's wages for most of the period he was laid up. Tickets to a game generally cost fifteen cents and newspapers reported a crowd of about three thousand. After deducting ten percent for expenses, Fred received around $400. In 1903, laborers in manufacturing industries worked on average fifty-seven hours a week and earned $1.23 an hour for a take-home pay of about $71. Of course, these are very rough calculations, but it does seem that the payout covered just about six weeks of work.

After Fred's injury it becomes more difficult to track the brothers' careers. They were getting older; in 1903 Oliver was over thirty and Fred was nearly twenty-eight. At the same time, more athletes with the surname Watson begin appearing in match reports, and unless a first name or initial is listed, it is impossible to confirm who was playing. The most extreme example came in a match played at the Dexter Street grounds between Pawtucket and Howard & Bullough on March 18, 1905. No less than four Watsons lined up for Pawtucket, with two of them almost certainly Oliver and Fred. The final notice that can be reliably attributed to the Watson brothers appeared in 1906. A few years earlier a group of teams linked to industrial concerns formed the Amateur Shop Association Football League in Pawtucket. One of the teams, Howard & Bullough, would go on to capture the American Cup in 1911. On November 4, 1906, a team from the Eastern Bolt Company defeated the Pawtucket Manufacturing Company squad by a score of 8–0. By this time Fred probably was working for Eastern, and two Watsons appeared on the team sheet, one in Fred's usual spot at the back and another in the forward line, Oliver's most common position.

Little is known about Oliver's life off the pitch. He was an expert pressman and bolt maker at the Standard Nut and Bolt Co. of Valley Falls, Rhode Island. He never married and died of heart disease on May 22, 1925. We know a bit more about Fred, who worked at the Haskell Bolt Company and later the Eastern Bolt Company. On May 19, 1901, he married Elsie L. Watts in New Bedford, Massachusetts. At some point before 1910, they bought a small house located at 942 Roger Williams Avenue in the Rumford district of Pawtucket. The structure was torn down sometime around 1970 and the site is now the parking lot of a bank. He likely continued to be involved in music, as Elsie played the harp, was part of Professor De

Santo's String Orchestra, and sang in her church choir. The couple were members of Wadsworth-Episcopal Church, Providence County Kennel Club, and the Algonquin Council of Indians. The Council formed after historian Thomas W. Bicknell organized a general meeting of associated tribes in Providence on December 13, 1923. The group aimed to restore Native American voices and erect monuments to their achievements in Rhode Island and elsewhere. Elsie died on March 2, 1931, in Pawtucket. Fred married again in Attleboro, Massachusetts, on June 30, 1934, to Dora C. (Dorsey) Brown. Fred died on December 22, 1941, and Dora on May 11, 1968. Fred had no children from either marriage.

Notes

1. Haywood, *Let Us Make Men*, 5.
2. MeasuringWorth.com.
3. Nelson, *Education and Democracy*, 10.
4. "Pawtucket," *Providence Journal*, June 5, 1894.
5. "On the Wane," *Fall River Globe*, December 24, 1894.
6. "Exciting Contest," *Pawtucket Evening Times*, April 22, 1895.
7. Farnsworth, "The Rise and the Fall."
8. "Foot Ball Notes," *Pawtucket Evening Times*, October 24, 1895.
9. "Cup-Tie Ended in a Tie," *Fall River Globe*, November 11, 1895.
10. "Pawtucket Team Made an Excellent Showing against Fall River Floats," *Pawtucket Evening Times*, October 31, 1898.
11. "Rovers Were Badly Beaten," *Pawtucket Times*, November 27, 1899.
12. "Played in the Snow," *Fall River Daily Evening News*, December 9, 1901.
13. "East End Echoes," *Fall River Globe*, December 30, 1901.
14. "East End Echoes," *Fall River Globe*, March 13, 1902.

Sources

Carter, Susan B., et al., eds. *Historical Statistics of the United States* Millennial Edition Online. Cambridge University Press, 2006.

Dahn, Eurie. *Jim Crow Networks. African American Periodical Cultures*. Amherst: University of Massachusetts Press, 2021.

Farnsworth, Ed, and Brian D. Bunk. "Gentlemen of Color: Oliver and Fred Watson and New England Black Soccer." In *Race and Resistance in Boston: A Contested Sports History*, edited by Douglas Stark and Robert Cvornyek, 67–85. Lincoln: University of Nebraska Press, 2024.

Farnsworth, Ed. "The Rise and the Fall: Fall River and Pawtucket Soccer, 1883–1896." *Society for American Soccer History*, February 1, 2022. https://www.ussoccerhistory.org/the-rise-and-fall-of-organized-soccer-in-fall-river-and-pawtucket-1883–1896.

Haywood, D'Weston. *Let Us Make Men: The Twentieth-Century Black Press and a Manly Vision for Racial Advancement*. Durham: The University of North Carolina Press, 2018.

Lincoln, C. Eric, and Lawrence H. Mamiya. *The Black Church in the African American Experience*. Durham: Duke University Press, 1990.

Mitchell, Andy. "John Walker, A Black Professional in the Scottish and English Leagues." *Scottish Sport History*, October 1, 2020. https://www.scottishsporthistory.com/sports-history-news-and-blog/john-walker-a-black-professional-in-the-scottish-and-english-leagues.

Mitchell, Andy. "The Lion Tamer's Son from Bournemouth: The Extraordinary Tale of an Early Black Footballer." *Scottish Sport History*, July 6, 2019. https://www.scottishsporthistory.com/sports-history-news-and-blog/the-lion-tamers-son-from-bournemouth-the-extraordinary-tale-of-an-early-black-footballer.

Mitchell, Andy. "Scotland's First Black Footballer: Robert Walker, the 'Curly-Haired Son of Africa.'" *Scottish Sport History*, December 10, 2020. https://www.scottishsporthistory.com/sports-history-news-and-blog/scotlands-first-black-footballer-robert-walker-the-curly-haired-son-of-africa.

Mitchell, Andy. *The Men Who Made Scotland: The Definitive Who's Who of Scottish Football Internationalists, 1872–1939*. Dunblane: Andy Mitchell Media, 2021.

Mitchell, Andy. "Willie Clarke—Scotland's Second Black Internationalist." *Scottish Sport History,* October 5, 2010. https://www.scottishsporthistory.com/sports-history-news-and-blog/willie-clarke-scotlands-second-black-internationalist.

Nelson, Adam R. *Education and Democracy: The Meaning of Alexander Meiklejohn, 1872–1964*. Madison: University of Wisconsin Press, 2001.

Vasili, Phil. *The First Black Footballer: Arthur Wharton, 1865–1930: An Absence of Memory.* Abingdon: Frank Cass Publishers, 1998.

Walker, Llew. *A Straggling Life: Andrew Watson, the Story of the World's First Black International Footballer*. Worthing: Pitch Publishing, 2021.

NEWSPAPERS

Fall River Daily Herald
Fall River Daily News
Fall River Globe
Pawtucket City Directory
Pawtucket Evening Bulletin
Pawtucket Evening Times
Pawtucket Times
Pawtucket Tribune
Providence Journal
Providence News

WEBSITES

Ancestry.com
FamilySearch.org
MeasuringWorth.com

2

Soccer and Stone

Barre, Vermont

Barre is a small city in north central Vermont, located about seven miles from the state capital of Montpelier. The ghosts of Barre's industrial past are less visible today than in other New England towns. The hulking brick mills that dominated those places both architecturally and economically were never built here. Although the scars of industrialization are harder to see, they do exist if you know where to look. Perhaps the saddest remnants are found in Hope Cemetery, where the dates carved into the gravestones show that too many men died too young. The deepest wounds are in the hills outside of town, where they dug granite in quarries that descend hundreds of feet into the ground. Entering the city, you can still find the sheds where the stone was polished and carved. One shaped like a horseshoe sits on Blackwell Street and just about a half mile away, a circle shed rests in a Burnham Street parking lot. The more common straight sheds are relatively plentiful, and you can visit several just a few steps off Blackwell Street.

Unlike mill towns where fortunes were made in cotton, wool, and paper, it took harder stuff to turn a profit in Barre. Extracted from the soil and worked in the sheds, granite was the foundation of wealth in north central Vermont. The first quarry opened before the American Civil War, but the completion of the railroad in 1888 marked the true beginning of the industry. Now the heavy stones could be more easily moved from the hills to the town and from the town to locations all over the country. Soon Barre produced more granite than almost any other place on Earth and began calling itself the Granite Capital of the World. During the late nineteenth and early twentieth centuries, the town underwent a tremendous period of growth. Between 1880 and 1910, the city's population increased from around two thousand to almost fifteen thousand. Many of these new arrivals came from Scotland, especially the area around Aberdeen, and took jobs as lumpers, polishers, and stonecutters. The immigrants also brought traditions of social organization and recreation. Barre's Clan Gordon became an important part of local life and encouraged the development of a soccer community in the city. The early soccer history of Vermont revolves around a single team: the Barre Rangers. The club dominated local competition during the late nineteenth century and did well against domestic and international sides. In addition to supporting the Rangers, the annual clan picnic featured a five-a-side soccer tournament billed as the championship of Vermont.

According to a later history, the Rangers formed in 1889, but a newspaper report from October 1890 announced the creation of a new, unnamed soccer team in Barre. The story listed a slate of officers, and since many of them were later associated with the Rangers, it is reasonable to conclude that the actual founding date of the club was 1890. Within a year the side had joined the American Football Association (AFA) and seemed poised to take part in the organization's Cup competition. In a prelude to the start of the Cup—and perhaps to test their mettle—the Rangers travelled to Pawtucket, Rhode Island, to face the Free Wanderers on November 7, 1891. The visitors were outclassed 5–0, although the *Fall River Daily Evening News* declared the team had potential. In January 1892, they were scheduled to play their first American Cup match against the Conanicuts of Fall River, Massachusetts, but had to forfeit because there was two feet of snow on the ground in Barre. Another planned home contest against Pawtucket Thistle in October 1892 did not take place after the visitors failed to raise enough money to make the trip. The squad entered the 1893 American Cup but again failed to play a single game. Following these scheduled matches, the Rangers seem to have withdrawn from the competition and perhaps from the AFA itself, because there are no confirmed interactions beyond 1892. Reasons for this may include the distances between central Vermont and other clubs of the AFA, as well as consistent weather-related issues. Local competition was lacking in the 1890s and the only regular matches Rangers played with area sides were against a team called the Burns Club. Little information can be found about the Burns Club, but most of the players were granite workers like their rivals.

Granite originates deep in the earth. Magma flows upwards and cools to create long columns of stone called plutons. Over time, erosion and the actions of glaciers worked to expose the rock. Composed of three main ingredients—feldspar, quartz, and mica—much of the granite found near Barre is classified as monument grade. The small crystals within the stone make it especially suitable for polishing and give it a hardness that resists wear. Before it can become a monument, however, it needs to be taken from the ground. The quarry men drilled holes, blasted, and split the rock before using a boom derrick to move each block to the edge of the site. After being trimmed, the stone was loaded onto railroad flatcars and taken to the finishing sheds. Before the arrival of the railroad, it took the power of men, horses, and oxen to move each block. A five-by-five-by-ten-foot block could weigh nearly twenty-one tons and had to be transported with great care. Originally, this was done by teams of animals pulling sleds that moved slowly on wooden rollers.

Stonecutters were the most numerous of the workers in the shed, although others were involved in moving, shaping, surfacing, and polishing the granite. The cutters stood all day at a workstation or banker, using practically their whole bodies to shape the stone. The sheds were constantly filled with the wrenching sound of the gang saw and the humming drone of pneumatic tools. The quarries and sheds also had whistles that marked out workday milestones like the start and end of a shift. They operated slightly out of sync with one another so that each day a cascading wave of notes washed over the town. The sheds overflowed with dust. The stonecutters and carvers spent their days enveloped in clouds of rock particles. Working without masks, safety goggles, or filtering technology, the dust soon filled their lungs. The result was silicosis, colloquially known as Stonecutters TB. It was deadly, and it killed men before their time. In 1900 the average age of death for men in the United States was fifty, but in Barre it was forty-two. A study published in 1923 showed that in the first two decades of the twentieth century, the affliction caused the death of 86 percent of stonecutters. Working under such conditions makes it all the more remarkable that some of them chose to play soccer. It is astonishing that they could run at all in wool jerseys on rough, nearly grassless pitches, chasing a heavy leather ball.

On November 30, 1893, Rangers defeated a team called Victoria United by the score of 1–0 in what the *Vermont Watchman and State Journal* called "the finest exhibition of Association foot-ball ever seen in Vermont."[1] As with the Burns Club, little is known about Victoria United except they may have come from nearby Montpelier, where the newspaper was based. The name could have been taken as an homage to the Scottish club of the same name that had formed in Aberdeen in 1889. A later newspaper report claimed that longtime Rangers player William Jopp had lined up for the Scottish Victoria United before coming to the United States. The same story also listed Orion as another of Jopp's former sides. In 1903, Victoria United, Orion, and another club merged to form Aberdeen FC, a team that currently plays in the Scottish Premiership. Due to the overall lack of clubs in Vermont, Rangers soon began looking outside the state for opponents. At times squads came from places like Massachusetts, New Hampshire, and Connecticut or from across the border in Canada. The earliest documented international clash took place on July 4, 1895, against Scottish Athletic Club of Montreal. Rangers scored after two minutes and went on to capture a 3–2 victory. A month later at the Clan Gordon picnic, Rangers once again bested Scottish AC, this time with a more comfortable score line of 4–0. The match seems to have ignited a brief period of club building in the area, as newspapers reported on new teams with names such as Granite City and Thistles. Such growth proved ephemeral and there is no evidence that Granite City played any matches at all; the only recorded Thistle game in September 1895 resulted in a lopsided 11–0 win for Rangers. The Barre side's winning ways continued as they defeated the Mohawk club from Montreal 6–0 as part of a Labor Day celebration sponsored by the Granite Cutters' National Union.

The union formed in 1886 and made Barre its headquarters in 1903. By the early twentieth century, over 90 percent of the workforce was unionized. Most of the shops in Barre were small- and medium-size, often employing just fifteen to twenty stonecutters. The general lack of exclusive clubs and other associations meant that the social distance between the manufacturers and the laborers was not as great as in other industrialized cities. In addition, many of the business owners had begun as stonecutters before launching firms of their own. Such factors did not eliminate labor disputes and major actions took place in 1903, 1908, 1909, and 1915. Indeed, the town had a bit of a rough edge at times, a consequence of a bachelor culture and the debilitating nature of the work. An Italian carver explained it like this: "You have to drink some if you work with granite. The damn silica kills you anyway. All the stonecutters like to drink. Men that work hard like they work have to drink. They all die young."[2] Stonecutters earned a relatively high wage for the time, and many spent freely at saloons, pool halls, and gambling dens. An unmarried Spanish granite worker summed up the life:

> We may be rough and tough, we swear a lot, drink a lot, and we don't hide what we do. We got blood in our veins instead of water. We do a man's work and lead a man's life. Maybe we're wild, maybe we're crazy . . . At least by God, we're alive—while we live.[3]

Many in the workforce were also highly politicized, leading scholar David R. Seager to comment that "Barre has perhaps the most militant working-class history of any Vermont city."[4] Sporadic acts of political violence included the murder of the police chief by anarchists in 1900 and the shooting of talented carver Elia Corti three years later. National labor leaders, including Emma Goldman, William "Big Bill" Haywood, and Eugene Debs, visited Barre and the city elected the state's first Socialist mayor in 1912.

On October 4, 1895, the Rangers players came to the home of William and Margaret "Maggie" Reaside. The purpose of the visit was to honor Maggie, who was described as "an enthusiastic admirer of the teams' good work."[5] In other words, she was a Rangers superfan. It is unusual for newspaper stories from this era to mention supporters, and there is no other example of a female fan being publicly acknowledged by a local team. In recognition of her efforts, the club gifted her a rocking chair. Maggie had a difficult life, and one hopes that the rocker served both as a place of respite and a reminder of the team she loved. Although her family's roots were in Northern Ireland, Margaret Gamble Reaside was born on February 6, 1864, in Airdrie, North Lanarkshire, Scotland. In 1883 she married William Reaside, who had been born in Stevenston, Scotland, in 1861. The pair must have known each other for a few years prior, as they were the witnesses when Maggie's sister Sarah married William's brother Robert in 1881. William and Maggie immigrated to the United States in 1884, settling in Barre where he worked in the stone sheds as a polisher. At least five of her nine siblings, along with her parents, also settled in Vermont. William had been inducted into Clan Gordon in June 1884 and Maggie was active in the Ladies of Clan Gordon. In just over twenty years, she gave birth to ten children: Robert, William M., Malcolm, Harry, Elizabeth, Janet, Isabelle, Thomas Henry, John, and William H. Tragically, only four of them lived to adulthood. Most of them passed away as small children except the eldest, Robert James, who died of tuberculosis when he was fourteen.

It is difficult to know why so many of Maggie's children died so young. Mortality rates had been in decline during the final decades of the nineteenth century but even so, nearly 20 percent of babies perished before the age of five. That still would not explain why the Reaside children died at twice the national average. Many of the factors that determined child mortality during this period favored the family: they were white, British, and literate, and Maggie did not work outside of the home. Still, residing in New England tended to be deadlier than the national average, and living in an urban area, defined as over five thousand inhabitants, also raised mortality rates. The causes of death provide a little more information. Infectious disease was the biggest killer of children during this period and at least two of the Reaside children—Robert and Harry—suffered from a respiratory illness. The cause listed for Isabelle, "convulsions," killed about

4 percent of infants nationally. The diagnosis is imprecise, however, and the convulsions were likely the result of some other infection or condition. The more general terms listed for William M., "weakness" and John C., "malnutrition," also point to other ailments, possibly gastrointestinal in nature. Such maladies were to blame for the deaths of a quarter of infants in the late nineteenth century. As scholars Samuel H. Preston and Michael R. Haines point out, another factor to consider was the absence of medical care during pregnancy and childbirth since "even by the standards of the time, obstetrics seemed backwards."[6] Preventative care during pregnancy was virtually nonexistent, and a high percentage of infant deaths could be attributed to issues that occurred during childbirth. Perhaps it was some consolation that in Barre she was surrounded by a large extended family as well as her compatriots in Clan Gordon. After Maggie died of dysentery on February 5, 1909, her funeral was well attended by family and community members. "There was a great profusion of beautiful flowers, showing the love and esteem in which the deceased was held by her many friends."[7]

The Rangers concluded the 1895 season in triumphant form, winning all four matches they played while outscoring opponents 22–2. The following campaign began with the club's annual dance, held in March 1896. In June of that same year, the team announced that it had signed a lease for a lot behind the City Hotel on Main Street in downtown Barre. Located between Church and Elm Streets, the Rangers erected a high fence and used the space for both soccer and baseball games. The new park was soon put to use as Scottish AC once again came to town for the area's Independence Day celebrations. Barre's mayor kicked off the game before a crowd of one thousand, who were sent home happy after Rangers cruised to a 4–0 victory. A month later at the annual Clan Gordon picnic, the team drew 3–3 with visiting side the Light Blues of Manchester, New Hampshire. That same month, notice appeared in the newspaper that Rangers had moved their headquarters from the Quinlan Building to a store owned by an Italian grocer named Angelo Scampini.

Many of Barre's earliest stonecutters came from Scotland, but the population of Italian workers soon equaled that of the first immigrants. In 1900, Scots comprised about 30 percent of the workforce, while Italians made up nearly 24 percent. Ten years later the percentages were almost completely reversed, and Italians had become the largest ethnic group in the city. By 1908 the Italian Athletic Club (IAC) had 750 members, although they never seemed to take up soccer. Instead, the IAC focused on traditional recreations such as bocce along with US favorites, including gridiron football and baseball. Scampini became an important pillar of the Italian community, welcoming new arrivals and serving as a translator. He was born in Samarate, a small town about fifty miles northwest of Milan. In 1899, he settled in Barre and soon leased land to open a store selling tobacco and groceries. The site became something of a social hub for the rapidly increasing Italian population in the area. In addition to his shop, Scampini was also an entrepreneur in recreational activities. The backroom of the grocery doubled as a pool hall and peep show, diplomatically titled "Dr. Man's Grand Museum of Anatomy," and he installed a merry-go-round on site.[8] Scampini himself was also a showman, performing as a magician and hypnotist at the Barre Opera House. In 1904, he built a new structure, dubbed Scampini Block. Designed as a showpiece of local granite, the building housed a storefront at street level and a third-floor assembly hall, where Rangers held their meetings.

As the 1896 season wore on, the team's fans must have been stunned when Rangers lost two straight matches. The first came at the hands of the Holyoke Rangers from Western Massachusetts. One area newspaper called it the first-ever loss for the men from Barre. A month later they again fell, this time in an away match played at Quincy, Massachusetts. The *Granite City Leader* called the 4–2 loss "one of the roughest games of football on record," claiming that few players escaped injury and specifically noting that "a dirty piece of work was perpetrated on Chessor."[9] Order was soon restored as Rangers handily beat the Burns club in two matches, the first by a score of 3–0 and the second 9–2. In December 1896, Clan Gordon donated a trophy for local teams to play for at their annual summer picnic held in early August. Inviting out-of-town squads, as had been the practice, was too costly, requiring that the organization pay transportation fees and provide the visiting team a guarantee. The silver trophy, valued at fifty dollars (about two thousand dollars today), stood nearly two feet high and was crowned with a bowl a foot and a half in diameter. One side of the bowl featured a blank plate topped by a stag's head surrounded by blooming thistles. Along with a space for the winning team names, there was an inscription that read "Presented by Clan Gordon No. 12 O. S. C." along with the Clan's motto "Bydand," meaning abiding or steadfast. The reverse side featured a St. Andrew's cross, and the bowl's lid was topped by a soccer ball.[10] The first match for the new cup took place on August 7, 1897. On a perfect summer day, the Burns club defeated the Clan Gordon side 1–0 to take home the trophy. Players from Barre Rangers appeared in the lineups for both teams, perhaps to make it a more competitive contest. The undisputed man of the match was Burns goalkeeper William Rust. During the first half, Rust made a number of saves that kept the game scoreless and drew repeated applause from spectators. After Burns scored the opening goal, earning the squad a box of cigars offered by a local resident, Rust made sure the tally held up by earning a clean sheet.

William Rust was born in Aberdeen, Scotland, on June 26, 1877, and came to the United States when he was sixteen years old. His father had been a mason and Rust began his career as a journeyman stonecutter until he joined Company E of the 1st Vermont Volunteer Regiment in 1898. Soon after forming in May, the unit was sent to Camp Thomas, located on the Civil War battlefield of Chickamauga in northwestern Georgia. Conditions in the camp were horrific, as nearly sixty thousand soldiers and fifteen thousand horses and mules lived and drilled on site. The dense clay soil prevented moisture from being absorbed into the ground and, when combined with the heat and humidity, created a hothouse of disease and misery. Rust caught malaria and spent much of August in the hospital. Following the conclusion of hostilities with Spain, he and the other Vermonters returned home and were mustered out in October and November. When he arrived back in Barre, one newspaper described him as "a skeleton of his former self."[11] Despite his changed appearance, Rust seemed a popular figure in town, undoubtedly due in part to his prowess on the soccer pitch. In late 1898, the *Barre Evening Times* ran a contest to determine the "Most Popular Stone Cutter" and Rust finished in the top ten. Two years later, he married Elizabeth "Lizzie" May Park, whose father was a partner in the granite manufacturing firm of Park & Dunbar. Sadly, Lizzie died in 1902 at the age of twenty-two, just ten days after giving birth to the couple's first child, Evelyn May. The cause of death was listed as chronic kidney disease, a condition that can increase the risk to both mother and baby during pregnancy and childbirth. Rust eventually remarried another daughter of a granite company owner. Margaret Church Brown's parents were William and Caroline Brown. Margaret was a native-born Vermonter, but her father came from Aberdeen and arrived in the United States in 1878. After Rust joined the firm (before or after the marriage, one wonders), the name was changed to Rust & Brown. Eventually, Rust's father-in-law sold his share of the company, and it became Rust & Brew. Throughout these years, William Rust continued to play soccer, sometimes intermittently, for Rangers. Initially, he stayed in goal but afterward lined up at forward. The last documented match Rust played in Barre was as part of a five-a-side team called the Crescents, who won the championship of Vermont at the Clan Gordon picnic on August 3, 1907. The Rust family eventually relocated to Los Angeles, California, where William died in 1919.

Around the turn of the twentieth century, the Barre Rangers experienced some turnover in membership, welcoming ten new recruits in the summer of 1899. One of the squad's veterans, James Lamont, briefly returned to Scotland, where he reportedly signed a professional contract with Aberdeen F.C. A player with the same surname appeared in a friendly for the club against Victoria United on August 17, 1899, but it is impossible to know if this was James. By 1900, however, Lamont, along with his brother Alexander, had returned to Vermont, where he served as the best man at the wedding of his Ranger compatriot William Jopp. Such activities were not uncommon among teammates, who, in addition to holding regular banquets and dances, often attended the funerals or weddings of their comrades and family members. In 1901, reports indicated that the Rangers might participate in the soccer tournament held at the Pan-American Exposition in Buffalo, New York. When they received a formal invitation from event organizers, they were also given notice that no funds were available to cover team expenses. As with many other clubs, the lack of financial support meant that Rangers did not participate. In the early years of the new century, Rangers continued to play local teams, especially

Bon Accord FC, five-a-side champions of Vermont, 1905. (Author's collection)

from the cities of Northfield and Hardwick, and faced off against visiting Canadian sides, including Strathcona, Valleyfield, and Westmount.

In 1904, Rangers inaugurated new grounds situated at the corner of Berlin and Smith Streets, just a stone's throw from the Canton Brothers granite shed. The property was fenced although it was a bit ramshackle, with plenty of peeking spaces for spectators who wished to avoid paying an entrance fee. For those who bought a ticket, there was a covered grandstand with room enough for several hundred fans. Bleachers alongside both ends of the stand could accommodate dozens more. The same year Rangers opened the new ballpark, they also welcomed the appearance of a rival side in their home city: the Bon Accord Football Club. The squad's name was probably taken from the motto of the city of Aberdeen and not from the soccer team that suffered the worst defeat in Scottish football history, losing to Arbroath 36–0 on September 12, 1885. Also in 1904, Angelo Scampini announced that he was donating a trophy to be awarded for a future competition. The first campaign for the Scampini Cup

The Berlin Street grounds opened in 1904 and hosted both soccer and baseball games. (Courtesy of the Vermont Historical Society.)

was something of a non-event, although it did spark a minor controversy. The Rangers defeated the Bon Accords two out of three matches to claim the title. A team from Northfield, however, saw that Rangers were being advertised as champions of Vermont and wrote in to ask how this could be since they had twice defeated the club from Barre. The Rangers' secretary responded, stating that they had invited squads to play for the Scampini Cup and the only team that took up the challenge was the Bon Accords.

In 1905, Northfield agreed to join Rangers and Bon Accord in the competition, now dubbed the Vermont Foot Ball League. The winner took home the cup and was crowned champions of the state. The league contest ended up being a tight affair, and by mid-September the teams all had the same record. In early October, the Rangers' 4–2 win over Northfield set up

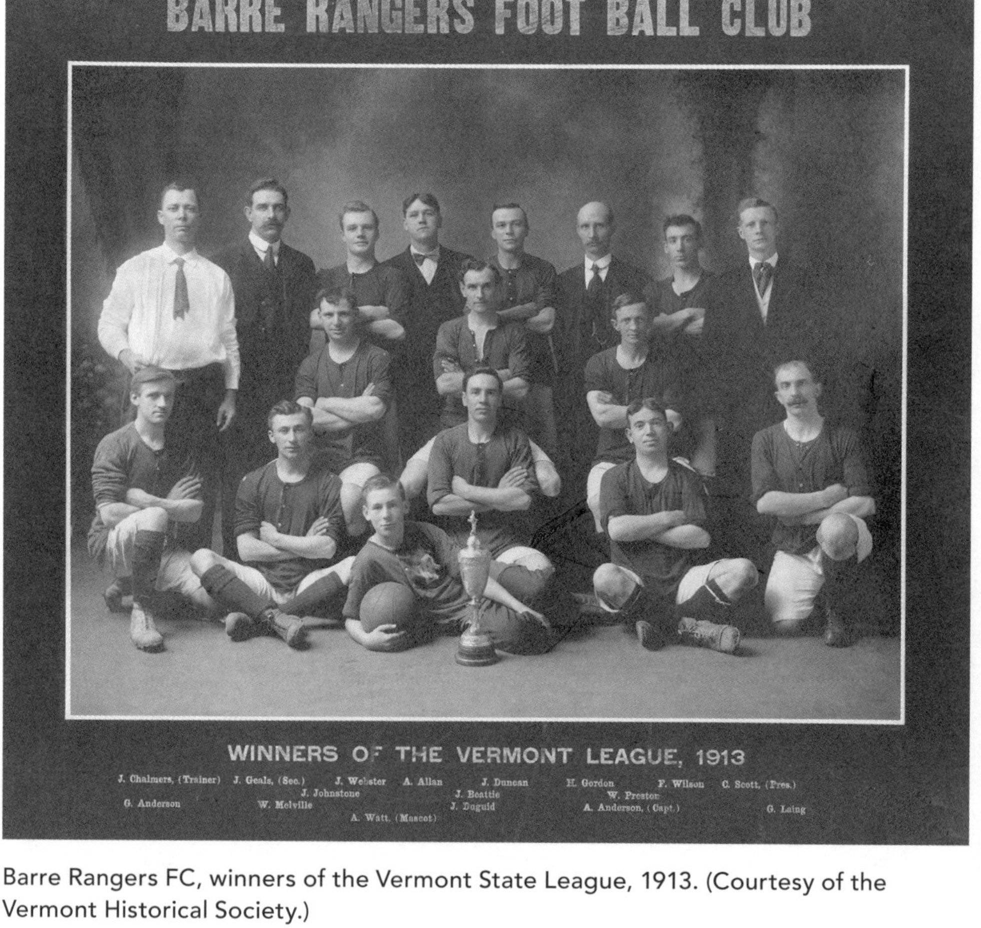

Barre Rangers FC, winners of the Vermont State League, 1913. (Courtesy of the Vermont Historical Society.)

a title decider with their local rivals. Bon Accord captured the Scampini Cup along with the state championship after a stunning 4–3 victory on October 7, 1905. The *Barre Daily Times* called the match "as brilliant and exciting a victory as was ever seen in the history of association football in this city."[12] In the seventieth minute, Rangers held on to what seemed a comfortable 2–0 lead, with the second goal coming from the boot of William Rust. The Bon Accords stormed back, levelling the score before a Rangers tally once again put them on top. Soon after, the Bon Accords clawed one back before netting the winner in the eighty-second minute.

An expanded roster of teams competed for the Scampini Cup in 1906. The sides included Northfield, Hardwick, Rangers, Bon Accord, and a new club known as Green Mountain. The latter team had signed up former members of both Barre squads, including such local legends as William Rust and William Jopp. The veterans proved they still had something left as they captured the title following a 1–0 win over Hardwick. Green Mountain finished with a 5-2-2 record, three points ahead of the second-place side. The season seemed to be the high point of the competition, and it attracted less attention from the press over the next decade. Rangers captured three straight titles between 1907 and 1910 and generally dominated the league in the years that followed. Eleven versus eleven matches gradually became rarer, although the five-a-side tournament continued as part of the annual Clan Gordon picnic. In addition to the honor of being crowned state champions, the winning team also received cash, except one year when the prize consisted of five leather suitcases. During World War I, at least a dozen members of the Bon Accords took up arms. The community supported them with fundraisers and by sending care packages of cigarettes overseas. In the fall of 1918, the city suffered horribly from the Spanish Flu epidemic. Within just three weeks, two hundred people had died of the disease, in part because the silicosis affecting many stonecutters made them more susceptible to influenza. Authorities closed local schools and churches; saloons and theaters also shut down. A shortage of doctors meant that medical students from the University of Vermont arrived to assist patients. The war in Europe, combined with the epidemic, brought the early era of soccer in Vermont to a close.

Notes

1. "Barre," *Vermont Watchman and State Journal*, December 6, 1893.
2. Tomasi and Richmond, "I can Laugh at the Granite," 293.
3. Tomasi and Richmond, "Spanish Granite Worker," 276.
4. Seager, "Barre, Vermont Granite Workers," 63.

5. "The Granite City," *Granite City Leader,* October 5, 1895.
6. Preston and Haines, *Fatal Years*, 14.
7. "Mrs. Reaside's Funeral," *Barre Daily Times*, February 8, 1909.
8. National Register of Historical Places Registration Form, Scampini Block, 2007.
9. "The Granite City," *Granite City Leader*, October 3, 1896.
10. "Clan Gordon Football Trophy," *Granite City Leader*, December 5, 1896.
11. Quoted in Heller, "The Boys from Barre," 135.
12. "Bon-Accords Champions," *Barry Daily Times*, October 9, 1905.

Sources

Aberdeen Football Club. "Player Archive." Accessed March, 8, 2022. https://www.afc.co.uk/teams/player-archive/.

Barclay, William. "Barre's Scotch Population." Typed manuscript, 1936. Vermont Historic Society, Barre City, Vermont.

Barre History Collection. Clan Gordon No. 12. Records, 1884–1977. BHC 57:1–5; BHC 65:1–2. Vermont Historical Society, Barre City, Vermont.

Brayley, Arthur W. *History of the Granite Industry of New England*. Boston: National Association of Granite Industrialists of the United States, 1913.

Edwards, Steven A. "The Aberdonians Who Became Football Champions . . . of Vermont." Unpublished essay. Vermont Historical Society, Barre City, Vermont.

Heller, Paul. *More Granite City Tales: Writings on the History of Barre Vermont*. Self-published, 2014.

Heller, Paul. "The First Italian . . . in Barre." *Times Argus Online*, October 30, 2018. https://www.timesargus.com/news/the-first-italian-in-barre/article_1d4f71c5-a8ca-5e44-841f-802109c34880.html.

McNeil, Charles A. "Carved from Stone? Community Life and Work in Barre, Vermont, 1900–1922." PhD diss., McGill University, 1989.

National Register of Historic Places. Registration Form, "Scampini Block." 2007. Accessed March 31, 2022. https://npgallery.nps.gov/NRHP/GetAsset/NRHP/07000160_text.

Preston, Samuel H., and Michael R. Haines. *Fatal Years: Child Mortality in Late-Nineteenth Century America*. Princeton: Princeton University Press, 1991.

Seager, David R. "Barre, Vermont Granite Workers and the Struggle against Silicosis, 1890–1960." *Labor History* 42, no. 1 (2001): 61–79.

Tomasi, Mari, and Roaldus Richmond. *Men Against Granite*. Edited by Alfred Rosa and Mark Wanner. Shelburne, VT: The New England Press, 2004.

Weir, Robert E. "Solid Men in the Granite City: Municipal Socialism in Barre, Vermont, 1916–1931." *Vermont History* 83, no. 1 (Winter/Spring 2015): 43–81.

Wood, Paul. "The Architecture of the Granite Shed." *Times Argus Online*, October 17, 2008. https://www.timesargus.com/news/the

-architecture-of-the-granite-shed/article_a2349802-e02c-5324-9a1e-b9ce71dc7275.html.

Wood, Paul. "Tools and Machinery of the Granite Industry." *The Chronicle* 59, no. 2 (June 2006): 37–52.

Wood, Paul. "Tools and Machinery of the Granite Industry, Part II." *The Chronicle* 59, no. 3 (September 2006): 81–96.

Wood, Paul. "Tools and Machinery of the Granite Industry, Part III." *The Chronicle* 59, no. 4 (December 2006): 130–151.

Wood, Paul. "Tools and Machinery of the Granite Industry, Part IV." *The Chronicle* 60, no. 1 (March 2007): 10–35.

NEWSPAPERS

Argus and Patriot (Montpelier)
Barre Daily Times
Barre Evening Telegram
Burlington Free Press
Fall River Daily Herald
Fall River Globe
Gazette (Montreal)
Granite City Leader (Barre)
Hardwick Gazette
Montpelier Evening Argus
Rutland Daily Herald
Vermont Watchman and State Journal (Montpelier)

WEBSITES

Ancestry.com
Familysearch.org
MeasuringWorth.com

3

Soccer in Black and White

Scranton, Pennsylvania

If you travelled to the Lackawanna Valley in Northeastern Pennsylvania around 1900, the first thing you would notice were the coal breakers. The immense structures dotted the landscape like medieval cathedrals in Europe except they were made of wood and steel, not stone. The eyes of the people who visited the churches were naturally drawn above, first to the vaulted ceilings but ultimately beyond to the kingdom of heaven. In contrast, the men and boys who labored in the breakers looked below to the rich veins of anthracite coal that fed the machine that gave them a livelihood. Unlike bituminous coal, anthracite would only burn efficiently if the lumps were of similar sizes and so it had to be sorted before it went to market. The coal was first dumped over iron bars to remove the largest pieces. Next, it passed through a cylindrical revolving screen before the intermediate chunks were broken up and sent to be screened again. The anthracite of various sizes fell into chutes and onto storage bins. While in the chutes, breaker boys removed small pieces of rock and slate by hand. It was cruel work, hot as hell in summer and freezing cold in winter. Injuries were common, and one scarred old-timer who worked at a breaker in Swoyersville, Pennsylvania, said the men nicknamed it the "Bucket of Blood."[1]

Eventually, the usable coal was moved to rail cars, while the leftovers were sent to a culm dump. As time went on, the culm banks grew taller and taller, looming over the countryside and the edges of cities like gritty warts. The medieval churches were not just about stone, they could also be filled with light, filtered through colorful panes of stained glass. The breakers too had windows, but they were usually small and offered little in terms of visual interest perhaps save for the view. The industrialized

Lackawanna Valley, however, did have things of delicate beauty. These could not be found in the anthracite fields but rather were manufactured in the factories of Wilkes-Barre and Scranton. The workers in these firms did not produce or process hard coal; instead they made fine lace.

The Lackawanna River begins at Stillwater Lake and runs forty-two miles south-southwest before joining the Susquehanna River. The original inhabitants of the region were Lenape Haki-nk, and the name of the waterway, translated as "stream that forks," comes from the Delaware language.[2] In some regions the Lenape people, also known as Delaware, played a version of football that included both men and women. The female players were allowed to kick and carry the ball, but men could use only their feet. No sources have survived to definitively prove that the Lenape of the Lackawanna Valley played such games, but it would not have been

The Holden breaker, Taylor, Pennsylvania, in 1910. (Courtesy of the Hagley Museum and Library. Holden Breaker, 1910, GL 1990, box 1, Delaware, Lackawanna & Western Railroad Co. Coal Department photographs (Accession 1990.267), Audiovisual Collections and Digital Initiatives Department, Hagley Museum and Library, Wilmington, DE 19807.)

impossible. Once European-American settlers took the land, they established communities along the banks of the river. Eventually, the Lackawanna River flowed past boroughs (the Pennsylvania term for towns) such as Jermyn, Throop, Old Forge, Vandling, and Scranton. It was these settlements and others that gave rise to the region's soccer teams. The early history of soccer in the Lackawanna Valley saw regular competition during the late nineteenth and early twentieth centuries. Even though games were played almost continuously throughout the period, formal, organized competition lasted only for a short time and the region produced just one top-class side: the Scranton Lace Works team.

Scranton, the area's largest city, began as a small village known as Dark Hollow. It would cycle through a few names over the years: Slocum Hollow,

The Hampton colliery breaker looms over the countryside near Scranton. Culm banks can be seen at the left and right of the structure. (Courtesy of the Hagley Museum and Library. Archibald, Hampton, and Continental collieries, 1908, GL 1990, box 1, Delaware, Lackawanna & Western Railroad Co. Coal Department photographs (Accession 1990.267), Audiovisual Collections and Digital Initiatives Department, Hagley Museum and Library, Wilmington, DE 19807.)

Harrison, and Scrantonia before settling on Scranton. It was originally an agricultural area, but the presence of iron ore deposits led to efforts at industrialization. In 1840, William Henry and Edward Armstrong bought land in the area, hoping to start an iron foundry. After the death of his partner, Henry offered his son-in-law, Seldon Scranton, and Seldon's brother George a chance to invest in the project. The initial years were marked by failure, but the operation turned profitable by manufacturing T-rails for the New York and Erie Railroad. While the area lacked quality reserves of iron ore, it did offer rich veins of anthracite coal. Anthracite coal is the top-ranked coal because it has a higher carbon content and fewer impurities than bituminous coal. Eventually, coal mining became the most important industry in the region, attracting workers from around the world. These immigrants brought soccer with them and provided the human resources to work the shafts and fill the team sheets.

During the nineteenth century, many of the workers came from Wales and Ireland. The cultural echoes of these groups can still be found in the miners' ballads chronicling their life and (mostly hard) times. These tunes were incredibly popular and are still performed today. The earliest mentions of football in the area are also linked to these nationalities, especially the Irish. In 1874, the Catholic Young Men's Society of Scranton hosted a picnic in honor of national delegates to the Irish Catholic Benevolent Union, who were meeting in the city. The festivities included a "foot ball match" that featured as many as two hundred participants.[3] These types of physical contests would have been familiar to readers, since games had been played on the same site since at least 1871. Formal, organized soccer only emerged in the mid-1880s. Challenge notices began to appear in the summer and fall of 1885. The Jermyn Football Club challenged any side in the county to a match with a five-dollar football as the prize. A few months later, the Scranton Caledonian Football Club held a meeting, elected officers, and named a team captain. According to the notice, the club secretary would try to arrange games with teams from Wilkes-Barre, Pittston, Pleasant Valley, and Olyphant. No match reports from this period have been found, but the evidence suggests that clubs had formed and were playing matches.

An important game took place on January 1, 1891. Despite earlier activity, the New Year's Day contest is the earliest documented soccer match in the area. It is also significant because it featured a side that became the dominant team in the region: Scranton Lace Works. The contest pitted the Lace Works squad against the Shamrocks of Plains, Pennsylvania. The Lacemen captured the honors with a 3–1 victory. The Scranton Lace Curtain Manufacturing Company began in 1890 when a small group of experienced English workers set up shop with fifteen Heathcoat looms brought over from Great Britain. The devices were named for John Heathcoat, an inventor whose tinkering made machine-produced lace possible. The firm's output was known as Nottingham lace, so called because it had been initially developed in the English city of the same name. At first the Lace Works struggled and was only saved after an influx of money from local investors, including J. Benjamin Dimmick and Henry Belin Jr. After reorganizing, the company was reborn in 1897 and earned $236,000 in sales that year. By 1905 those figures had more than doubled to over $550,000. Over time, the Scranton Lace Works became the world's leading producer of Nottingham lace, fabricating a myriad of products, including napkins, tablecloths, and curtains. If your grandmother's house had lace curtains or a tablecloth, odds are they came from Scranton. The company continued operations until 2002, when the factory was abruptly shut down midshift. The buildings still stand and, like many industrial mills, have been converted into luxury apartments.

Although 1891 was an important date due to the appearance of the Lace Works team, it would take a few years before organized competition began in the area. In February 1893, the Luzerne and Lackawanna Counties Foot Ball Association met to organize a soccer tournament. It is unclear from the reports if this group had been previously established, or if it was a newly created association. Six teams—Wilkes-Barre, Scranton, Avoca, Miller's Grove, Shamrocks, and Pleasant Valley—competed for the T. C. Parker Cup. The man who donated the prize, Captain Thomas C. Parker, was born in 1850 in Aston, England, a section of the West Midlands city of Birmingham. The son of a goldsmith, Parker was one of nine children. He arrived in the US in 1864 and established himself as a jeweler and watchmaker in Wilkes-Barre. Parker also served in the Wyoming Artillery, part of the Pennsylvania National Guard, enlisting in 1876. Eventually, he was promoted to the rank of Captain before being discharged in 1881. By the end of April 1893, the Parker Cup competition came down to two finalists: Pleasant Valley and Wilkes-Barre. Unfortunately, no description of the final match has been found and the winner of the Parker Cup remains unknown. The competition seems to have been a one-off, and soccer in the Lackawanna Valley soon reverted to its previous casual state. As before, the nature of play involved teams from various boroughs organizing teams and challenging other squads. These sides came from places such as Scranton, Vandling, Taylor, Avoca, and Peckville. Although it seems unlikely an organized league existed, the sides did contest some type of informal championship.

Thomas Parker's willingness to donate a cup was not unusual and he regularly contributed prizes to various types of contests, including regimental marksmanship, choir competitions, and ladies' recitation. The latter two events took place as part of a local *eisteddfod,* a traditional Welsh festival of poetry and song. The decision to provide a cup for association football reveals how the sport was intertwined with other aspects of community life. It also illustrates the contributions of Welsh immigrants to the culture of the region, including soccer. In many parts of the country, it was not uncommon for Scottish- or English-born players to take the lead in organizing teams and leagues. Perhaps owing to the wider popularity of rugby in Wales, along with lower numbers of newcomers overall, Welsh immigrants did not usually play a significant role in US soccer communities. The situation was different in the Lackawanna Valley. A selection of players on the Scranton Lace Works team had roots in Wales. Goalkeeper William Bonna, for example, was born in Aberdare on July 1, 1873. A miner by trade, he undoubtedly came to Pennsylvania in search of work underground. Such labor was not without risk and in April 1904, Bonna fell forty-five feet down the Tripp shaft of the Diamond colliery.

Accidents were common in the coalfields, and hundreds of mine workers perished on the job during this period. Estimates suggest that over 1,000 died and another 1,700 were severely injured between 1851 and 1915. The earliest and perhaps best-known high-casualty event took place on September 6, 1869, at the Avondale mine in Plymouth. The official narrative concluded that it began as an accidental fire in the furnace below ground that soon spread to the wooden supports of the shaft. The flames moved to the breaker located directly atop the mine and because fire consumed the only exit, 108 men were trapped below and suffocated. Other accounts from the period, however, claimed that the fire was deliberately set. In their re-evaluation of the available evidence, Robert P. Wolensky and Joseph M. Keating conclude "a majority of witnesses who expressed a view did not support the furnace hypothesis and were supportive either directly or indirectly of the incendiary explanation."[4] The disaster spurred reforms in the industry, although many of them were ignored or circumvented. It also encouraged the formation of benevolent associations and eventually unions. The miners who died left behind seventy-two widows and over 150 children without fathers. It was also commemorated in song. Created by an unknown author, the ballad "The Avondale Mine Disaster" is one of the most enduring legacies of the incident. It begins with an exhortation to remember:

Good Christians all, both great and small,
I pray ye lend an ear,
And listen with attention while
The truth I will declare;
When you hear this lamentation,
It will cause you to weep and wail,
About the suffocation
In the mines of Avondale.[5]

Many of the dead were of Irish or Welsh descent, including two would-be rescuers who voluntarily entered the mine after the accident. They also perished, raising the total lost to 110 souls. Unfortunately, Avondale was not the only major tragedy to hit the region. In June 1896, the Newton Coal Company's Twin Shaft in Pittston collapsed, killing fifty-eight miners. The explosion knocked people from their beds and rattled windows across town. This time the dead were mainly Irish and Lithuanian miners whose bodies remain entombed where they fell. A song called "The Miners' Fate" lamented that their families and friends were unable to properly say goodbye.

Unlike the miners at Avondale and Twin Shaft, William Bonna survived his fall because he landed in sump water. Bonna's presence in the mines showed that, although their numbers had been in decline since the end of the nineteenth century, the Welsh remained an important part of the region's community. Some years before the goalkeeper's accident, an immigrant with the same surname, Henry Bonna, recited an original poem in Welsh at an *eisteddfod* held in the borough of Taylor. Such events became key locations for Welsh residents who wished to preserve aspects of the native land and culture. George W. Bowen was a Pennsylvania miner and poet from Wales who published *The Legend of the Mines and Other Poems* in 1901. Like Henry Bonna, he used verse to recall his birthplace, penning sentimental works such as "St. David's Day."

And thou, Dear Gwalia, home of Song,
Though roaming far from thee,
The murmuring Cynon gliding long,
Still sings her song to me.
Forgive, Sweet Land! thy alien son,
Whom home-love leads astray;
I'll think of thee, and Wales has one
On this St. David's Day.[6]

The informal structure of soccer competition in the region remained unchanged until after the turn of the twentieth century. In March 1904, the

Tribune reported that employees of the Scranton Lace Works had formed an athletic association. The workers planned to field cricket, baseball, and soccer teams. These types of sporting organizations were common in industrial firms at the time. It is unknown how much, if any, financial support the group received from the company itself. A team had been playing under the name of Scranton Lace Works for over a decade and it is unclear what changed with this new organization. Taking red as their primary color, fans encouraged the squad by yelling the team's slogan: "Play up, Reds!"[7] Such a choice may have been inspired by the colors of Nottingham Forest FC, an English soccer club founded in 1865 and known as the Reds. The Scranton Lacemen competed with other local teams, including Wilkes-Barre Lace Works, Vandling, and Old Forge. The Swift Winds of Old Forge emerged as one of the Lace Works' strongest rivals during this period. The two clubs played a charity match on Thanksgiving 1905 to benefit the Home for the Friendless and St. Joseph's Foundling Home. One newspaper called the match "the first real big game of association or English style foot ball played in this city."[8] Unfortunately, bitter cold kept attendance down as the Swift Winds defeated the Lacemen 3–1.

Despite not playing in a formal league, the Lace Works team decided to test themselves against outside competition at the close of 1905. They travelled to Philadelphia to take on the British-American and Albion squads of that city. The visitors triumphed in the first match, shutting out the British-Americans 2–0 in front of a crowd of 2,000 on December 30, 1905. In the second match versus Albion, the Lace Works fell 3–2 after goalkeeper Bonna dropped the wet ball, allowing the home side to score the winning goal. Overall, the Lacemen seemed pleased with their showing against the big city sides and the victory against the British-Americans would be talked about for years afterward. It was the only time in this period that a team from the Lackawanna Valley ventured outside of the region for a soccer match. It is unknown why they had such little formal contact with other Pennsylvania soccer communities. Philadelphia had a long history playing the sport, with reports of games first appearing in the late 1870s. The earliest league organized in 1889, and the city soon emerged as one of the county's great soccer playing areas. The first soccer match in Pittsburgh took place on October 6, 1885, and the earliest formal competition began five years later. The game experienced ups and downs over the next few decades, but by the early twentieth century, western Pennsylvania also had a thriving soccer scene.

A key figure for the Scranton Lace Works Club was manager Francis "Frank" Goodall. Born on March 12, 1871, in Nottingham, England, he arrived in the US in 1882. He worked at the company as a weaver. Although he did not play competitive soccer himself, Goodall was deeply involved with the sport in the region. In addition to managing the Lace Works team, he served as treasurer and secretary of the Anthracite Association Football League (AAFL) when it formed in 1906. Goodall's participation in soccer was part of his overall commitment to assisting his community in various ways. He represented Scranton as a delegate to the Chartered Society of Amalgamated Lace Operators of America's annual convention in 1904. The group organized in 1892 and had over 350 members across the country, nearly 75 percent of the total workforce in the United Sates. The general aims of the union included the "endeavor to avoid labor conflicts and their attendant bitterness and pecuniary loss by resorting to conciliation in the settlement of all disputes concerning wages and condition of employment."[9] Goodall was elected assistant secretary of the Brotherhood of St. Andrew, an association linked to the Church of the Good Shepherd where he served as a vestryman. Later, Goodall switched positions at the Lace Works, becoming welfare director, a job he held for more than two decades before his death in 1939.

The 1906–07 Scranton Lace Works team, featuring George Parry, seated to the right of the player holding the ball; Frank Goodall, in a suit, second row, second from the right; and William Bonna, standing, fifth from the left. (Author's collection)

The AAFL first came together in 1906, perhaps inspired by the Lace Works' mostly successful trip to Philadelphia. The league started the inaugural season with seven teams: Wilkes-Barre, Old Forge, Scranton Lace Works, Peckville, Nanticoke, Vandling, and Plymouth. By the fall, the competition had grown to eight as squads from Throop and Forty Fort joined and Vandling withdrew. As in other parts of the US during this period, the AAFL faced challenges regarding the integrity of the competition. In October 1906, the Lace Works travelled to Plymouth for a match only to discover that their scheduled opponent had disbanded. When the Wilkes-Barre team threatened to withdraw from the league over accusations of referee bias, the problem was resolved thanks to the negotiating skills of Frank Goodall and another league official. Despite such problems, the first season of the AAFL was mostly deemed a success. Ultimately, the Lace Works team finished top of the table during 1906–07 and would go on to claim the title the following season as well.

The company seemed pleased with the play of the soccer team and saw it as a means of maintaining labor peace at the firm. On February 3, 1906, the club held its annual banquet with J. Benjamin Dimmick, president of the Lace Works, as the guest of honor. He took the occasion to announce the donation of a silver cup for the first team to win the league three years in a row. Lace Works General Manager Paul Belin gave a speech titled "Good Fellowship" that praised the harmonious relationship between management and employees at the plant. Belin later provided a trophy to be awarded to the league winners. The club's meeting for 1907 offered similar fare. Forty-two guests met at the Hotel Terrance, described as "one of the leading hostelries of the city," with Frank Goodall serving as toastmaster.[10] Dimmick, now mayor of Scranton, was the official host although he was unable to attend due to illness. Paul Belin took over the duties and spoke on "loyalty," emphasizing that fans should stand behind the team even when they lost. Other speeches expressed similar notions of fellowship and the moral value of sport. William Smith, speaking on "honesty in sports," declared that "I honestly believe that the honest and gentlemanly way in which the Lace Works team play their games is in no small measure responsible for the proud position they hold, that of an unbeaten team."[11]

One player in attendance that night was center forward George Parry. Born in Wales on November 25, 1873, he came to the US when he was about fifteen years old. Parry was a prolific striker who first attracted attention in footballing circles when he starred for the Butler Slope team as they defeated the Thomas Shaft squad 8–1 in November 1905. It was not his first club, however; the match report noted that he had previously played for the Black Diamond squad. All three of these teams were named for coal mines and Parry himself worked the seams. He may have been employed at the Black Diamond colliery in 1897 when a fire consumed the breaker. The loss was estimated at between $50,000 and $100,000 ($1.9-$3.9 million today) and its destruction threw six hundred men out of work.[12] Well-known performer Cornelius "Con" Carbon wrote at least two songs commemorating the event. Carbon was the greatest of the coalfield bards, blessed with a fine voice and a gift for storytelling. He also had a talent for articulating the hopes and anxieties of the miners in song. The chorus of his tune "When the Black Diamond Breaker Was Burned to the Ground" simply, but emotionally, communicates the impact of the fire:

> Times are hard as can be,
> And meat in the house is a rare thing to see;
> To a bare empty table I have to sit down
> Since the Black Diamond breaker was burned to the ground.[13]

Although its tone reflects a certain wry humor, the final verse reveals how the closing of the mine reverberated throughout the community:

> For grub I owe thirty at Mackin's cash store,
> And beyant at McLaughlin's I owe twenty more.
> Tigue the shoemaker I owe for my shoes,
> O'Day and Jim Mundy I owe for my booze,
> Not speakin' a word of what I owe lower down
> Since the Black Diamond breaker was burned to the ground.[14]

George Parry was not one of the unfortunate workers who perished in a workplace accident, but his job as a miner probably contributed to his early demise in 1932 at age fifty-eight. The cause listed on the death certificate was pulmonary tuberculosis, a condition prevalent in miners due to long-term exposure to carbon and quartz dust. In 1906, however, Parry was at the top of his game, leading the line for the Lace Works team, even though he was not employed by the firm. His goals helped the Lacemen capture the championship of the AAFL. One local paper suggested that he was a "credible candidate" for the US team that was scheduled to travel to England.[15]

The movement of players from team to team showed that clubs and fans took the competition seriously and sought to improve their squads in any way possible. After Peckville lost 4–0 in October 1906, they sat tied for bottom in the league and the *Tribune* newspaper called out management, complaining that they had made no effort to strengthen the squad over the summer. To make matters worse, the manager of the team was also vice president of the AAFL, and the dismal play of his squad threatened to kill interest in the league. The article implored him to do something to salvage the season: "Brace up, Taylor, and get at least a few good men."[16] Prior to the start of the 1907 season, it was reported that team managers were travelling abroad in search of players. The article noted that the boss of the Scranton Rangers, a team composed entirely of Scots, was currently in Scotland recruiting athletes. Although generally a positive thing, the competitiveness of the league may ultimately have contributed to its undoing.

After two relatively successful seasons between 1906 and 1908, the organization struggled to continue. One newspaper, reporting on efforts to revive the AAFL in 1911, noted that the use of outside players had hampered the league's development. The article concluded that rules needed to be put in place "to keep the professional side of the game as much as possible in the background."[17] Such a notice implies that the recruitment of non-employee players like George Parry may have involved payments apart from regular working wages. Reports from fall 1911 noted that up to eight teams, including the Young Men's Bible Class from the Church of the Good Shepherd in Scranton, planned to reestablish the AAFL. By October, six teams were confirmed participants and a schedule drawn up. Just days before kickoff, however, the fixtures were put on hold because the teams could not agree on the league rules. As a result, the AAFL never got going and the sport returned to its previous state, featuring challenge matches between teams from a variety of boroughs.

The lack of an organized league meant that over the next few years, the newspaper columns were filled with contested claims to the championship of the region. In January 1912, the Forty Fort soccer team called themselves champions of the three counties, but Old Forge disputed the claim. The following season, the Mott Haven squad asserted they had won, and in the fall of 1913, a side known as the Glennons declared themselves champions. The team may have been linked to the Joseph H. Glennon Brewery company of Pittston. Unlike earlier squads in the region save the Scranton Rangers, the Glennons' players came almost exclusively from Scotland. The squad finished top of the table again in 1914 and celebrated at the home of manager John Manley. The evening featured bagpipe music and songs, including "Reminiscences of Scotland." After attempts to continue the league in 1915 failed, organized soccer in the region virtually disappeared until after World War I.

Notes

1. Rushton, *Relics of Anthracite*, 57.
2. Gannett, *The Origin of Certain Place Names*, 178.
3. "Picnic of Catholic Societies," *Scranton Tribune*, August 7, 1874.
4. Wolensky and Keating, *Tragedy at Avondale*, 28.
5. Korson, *Minstrels of the Mine Patch*, 189.
6. Bowen, *Legend of the Mines*, 30.
7. "Saturday's Game to Settle Championship," *Scranton Tribune*, April 25, 1907.
8. "Lace Workers and Swift Winds Will Play Football for Charity," *Scranton Times-Tribune*, November 29, 1905.
9. "The Chartered Society of the Amalgamated Lace Curtain Operators of America," *Reports of the Industrial Commission on Labor Organizations*, 72.
10. Hitchcock, *History of Scranton*, vol. 1, 152.
11. "Lace Workers Dined," *Scranton Tribune*, December 9, 1907.
12. MeasuringWorth.com.
13. Korson, *Minstrels of the Mine Patch*, 31.
14. Korson, *Minstrels of the Mine Patch*, 32.
15. "Successful Season," *Scranton Tribune*, November 17, 1906.
16. "Peckville," *Scranton Tribune*, October 15, 1906.
17. "Plan to Organize a Soccer League," *Scranton Truth*, September 7, 1911.

Sources

Archibald, Hampton, and Continental collieries, 1908, GL 1990, Box 1, Delaware, Lackawanna & Western Railroad Co. Coal Department photographs (Accession 1990.267), Audiovisual Collections and Digital Initiatives Department, Hagley Museum and Library, Wilmington, DE 19807.

Bowen, George W. *The Legend of the Mines and Other Poems*. Scranton: Press of the Republican, 1901.

Bunk, Brian D. *From Football to Soccer: The Early History of the Beautiful Game in the United States*. Urbana: University of Illinois Press, 2021.

Conlogue, Bill. *Undermined in Coal Country: On the Measures in a Working Land*. Baltimore: Johns Hopkins University Press, 2017.

Farnsworth, Ed. "The Origins of Soccer in Philadelphia, Part 6, the First League." *The Philly Soccer Page*. December 1, 2014. https://phillysoccerpage.net/2014/12/01/the-origins-of-soccer-in-philadelphia-part-6-the-first-league/comment-page-1/.

Gannett, Henry. *The Origin of Certain Place Names in the United States*. Washington, DC: Government Printing Office, 1905.

Healy, R. G. *The Pennsylvania Anthracite Coal Industry, 1860–1902*. Scranton: University of Scranton Press, 2007.

Hitchcock, Frederick L. *History of Scranton and Its People*. 2 vols. New York: Lewis Historical Publishing Co., 1914.

Holden Breaker, 1910, GL 1990, Box 1, Delaware, Lackawanna & Western Railroad Co. Coal Department photographs (Accession 1990.267), Audiovisual Collections and Digital Initiatives Department, Hagley Museum and Library, Wilmington, DE 19807.

Korson, George. *Minstrels of the Mine Patch: Songs and Stories of the Anthracite Industry*. Philadelphia: University of Pennsylvania Press, 1938.

Reports of the Industrial Commission on Labor Organizations. Vol. 27. Washington, DC, 1901.

Rushton, Michael G. *Relics of Anthracite in Northeastern Pennsylvania*. Charleston, SC: America Through Time, 2018.

Wolensky, Robert P., and Joseph M. Keating. *Tragedy at Avondale: The Causes, Consequences, and Legacy of the Pennsylvania Anthracite Coal Industry's Most Deadly Mining Disaster, September 6, 1869*. Easton, PA: Canal History and Technology Press, 2008.

NEWSPAPERS

Evening News (Scranton)
Morning Republican (Scranton)
Philadelphia Inquirer
Scranton Times-Tribune
Scranton Tribune
Scranton Truth
Sunday News
Wilkes-Barre Record
Wilkes-Barre Times Leader
Wilkes-Barre Tribune

WEBSITES

Ancestry.com
MeasuringWorth.com

4

Chasing Nomads

Buffalo, New York

The photograph itself is unremarkable. Like many images from the early history of soccer in the United States, it shows eleven players along with various other folks posed on a field. The lower left-hand corner is inscribed with the name of the club and the date—1908. The team was called the Nomads and they were from Buffalo, New York. What makes the photo unique for the period is that one of the players, seated in the second row on the far right, is of African descent. Information on Black players during this period is almost nonexistent. Fred and Oliver Watson of Pawtucket, Rhode Island, are the earliest known African American soccer players in US history. Their careers spanned from 1894 to approximately 1906, ending just before the player appears in the team photo from Buffalo. Around the same time, evidence suggests that Black players, mostly immigrants from the Caribbean, began organizing teams in and around New York City. Later, schoolboys in Springfield, Massachusetts, Brooklyn, New York, and Chicago, Illinois, also took up the game. Few of these young players seemed to stick with the sport long term. Even in Great Britain, the number of known players of African descent in these years is only a handful. Having a Black player on an otherwise all-white team of adult men was rare in this period, and it is important to try and identify who he was. His presence broadens our understanding of who played the game in the United States during this period, and knowing more about him would help to build a more complete picture. It turns out, however, that putting a name to the face is extremely difficult.

Part of the problem involves the general challenges of researching Black lives in early twentieth-century United States. Systemic racism and widespread segregation meant that documents and photographs were not preserved. Many of the sources usually employed to understand the histories and experiences of soccer players are not as reliable for non-white athletes. Official records can be inconsistent and incomplete. Stories about Black folks in white newspapers were not common and often focused on accidents, criminal activity, or popular sports such as boxing and baseball. The emergence of the Black press aimed, in part, to provide more widespread coverage of these communities and to counter negative stereotypes. Although widely disseminated across the country, many of the most popular Black newspapers were centered on large urban communities such as Chicago, Pittsburgh, and New York City. Black baseball teams attracted some attention from the Buffalo media, but African American newspapers in the city only emerged at least a decade after the 1908 photograph. The task of identifying the player in the Nomads team photo is made more difficult by the typical challenges of identifying soccer players from this period. Generally, match reports and team sheets identify the athletes by surname only. At times this was supplemented by a first initial if two players had the same last name. More detailed accounts of club activities

The 1908 Buffalo Nomads. The player of African descent is seated in the second row, far right. (Author's collection)

or match previews sometimes reveal first names. All these factors make any identification tentative and so we must rely on educated guesses. In the case of the Nomads, the most convincing evidence suggests that the man in the photograph was named Walter Johnson.

Buffalo has a long history playing soccer-like games. One of the earliest documented football clubs formed in the city in 1858. It was organized by boys and announced in the local newspaper, but it is unclear if they played any matches or what rules they followed. A few years later advertisements printed in the *Buffalo Commercial* described a multiday event called the “Festival of the Flower Queen” that featured a football game along with other amusements. Formal notice of soccer games in the city only began to appear in the 1880s. One of the earliest teams organized in July 1885 and emerged out of the Buffalo Cycling Club. The members who formed the Buffalo Football Club may have seen the game as a way to keep in shape and prepare themselves for the racing calendar that generally began in the late summer and early fall. Rider William B. Milley competed mostly in one-mile races and played goalkeeper for the Buffalos’ soccer club. A florist by profession, he was born in New York, but his parents came from England. An offhand remark in the *Buffalo News* in 1886 stated that he was seven feet tall. If true, he would have struck an extraordinary figure between the sticks!

In the fall of 1885, the Buffalos and the Queen City Athletic Club played three matches to determine a city champion. The teams used various rules during the series, including rugby, soccer, and possibly intercollegiate football. Queen City won the first match by a score of 2–0. The sides played with ten men each in the following positions: six rushers, two halfbacks, one quarterback, and one goalkeeper. The tactic resembles the 2-3-5 soccer formation common for the time, but with only ten men. It also uses different terminology, employing rushers rather than forwards and a quarterback instead of a fullback. Perhaps they played rugby or a version of intercollegiate football, but the score suggests not. Maybe they played soccer, but whoever wrote the match report was unfamiliar with the game and used different position names. A week later the *Buffalo Times* gave notice the teams were meeting using the rugby rules. The final match of the series on September 30, 1885, ended in a 1–0 victory for Queen City, giving them the title.

By 1886 Buffalo FC was clearly dedicated to soccer and played most of its games against teams from Canada. They recovered from an early-season 9–0 drubbing at the hands of a Toronto side to secure a 4-2 record over the course of the spring and summer. For the next two years, the pattern continued as few other soccer teams emerged in the city of Buffalo. The number of games played dwindled, perhaps due to the absence of local competition. The squad had seven matches in 1885, six in 1886, and just three in 1887. Despite looking very "picturesque" in their black and orange striped tops, white caps, and shorts with blue socks, they struggled to find opponents.[1] By 1889, Buffalo FC considered dropping soccer and taking up another football code.

Although they ultimately decided to continue at soccer, the dilemma may have signaled deeper tensions within the club. In January 1890, the *Buffalo Morning Express* quoted William J. P. Siepp that "internal discussions" had disrupted the team.[2] Siepp had been the original secretary of Buffalo FC when it formed in 1885. A notary and possibly a lawyer, he worked in various firms led by well-known local attorney Ansley Wilcox. The swearing-in ceremony of Teddy Roosevelt as president of the United States, after the assassination of William McKinley in Buffalo in 1901, took place in Wilcox's home library. Members of the old Buffalo FC side formed a new club called the Wanderers on March 24, 1890. It also seems to have been connected to a cycling club of the same name. Wanderers issued challenges in local newspapers, but once again most of the responses came from Canadians. The situation changed in August when a new team appeared called the Star Football Club.

During the fall of 1891, evidence suggests that several groups had organized football teams. It is hard to tell if they were exclusively soccer clubs or if they played by a variety of codes depending on the opponent. The *Buffalo Sunday Morning News* did little to clarify the situation by noting that both soccer and rugby were popular in the city. Wanderers merged with Star FC and competed against other teams, including the Queen City Athletic Club, Iroquois Athletic Club, 65th Regiment Athletic Association, and Ramblers. Match reports are scarce, but Star FC seemed to be the top club, finishing 1891 with a perfect 6-0 record while scoring thirty-four goals and giving up just four. New teams appeared in Buffalo the following year, with both the Jerseys and Niagaras playing matches. As was often the case in other locations, the rising popularity of soccer seemed to trouble fans of the intercollegiate game. One commentary appearing in the *Buffalo Courier* on November 7, 1892, asked why football clubs played soccer. Like many similar screeds, the piece disparaged soccer as a foreign game, declaring "Rugby-Union and Association Football belong to Canada, and they should be allowed to remain on the other side of the border. Be patriotic, ye local clubs, and play the American game."[3] Such animosity did little to discourage aficionados of the kicking game, and by 1893 a league had formed in the city composed of the Niagaras, Jerseys, Hawthorns, and Imperials. At least two of the sides—Niagaras and Imperials—had links to local hotels.

The competition came down to the Jerseys and Niagaras, but disagreement over the date of the final match meant no champion was crowned. Despite the season's underwhelming conclusion and the verdict by one sportswriter that excitement over the sport was less than "feverish," the same four squads began playing again in the spring and summer of 1894.[4] This time the Jerseys clinched the honors after an 8–3 win over the Hawthorns in front of 1,500 people on July 4, 1894. About ten days later, a Buffalo league select team lost 4–2 to the visiting Toronto Scots. It was a fine showing and signaled an improvement over the city's earliest results versus Toronto clubs. The match featured several players on the Canadian side who would soon be playing in the newly formed American League of Professional Football. These included a forward named Barkey and one of the McKendrick brothers from Detroit. The match report praised McKendrick's play in the backline, noting that his "brilliant defense saved a dozen goals."[5]

The promising showing against Toronto Scots and a generally successful league season seemed to indicate a rising trajectory for the sport in Buffalo. A sporting goods firm called Sweet and Johonnot donated a trophy to be awarded to the competition winner. Despite these positives, organized soccer in Buffalo collapsed in the years that followed. In the spring of 1895, the Iroquois Athletic Club met to prepare for the upcoming year. Soon they were challenging other local teams as well as Canadian sides. The offer was generally met with silence, especially by city clubs. Although newspaper reports indicated that other association football clubs existed in Buffalo, they could not seem to muster the effort to play any matches. As a result, just as had been the case a decade earlier, Iroquois AC mainly faced out of town sides.

By the fall of 1895, the Niagaras had reformed, and the two clubs launched a four-game series to determine a city champion. The Niagaras won the first two games, with Iroquois taking the last two. The results set the stage for a one-game title decider, something that would surely excite the Buffalo sporting community. In a repeat of the 1893 season, however, the final match never took place. After a newspaper column suggested that Niagaras could claim the title, Iroquois president Alf E. Tovey wrote in to dispute the notion. Tovey claimed that no game was scheduled for a couple of reasons. First, the football season ended at Thanksgiving. Second, the Niagaras had won the first two games in part because they took place at an open field. This allowed spectators to crowd the pitch and interfere with the match. The last two games, won by Iroquois, were held at an enclosed ground, which prevented the fans from impacting play and allowed the teams to charge admission. Despite his arguments, Tovey concluded that readers could make up their own minds about who the champion was. In the years that followed, soccer virtually disappeared from the fields and parks of Buffalo.

It would be over a decade before the sport made a comeback. On June 7, 1908, a simple notice appeared in the *Buffalo Enquirer*: "The Nomad Association football team would like to hear from three or four good players" as well as "a first-class goal keeper."[6] The note asked interested parties to contact John Bray of the E. R. Thomas Motor Co. The Thomas company had been founded in 1900 and, in a link to soccer's distant origins in Buffalo, originally manufactured motorized bicycles. In 1902, Thomas began making automobiles aimed primarily at well-heeled consumers. Author Dermot Cole noted that at the time, a Ford Model T cost around $850 while a Thomas Flyer was priced at $4,000. In addition to being expensive, the production process was slow; at its peak in 1909, only around one thousand were made. In comparison, that same year Ford made nearly eighteen thousand automobiles and Buick shipped just over fourteen thousand. As a result, Thomas vehicles never sold as well as the other manufacturers. In addition to high costs and low availability, the cars were underpowered and had chronic mechanical problems. Still, they had some devoted fans and in 1908, the same year Bray posted his notice, a Thomas Flyer won the New York to Paris around-the-world race. It was the first time a US-built car had won a major international race. Originally, the winning company would be awarded the *Coupe de Monde* or World Cup, but this was eventually dropped. Two years after the race, Thomas Motors was given a six-foot, six-inch trophy that weighed sixteen hundred pounds. The towering prize featured a bronze globe with the route of the race inscribed in silver set atop a base of pink and green marble. Perched on the globe was a magnificent eagle. Unfortunately, both the winning car and the trophy were sold as part of bankruptcy proceedings when Thomas Motors went under in 1919. The car has since been restored and is part of the collection of the National Automobile Museum in Reno, Nevada.

In the summer of 1908, however, the demise of the company was over a decade away. As noted in the *Buffalo Enquirer*, the Nomad soccer club had close links to the car company and on a few occasions, they were referred to in the press as Thomas Football Club or the Thomas Eleven. John B. Bray, who seems to have been the organizer of the squad, was born in England in 1889 and arrived in the United States in 1906. He worked in the stockroom at the Thomas Motor Co. The Nomads played their first match on June 17, 1908, against the Lundy's Lane team of Niagara Falls, Ontario. They lost 4–0 to the Canadians, who were reigning champions of the district. The match report also included another message from Bray stating that any player who wished to try out should join the club at practice. This set up a pattern for the Nomads, as the club was constantly on the lookout for more talented athletes. In July they arranged for better practice facilities with the hope that improved conditions would attract more players. Two months later, as the club prepared for the fall season, they remained "anxious to hear from some good players."[7] At the end of what turned out to be a disappointing fall campaign, the club announced that while the core of the group was solid, they were still in need of three or four players of quality. Such an approach explains why over the course of 1908 and 1909, at least thirty-eight men either played for the Nomads or were listed on potential lineups for matches. It might also indicate why the team was open to fielding a Black player.

At the time, race relations in Buffalo were generally amicable, although tensions rose as the African American population grew. The Black population of Buffalo numbered just over 1,200, less than 1 percent of the citywide total in 1905. It advanced slowly over the next decade before rising quickly during and after World War I. The community was on the younger side, with nearly three-quarters of residents under the age of forty-five. Although a Black district existed in the city, many neighborhoods remained integrated and there was no organized push for widespread segregation. Historian Lillian Serece Williams writes that Buffalo provided some commercial opportunities for non-whites, although the system "generally relegated them to subordinate economic and social positions."[8] Many young men worked as waiters, bootblacks, or porters in hotel and club rooms. A young Black man in the city during the time of the photograph, while not enjoying full freedoms, did not face the same racism and segregation that emerged in the following decades.

The first step in finding the name of the Black player was to look at who lined up for the team in 1908. Bray's notice from early June gives a starting point. There is also an endpoint because the *New York Courier* published the team photograph on November 13, 1908. Fortunately, the window can be narrowed down even further. On September 19 a report indicated that the Nomads expected new uniforms to arrive soon. They described the shirt colors as royal blue and white. Although the team photo is in black and white, the colors echo those in the newspaper report—dark shirts with a light band across the chest. Additional confirmation comes from *Spalding's Official Soccer Foot Ball Guide* published in 1908. The annual guides provided information on the year's soccer activities across the country and were also catalogs showcasing the company's products. The 1908 edition of the pamphlet contains a listing for worsted wool soccer shirts in royal blue with a six-inch white band around the body. The color exactly matches those ordered by Nomad's management and the drawing in the catalog is identical to the shirts in the photograph. Even the distinctive turtle-neck collar is the same. Two price options were available: $3.25 each for model No. 10 PW or $2.75 for version No. 12 PW. The club could have used the catalog or ordered the kit through the A. G. Spalding company store at 611 Main Street in downtown Buffalo. The arrival date of the new shirts indicates the photo was taken between late September and mid-November 1908.

During this period, the Nomads played at least six matches where names of players appeared in the newspaper. It may be possible to narrow this still further since on October 17, a story indicated that the Nomads squad was set for the season. After searching for quality players and trying out different lineups, the team had settled on a regular eleven. It makes sense that a club would arrange for a team photograph only after new uniforms arrived and the roster was finalized. Trusting this assumption leaves only three team sheets to examine. A total of eighteen names are included in those reports. Some of them, such as the brothers Robert and Samuel Blake, appeared in two matches and one match respectively. Both had been born in England and both worked in the automotive industry—Robert as a private chauffeur and Samuel as a lathe hand. Another player who appeared in two games is harder to identify with certainty. It was likely William Walmsley, who was born in Paisley, Scotland, in 1884. Two names appeared in a match report dated November 3, 1908—Owen and Lyttle. This was the only time the names were connected to the Nomads. The team listing for the day contains several errors and it's possible that one or both names are misspelled. Owen could be a version of Hogan, the last name of two brothers who regularly turned out for the Nomads. It could also be a reference to Owen Smythe, who is discussed below. Searching genealogical databases for Blake, Walmsley, Owen, and Lyttle results in no plausible matches to any Black, male residents of the city.

After eliminating the marginal players, we can examine those who both had appeared in the key matches and been part of the club since its founding in June 1908. Nearly all the players came from abroad. John Bray, James Fishenden, Thomas Kendrick, Archie Goodall, and Oswald Askin were all born in England. Patrick and John Hogan originally came from Ireland and Jack MacPherson from Scotland. Alfred Wilson was born in Buffalo, but his parents immigrated from the United Kingdom. All these men can be ruled out because they were listed as white in census and other records.

In addition, Bray, Fishenden, Askin, Walmsley, and the Hogan brothers appear in a team photo from 1910 that does not include the Black player. That leaves only three or four possible names: Smith or Smythe, Kelly, and Johnson. Focusing on a few main factors can help narrow the search. First, because nearly all the other Nomads had been born overseas, it was probably true of the Black player as well. Given the fact that soccer had been absent from Buffalo for years before 1908, it's unlikely that someone would have picked up the game without a connection to a place where it was regularly played. The second thing linking many of the Nomads was the automotive industry. Along with birthplace, working on or around cars provided connections that might lead someone to take up soccer. John Bray, Patrick Hogan, and Alfred Wilson worked at an automobile factory and Thomas Kendrick was a mechanic.

The surname Smith appears in just a single match for the club in 1908, while Smythe shows up in three. It's reasonable to conclude that the actual name was Smythe because another newspaper story on the team notes that the player was a cricket coach in the old country. Owen Smythe was born in England in 1881 and was an electrician by trade. He is known to have played for Buffalo Rangers in 1910 and so was probably the same man who lined up for the Nomads two years earlier. A player with the surname Kelly appears in Nomads matches as early as July 1908. One clue to his identity comes in a newspaper article from August 29, 1909. The story gave notice of the Nomads' annual meeting and included a list of people invited to attend. Among the names listed is T. Kelly. Several previously identified Nomads from the prior season, including Bray, Askin, Hogan, MacPherson, and Walmsley, were also on the list. Searching the genealogy databases yields Thomas Kelly or Kelley, a white man born in Ireland in 1887 who came to the United States in 1904. He fits the profile of someone born overseas, but he worked at a piano factory and not in the automobile industry. It turns out, however, that Jack MacPherson also worked at a piano factory and by 1910, the two men lived about a mile away from each other. While it's not possible to confirm they knew one another, it certainly is a solid guess.

After ruling out Smith/Smythe and Kelly as possible names for the Black player, it leaves only Johnson. Other evidence points toward Johnson being the correct surname. The name Johnson or the Black player do not appear in match reports after 1908 or in photographs of the Nomads taken in 1909, 1910, and 1912. He was not one of the people invited to the club's general meeting in 1909. Johnson is a common name with no shortage of Buffalonians of color that might be the right fit. For example, Henry B. Johnson was a cook born in Ohio in 1887 and Hunter Johnson was a club room porter from Virginia. While one of them could in theory be the player, they do not fit the general profile of the Nomads squad. Both men and their parents were born in the United States, and they did not work with automobiles.

Only Walter Johnson checks all the boxes. He was born in England in 1884 and came to the United States in 1906. The 1910 census reports his occupation as washer in a garage, and therefore he would have had contact with other people who worked around vehicles. The record lists him as being of mixed race, with both of his parents also born in England. Although it is difficult to say for certain, the player in the Nomads team photo appears to have a light complexion. By 1910 Johnson was living at 121 Chester Street with an African American family named Smith. There is also evidence that Johnson was an athlete. In April 1911, a boxing challenge appeared in the *Buffalo Courier* from Walt Johnston—note the spelling of the last name—of London, England. He wished to take on anyone at 142 pounds, a weight that fits the physical characteristics of the man in the team photo. Although the surname in the newspaper is spelled slightly different, the contact address listed for him was the Smith house at 121 Chester Street. A month later Johnston fought Battling Johnson to a six-round draw. In July of the same year, another boxer named Spike Webster answered a challenge from Walt Johnson, saying he would "meet the Englishman before any club wishing to stage the bout."[9]

However, things get more complicated after the 1908 season. In September 1909, the *Niagara Falls Gazette* noted that "Johnston, the Cuban" who played outside left for the local Wanderers, was quite the world traveler.[10] According to the paper, he had played soccer in the United States, England, South Africa, Australia, Argentina, and Cuba. He does not seem to have featured much for the Wanderers that season, and no additional information could be found. While it seems probable this was the same man who had been with the Nomads a few months earlier, his identification as a Cuban confuses things.

During the 1908 and 1909 seasons, the Nomads' main rival was another city club called the Rangers. The matches were tight affairs featuring two 0–0 draws and two Rangers 1–0 wins in 1908. The Nomads did have some success, capturing a trophy presented at the Scottish Games in August 1909. The prize, dubbed the Paterson Cup, had been donated by Andrew Mudison and Adam Paterson, two players from the early days of soccer in the city. That same month, the factory manager for the Thomas Motor Company, Frederick P. Nehrbas, donated a trophy to be played for by local teams from across the region. Over the next few seasons, teams from Buffalo, Rochester, and Niagara Falls, New York, competed for the honors. By early 1910 the squads decided to form a league, mostly because players kept making appearances for multiple clubs during the Nehrbas Cup competition. The Buffalo and District Association Football League (BDAFL) began play in the late summer and continued until the weather made outdoor games difficult. The Niagara Falls Wanderers proved the dominant force in the BDAFL winning the title in each of the organization's three seasons. During the colder months, Buffalo clubs also played indoors, sometimes fielding squads with less than eleven players. In what would prove the team's final hurrah, the Nomads took home the 74th Infantry Armory indoor games trophy in April 1912. The club's fortunes had been in a steady decline, finishing second bottom in the league in 1911 and narrowly avoiding being shut down. The Nomads formally disbanded a year later, when the BDAFL itself voted to dissolve. The 1911–12 season had been successful, and organizers thought the time was right to form a larger circuit. The Independent Association Football League formed in late August 1912 and included representatives from Erie, Pennsylvania,

The Niagara Falls Wanderers, champions of the Buffalo and District Association Football League, 1910–12. (Author's collection)

Buffalo, Jamestown, Tonawanda, and Niagara Falls, New York. The Buffalo clubs were consolidated into Buffalo City and Buffalo Corinthians.

As for Walter Johnson, his trail runs cold after just a few tidbits of information. He is absent from the 1915 New York State census and the 1920 federal count. Tracing Black Britons can be a challenging endeavor. Unlike the United States, the British government did not record race in official documentation, including census, birth, and baptismal records. Because Walter Johnson was a relatively common name, it is impractical to narrow down the possibilities through official documents without additional clues. As was the case in Buffalo, the spelling of a name such as Johnson or Johnston could vary over time, even in formal records. British newspapers are equally difficult to navigate, and no credible information about Johnson's life prior to his arrival in the United States has been found. During the nineteenth century, many Black citizens of England originally came from North America, Africa, or the West Indies. If one or more of Johnson's grandparents had relocated from the United States, it might explain why he came to the country in 1906. Historian Jeffrey Green has traced the lives of several formerly enslaved people from the United States named Johnson who settled in England. Although none of them have any clear links to the Nomads player, their stories reveal that Johnson was not an unusual name among Black residents of the United Kingdom.

Musician Frank Johnson spent a year touring England, and singer John Alexander Johnson lived in Birmingham from 1871 with his wife and three children. Robert Johnson was born into slavery in Kentucky but escaped and eventually studied medicine in Scotland. An enslaved man named James Alfred Johnson fled to England from his home state of North Carolina during the American Civil War. For a time, he worked as a boxer with a traveling show and later settled in Oldham, where he died in 1914. Because he stayed in the same area for several decades, it is possible to trace how details of his origins changed over time. In the 1871 census, his birthplace is listed as "North Carolina, America." Three decades later, in 1901, it had been transformed into "South America Carolina" with the word Brazil added by the enumerator.[11] James Johnson had no children and has no known connection to Walter, but the case is an example of how basic information can be unreliable even in governmental records.

It seems most likely that some member of Walter Johnson's family originally came from the United States, but he could have had links to the West Indies. If Johnson had roots in the English-speaking Caribbean, perhaps the Niagara Falls newspaper's description of him as Cuban was a misunderstanding. Another possibility is that for some people of African heritage during this period, passing as Spanish or Cuban became a way of avoiding discrimination. Baseball player Vincent Nava was a Mexican of African descent whose nickname—the Spanish catcher—helped enable his career as a professional. Writer James Weldon Johnson and poet Langston Hughes, both fluent Spanish speakers, noted that appearing to be Cuban was a way of avoiding Jim Crow segregation. For Walter Johnson, perhaps a Cuban identity allowed him to live under similar freedoms. Unfortunately, much of this is really guesswork and until more information comes to light, we can only speculate about the true background of the man in the team photo.

Notes

1. "Sports in Season," *Sunday Truth*, April 22, 1888.
2. "The Buffalo Athletic Club," *Buffalo Morning Express*, January 19, 1890.
3. "Sporting News," *Buffalo Courier*, November 7, 1892.
4. "Notes on Sports," *Buffalo Sunday Morning News*, April 22, 1894.
5. "Beaten By Team Play," *Buffalo Sunday Morning News*, July 15, 1894.
6. "Wants Football Players," *Buffalo Enquirer*, June 4, 1908.
7. "Association Football," *Buffalo Evening News*, September 1, 1908.
8. Williams, *Strangers in the Land of Paradise*, 30.
9. "Challenges," *Buffalo Courier*, July 2, 1911.
10. "Association Football," *Niagara Falls Gazette*, September 18, 1909.
11. Jeffrey Green, "135: James Johnson of North Carolina and Oldham 1847–1914."

Sources

Bressey, Caroline. "The Next Chapter: The Black Presence in the Nineteenth Century." In *Britain's Black Past*, edited by Gretchen H. Gerzina, 315–29. Liverpool: Liverpool University Press, 2020.

Bunk, Brian D. *From Football to Soccer: The Early History of the Beautiful Game in the United States*. Champaign, IL: Illinois University Press, 2021.

Burgos Jr., Adrian. *Playing America's Game: Baseball, Latinos, and the Color Line*. Berkeley: University of California Press, 2007.

Chater, Kathleen. "Genealogy and the Black Past." In *Britain's Black Past*, edited by Gretchen H. Gerzina, 31–42. Liverpool: Liverpool University Press, 2020.

Cole, Dermot. *Hard Driving: The 1908 Auto Race from New York to Paris*. New York: Random House, 1991.

Fryer, Peter. *Staying Power: The History of Black People in Britain*. London: Pluto Press, 2018.

Green, Jeffrey. "135: James Johnson of North Carolina and Oldham 1847–1914." *Jeffrey Green. Historian*. Accessed April 29, 2023. https://jeffreygreen.co.uk/135-james-johnson-of-north-carolina-and-oldham-1847-1914/.

Green, Jeffrey. *Black Americans in Victorian Britain.* Barnsley, UK: Pen and Sword Books, 2018.

Olusoga, David. *Black and British: A Forgotten History.* London: Macmillan, 2016.

Rampersand, Arnold. *The Life of Langston Hughes.* Vol. 1, *I, Too, Sing American: 1902–1941.* New York: Oxford University Press, 1986.

Watkins-Owens, Irma. *Blood Relations: Caribbean Immigrants and the Harlem Community, 1900–1930.* Bloomington: Indiana University Press, 1996.

Weldon Johnson, James. *Along This Way: The Autobiography of James Weldon Johnson.* Viking, 1933. Reprint, Da Capo Press, 1973.

Williams, Lillian Serece. *Strangers in the Land of Paradise: The Creation of an African American Community in Buffalo, 1900–1940.* Bloomington, IN: Indiana University Press, 2000.

NEWSPAPERS

Buffalo Commercial
Buffalo Courier
Buffalo Enquirer
Buffalo Evening News
Buffalo Morning Express
Buffalo News
Buffalo Sunday Morning News
Buffalo Sunday Truth
Buffalo Times
Niagara Falls Gazette

WEBSITE

Ancestry.com

5

Deering's Rangers in El Dorado

Miami, Florida

The mansion was designed to be approached from the bay. Boats made their way through a channel marked by buoys, gently gliding toward a two-story cement building covered in light pink stucco with square towers on either side. As it got closer, a breakwater designed to look like a massive stone boat appeared. Known as the Barge, it had a concrete foundation, was clad in local limestone, and finished with copious decoration. Gondola landings at the midships led to the main deck past four carved stone columns representing the tropics. At the prow, a pair of busty mermaids flanked a fat, open-mouthed catfish-like creature. The "sea girls," as they were referred to, were carved by A. Stirling Calder, father of Alexander the famous mobile designer. Initially, the figures were deemed too sexy, and the sculptor toned them down a bit.[1] After arriving on land, the eye wandered up to the gabled centerpiece, topped with a sundial and broken pediment. It also contained an inscription (in slightly flawed Latin): "Accept the gift of pleasure when it is given. Put serious things aside."[2]

In the early twentieth century, Miami, Florida, had many nicknames: El Dorado, the Magic City, Eden, and Fairyland, just to name a few. All of them had something in common, something that spoke to the imagined nature of the city. Miami was, according to historian Julio Capó, "a place where leisure and entertainment were central to every aspect of life."[3] At the heart of this fantasyland in South Florida was the mansion on the water called Vizcaya. It was the winter residence of James Deering, an industrialist from Chicago whose family made a fortune selling agricultural machinery. After merging with a rival company, the firm known as International Harvester controlled about 85 percent of the US market. Due to ongoing health issues, Deering essentially retired in 1908. After buying up land in Florida, he enlisted architect F. Burrall Hoffman, Jr. and designer Paul Chalfin to create Vizcaya. The house was extraordinary and decadent. It was built during a period when a small number of families like the Rockefellers, Vanderbilts, and Deerings spent enormous sums on so-called country houses. Although Vizcaya had a Spanish name, the overall vibe of the structure is Italian. The builders and designers sought inspiration from Italy but did not limit themselves to a single geographical place or historical period. Chalfin was responsible for the interiors and aimed to create "a historic sampler" of different places and eras.[4] Deering, who kept a close watch over the construction and decoration, spent lavishly. Its treasures included wrought iron gates from the Palazzo Pisani in Venice, a massive French Renaissance stone chimneypiece, and a fifteenth-century Spanish rug once owned by Don Fadrique Enríquez de Mendoza, grandfather of Ferdinand of Aragon. No final total was ever given, but the

James Deering's mansion, Vizcaya. (Courtesy of Vizcaya Museum and Garden Archives, Miami, Florida. *East Façade*. c. 1916. Photograph, CA07011, "Construction Photograph Albums," Vizcaya Museum and Gardens, Miami, Florida.)

cost of the house, apart from its contents, has been estimated at nearly $3 million, the equivalent of about $80 million today.[5]

The culture of pleasure in the city and at Vizcaya took place in overwhelmingly male spaces. Julio Capó argues that for wealthy tourists and part-time residents such as Deering, "This period saw the development of a distinct bachelor culture tied to the recreations and vices modern cities offered."[6] Miami boosters sought to attract white, male visitors with promises that the usual social norms did not apply, including in matters of sexuality and gender. One subculture included those who challenged and subverted traditional notions of appropriate masculine sexual desire. Chalfin lived openly with his partner Louis Coons, and the pair were guests for the first dinner party given at Vizcaya after its completion in December 1916. Deering never married and his sexual interests, or lack thereof, have been the cause of speculation both at the time and today. Artist John Singer Sargent, another lifelong bachelor, visited the estate in 1917 and created suggestive images of black Bahamian workers. At the height of construction, nearly one thousand people worked on the grounds, and while Vizcaya was largely completed when Sargent visited, the estate still employed a regular staff of around one hundred and fifty. These laborers formed a second distinct bachelor subculture. The seasonal migrants came from their homes in the Bahamas to work on the construction of railroads, highways, and buildings across the region. Their families remained on the islands, and while in the United States, they lived out their public and private lives almost exclusively in the close company of other men.

Soccer was a third male dominated subculture, one that also had close links to Vizcaya. Many of the players and administrators initially came to the United States from Great Britain. One important example of these connections was the Orr family. The patriarch, Alexander Orr, and his wife, Jessie Dawson Eadie, immigrated to the United States from Scotland with their large family in 1912. The pair had thirteen children, four daughters—Margaret, Jessie, Martha, and Elizabeth—and nine sons—Alexander Jr., Robert, George, John, MacNiven, William, James, Joseph, and Archibald. The eldest child, Margaret, was born in 1874, twenty-seven years before her youngest sibling, Archie. The father worked as a plumber and several of his sons followed him into the trade. In Miami, Alexander Jr. ran a plumbing and heating company that did work on the fountains and gardens at Vizcaya.

As a child, John Orr attended school in the Parkhead neighborhood of Glasgow, the home of Celtic Football Club and the stadium known as Celtic Park. Afterwards he studied at the Glasgow and West of Scotland Technical College, now known as the Royal College of Science and Technology. He went on to an apprenticeship as an ornamental plasterer before travelling to North America. After settling in South Florida, Orr operated his own contracting business specializing in the application and coloring of stucco. He worked on many prominent buildings in the city, including the Deering estate. Orr's firm completed the stucco work on the house and earned praise for the ability to give a gently weathered look to new material. Orr himself may have done much of the decorative plastering inside the mansion. In a letter dated May 10, 1917, Paul Chalfin praised his delicate modelling and use of color, declaring, "I fear that the photographs of the rooms in which your work appears will never do you justice."[7] In addition to working at Vizcaya, several of the Orr brothers took on leading roles in the development of Miami's soccer community. They served as players, referees, and administrators, helping to grow the game in South Florida.

Miami's young age—it was only incorporated in 1896—and its relatively small population meant that soccer was slow to develop in the area. It is not known when the first match was played, but occasional stories relating to the sport appeared in local newspapers as early as 1906. Such notices were usually wire reports of activities in other cities, including the visit of the English club Corinthians to New York City or reports of action at New England colleges. A longer story chronicled efforts by US officials to join the *Fédération Internationale de Football Association* (FIFA) in 1912, but the article did not seem to be the product of local reporting. A story in the *Miami Herald* on August 25, 1913, announced the formation of a soccer club in the city. Although no name was mentioned, the group claimed to have nearly thirty members and planned to sponsor multiple teams. They had already ordered a kit and hoped to visit different southern cities, including Jacksonville, Florida, and Savannah and Augusta, Georgia. Unfortunately, nothing more is known about this organization. One reason for the absence is that copies of the newspaper that published the story are not available for the remainder of 1913, and no other record has been found confirming the hoped-for tour. Issues become available again in January 1914, but no more information about this earliest club has been found.

In 1915, the *Miami News* reported that a group of men played "old time football" at Royal Palm Park on February 13. According to the article, some of the participants were members of the Britannia Club and most had ties to Vizcaya. One team was called "John Orr's Plasterers," and the other was described as men working on the Deering job.[8] Orr's side easily triumphed 7–1 in the sixty-minute game. A match report from another newspaper described the teams slightly differently, calling Orr's squad the Britannia Club and explaining that the other team was composed of stonecutters working at Vizcaya. Little is known of the Britannia Club, and although the group reportedly purchased land to build a clubhouse, nothing seems to have come of the plans. It is not surprising given the scale of the work at Deering's estate that the site had its own stone-carving operation. As in other parts of the United States, these stonecutters organized soccer teams as a form of recreation and friendly competition. Miami soccer aficionados also hoped to arrange a match versus Palm Beach, and if there was interest, to form a three-team league.

A week later the two sides played again, except now the team of stonecutters was known as Deering's Rangers. Many of the players came from Scotland, including Adam Cruickshanks and brothers Alexander and William Doig. The Britannia Club lineup included three Orrs—William, James, and Joe—while brother George served as a linesman. By March, an England versus Scotland match had been organized. William, James, and Joe Orr played for Scotland along with a father and son from Aberdeen named Francis and Frank Hendry. Listed as forward for the English squad was A. N. Other, who was not a real person but merely a placeholder that newspapers sometimes used when a team lineup was incomplete. The Scots ran out easy 5–1 winners, with the only English tally coming on a Scotland own goal.

The two squads, now called Deering's Rangers and the Miami Association Football Club, continued to play into the fall and winter of 1915. The Rangers' uniform consisted of white shirts with black shorts, while Miami AFC wore blue jerseys with white shorts. As the season wore on, the Rangers added several "lusty youngsters" and Miami picked up a reinforcement close to home, MacNiven Orr. They also signed a goalkeeper named W. Baader, who was described as an "old star."[9] In other communities, when teams began to acquire new players, it usually signaled an uptick in the level of competitiveness. This does not seem to have been the case in Miami. A match scheduled for Christmas Day in 1915 had to be canceled after one team did not show up. The reason given was that they had eaten too much holiday dinner. "How do you expect a man to chase himself all over a football field when his stomach is full of turkey?" said one unnamed player.[10] Generally, Miami AFC had the better of the rivalry, winning every game until January 29, 1916, when the Rangers took home the honors after a close fought 2–1 battle. Miami attacked from the opening whistle, but the Rangers' defense held strong. Soon the action was end to end and both keepers made quality saves to keep the game scoreless. A quick counterattack by the Rangers led to the opening goal as Arthur Southern scored with a curving shot just under the crossbar. After falling behind the Miami squad woke up, and they soon equalized. The score remained tied as the first half ended. Early in the second half,

Miami tested their opponents' defense, but they did not break. Rangers' winning goal came after Thomas Bilyard made a nice run into the corner before centering it for Daniel McKinnon's finish.

Games continued into the spring of 1916, and as the quality of play increased so did the crowds at Royal Palm Park. The clubs decided to hold a best-of-five series of matches to determine the city champion. The first took place on March 11, 1916, before a record crowd of 1,700 that included both local fans and tourists. William, James, Joe, and MacNiven Orr lined up for Miami. The players "seemed full of pop as they took the field," perhaps excited that gold medals would be awarded to the series winners.[11] Miami attacked early and only the skill of Rangers' goalkeeper Arthur Hoad kept them off the scoresheet. Hoad was nearly six feet tall, lanky with a fair complexion and slightly receding hairline. He was born in England on April 15, 1887, and as a young man lived in London while serving as a footman for Augustus John Debonnaire Monson, the ninth Baron Monson of Burton. After coming to Miami, Hoad worked as a valet at the Deering residence. It was William Orr who scored the winning goal, faking a pass before beating Hoad with a fierce shot. Ultimately, Miami AFC won three games in a row to sweep Rangers and capture the first city championship.

Matches between the teams were played under the auspices of the Seminole Athletic Association (SAA). The newly formed group hoped to build a clubhouse and organize a four-team soccer league in the city. On April 4, 1916, the SAA put on a banquet to celebrate the conclusion of the soccer season and toast victorious Miami AFC. Fifty members of the club met at the Boston Lunch Room to witness the presentation of the prizes to the teams. Although not in attendance, James Deering had provided gold medals for the champions and silver ones for the runners-up. The owner of Vizcaya was well liked by the people who worked on the estate, and they referred to him affectionately as "Mr. Jimmy."[12] The players also gifted a watch chain to George Orr for his service as referee. Alexander Orr Jr. gave a speech on how sports provided an outlet for the excess energy of young men. Such activities kept them away from "pursuits of a less beneficial nature."[13] William, George, and John Orr also gave speeches.

The theme of Alexander's talk and the prominent roles played by his family reveal something about the values and attitudes of the soccer-playing population. Despite Miami's reputation as a city of unrestrained hedonism, the Orrs represented more traditional values. The family was part of the white, Protestant community that wielded much of the economic and political power in the city. As in other areas of the United States, soccer became linked to that subculture, promoting manly exercise and competition as a moral good. Alexander Orr Jr. was a deacon at the Presbyterian church, president of the Miami Boy Scouts, and mayor of the city in 1940–41. John Orr served as a city commissioner and was an organizer of local branches of both the Shriners and the Masons. In the 1920s, he was a member of the Committee of 100, a group formed by local elites to transform the city into a place that epitomized wholesome family values. They pushed for law enforcement policies that, according to Julio Capó, "fueled xenophobic, racist, and class-based warfare in the urban center."[14] The Committee was partially a response to the increasing presence of organized crime figures in South Florida, including Al Capone. The Chicago mobster bought a house on Palm Island in 1928; among the neighbors who organized against his presence was John Orr. While not a member of the super-rich like James Deering, Orr had made a great deal of money thanks to his contracting work for wealthy clients. In addition to Vizcaya, his firm worked on other notable properties, including various landmark hotels and *El Jardin*, a mansion built for John Bindley, president of Pittsburgh Steel. When he died in 1932, Orr's estate was valued at $500,000, about $9.5 million today. His son Jack Orr served in the Florida House of Representatives and was elected mayor of Miami-Dade County in 1972.

By the end of 1916, the soccer community had expanded, and plans were made for a four-team league in the city. SAA president S. W. Bayles donated a gold cup to be given to the winner of the competition. The league squads included veteran clubs Miami AFC and "the husky lads from the Deering job," who had once again changed names, going from Rangers to Wanderers.[15] The two new clubs were the Vizcayas, made up of staff at the mansion, and a team called the Rovers. Each side had a distinct kit: Miami sported blue shirts with gold stripes; Wanderers a red top with white shorts; Rovers ran out in blue with a white band; and the Vizcayas wore navy tops with pale blue stripes. Deering offered space to have games on the grounds of his estate, although it is unclear if any were ever played there. The lack of matches at the site may have been because the Vizcaya squad quickly dropped out of the competition.

Led by William, Joe, James, and MacNiven Orr, Miami AFC jumped out to an early lead and seemed to be headed for a second straight title. The Rovers, however, also had an experienced side, including keeper Arthur Hoad. On April 12, 1917, the Rovers team met at the Boston Lunch Room for an end of season banquet. The team was full of confidence, having just beaten Miami in a 1–0 thriller about a month earlier. Around three thousand people turned out to Royal Palm Park on a gorgeous spring day, with temperatures in the mid-70s and just enough of a breeze to keep things cool. Once again Hoad played brilliantly as he "shut out the Miami boys, time and again, when it appeared they had a cinch in putting the ball over."[16] The team was convinced they would capture the league title with a victory over Miami on Saturday, April 14. Unfortunately, no report of the final match has been located and the winner of the league remains uncertain. One piece of evidence, however, suggests that Miami may have prevailed. A photograph of the team from this period shows them posing with two different trophies. It is possible that one was for the city championship in 1916 and the other was for the league crown in 1917. A few other matches were played to close out the season, including a bachelors versus benedicts, also known as the unmarried and the married, game, with the former winning 3–2.

Even as they competed for championships in Miami, World War I entered its third grueling year in Europe. The ongoing conflict eventually had an impact on the soccer community in Southern Florida, including on the Orr family. A few months after the title-deciding match, MacNiven Orr enlisted in the US military on June 7, 1917. During his two plus years in the army's 6th Engineers, Orr spent time in France where his unit participated in the Battles of the Somme, Marne, and Meuse Argonne. He was also stationed in occupied Germany following the conclusion of hostilities before being discharged on September 2, 1919. Although never wounded or decorated, he eventually was promoted to the rank of sergeant first class.

Miami AFC, c. 1917. (Author's collection)

Joe Orr signed up for the Canadian army in March 1918 and, like his older brother, served in an engineering unit. Just a few weeks into his service, Orr was hospitalized to remove his tonsils and a few months after that fell ill with influenza. Although not stated outright in his medical records, it may have been the Spanish flu, since the virus was introduced to Canada through major cities and Orr spent all his military service at the Engineering Training Depot in Saint-Jean-sur-Richelieu, Quebec, about twenty-five miles from Montreal. He was discharged on January 3, 1919, and returned to Miami. After the war, Joe was president of the Miami Chamber of Commerce and was the last of the soccer-playing Orr brothers when he died in 1968. Miami's soccer scene began relatively late and lasted only a few short years. As in communities in other parts of the United States, the earliest phase of soccer in the city ended during World War I.

Notes

1. Rybcynski and Olin, *Vizcaya*, 167.
2. Rybcynski and Olin, *Vizcaya*, 64.
3. Capó, *Welcome to Fairyland*, 1.
4. Rybcynski and Olin, *Vizcaya*, 65.
5. Contemporary values here and below calculated at www.meauringworth.com.
6. Capó, *Welcome to Fairyland*, 101.
7. Chalfin, Paul, letter to John B. Orr, reprinted in *Architectural Review* 5, no. 7 (July 1917): ix.
8. "Old Time Football Is Revived in Miami by Britannia Club Men," *Miami News*, February 15, 1915.
9. "Soccer Game at 2:30 Tuesday," *Miami Herald*, December 4, 1915; "Miami vs. the Deerings," *Miami Herald*, December 11, 1915.
10. "Too Much Turkey, So Couldn't Play Ball," *Miami Herald*, December 27, 1915.
11. "Miami Wins Soccor [*sic*] Game," *Miami Herald*, March 12, 1916.
12. Interview with Joe Orr, February 17, 1954, box 4, folder 20, record unit 7439, Robert Tyler Davis Papers, Smithsonian Institution Archives, Washington, DC.
13. "S. A. A. Feast Enthusiastic," *Miami Herald*, April 5, 1916.
14. Capó, *Welcome to Fairyland*, 245.
15. "Soccer Squads to Work Out Today," *Miami Herald*, December 16, 1916.
16. "Thousands at the Football Game between Miami Teams," *Miami News*, March 12, 1917.

Sources

Capó, Julio, Jr. *Welcome to Fairyland: Queer Miami before 1940*. Durham: University of North Carolina Press, 2017.

East Façade. c. 1916. Photograph, CA07011, "Construction Photograph Albums," Vizcaya Museum and Gardens, Miami, Florida.

Florida: The East Coast: Its Builders, Resources, Industries, Town and City Developments. Miami: Miami Herald, 1926.

Ling, Sally J. "Capone in Miami." *The Best of Boca Raton* 36, no. 6 (July/August, 2016): 78–85.

Rybcynski, Witold, and Laurie Olin. *Vizcaya: An American Villa and Its Makers*. Philadelphia: University of Pennsylvania Press, 2007.

NEWSPAPERS

Miami Herald
Miami News
Sarasota Herald
Tampa Tribune

WEBSITES

Ancestry.com
MeasuringWorth.com

6

Irish Shamrocks and Jewish Gyms

Cincinnati, Ohio

In the not too distant past, if you wanted to study the early history of soccer in the United States, you had to look at microfilm. Newspapers have always been and remain the best source of information on previous players, teams, and competitions. Before many of these papers had been digitized, the only way to access them was through microfilm copies. The first task was to locate the boxes that contained the correct reels. Often, they were stored in large metal cabinets with small labels affixed to the outside giving the title and dates. After pulling open the drawer, you saw the boxes, huddled together like chocolate truffles in a candy store case, a sticker on each listing the name and time period. You grabbed a couple of boxes; each reel covered a few months to a few years depending on the size and frequency of the paper. Next, you carried them to a machine and opened the first one. Each reel was tied with a slip of paper that had to be carefully removed before it could be placed in the reader. You clicked the power button, the screen flickered to life, and the fan began a low whirr. Even with a good deal of practice, it sometimes took a few tries to make sure the film was loaded in the correct way, otherwise the images would be upside down or backwards.

Now came the tedious part, scrolling through day after day of newspapers. For a while it was kind of cool to see advertisements for familiar products or the headlines of familiar stories. This got old pretty quickly, and it was hard not to lose focus as the black and white text flashed endlessly by. Every once in a while, however, something interesting turned up. Even the smallest story was cause for joy. The times when a missing match report or a detailed article filled gaps in your knowledge was like striking gold. One historian described how, after finding a much-needed story at the Newark Public Library, he calmly walked to the elevator and when the doors closed, he did a fist pump in celebration. Over time it became clear when the articles on soccer were going to be published, say on Friday before weekend matches or on Monday to review the results. Overall, the process was time-consuming and, no matter how carefully one looked, a lot would be missed.

The machines for microfilm have changed over the years, but the process remains the same. Digitization has revolutionized the search. Now it is a simple thing to comb through hundreds or even thousands of issues in a few hours. While this has made it easier to do the research, it is still not perfect. Not every issue for every paper is available and there are big gaps in some of those that have been uploaded to databases. The optical character recognition software can be imperfect, leading to dozens of false positives. For example, the word "success" often comes up in results for "soccer." The search process itself can be finicky, usually requiring multiple tries using slight variations on familiar terms. Finally, the quality of the scans can be poor, making stories unreadable. As a result, key information will still be missed, and the story imperfectly told. Although these complications impact every city, the issues seem especially challenging in the case of Cincinnati. The technical problems are compounded by the frustrating nature of soccer coverage in the city's two main English-language papers, the *Post* and the *Enquirer*. For many years, most of the stories published about the sport were brief announcements of upcoming games, scores, and notices of team meetings. At other times the papers reported lineups, but detailed match reports were not common, especially in the period after 1910. Although the city has a rich soccer history before 1920, it has been a challenge to uncover just how the game developed in southern Ohio.

As in other places around the country, Cincinnatians played football during the second half of the nineteenth century. In most cases the games were informal and if there was a set of rules guiding the contests, it has not been recorded. Perhaps the most famous football game in the city was the annual match played by alumni of Woodward College. The school shut down in 1851 and four years later a group of former students began meeting annually to reminisce about their younger days and play various childhood games, including football. The reunion happened each year for the next few decades, with the events usually recorded in detail by newspapers. Other football matches took place at picnics linked to the Irish independence movement. A few months after the conclusion of the American Civil War, advertisements for a "Grand Fenian Picnic" appeared in the pages of the *Enquirer*.[1] The aim of the event was to raise money to send rifles and trained soldiers to Ireland. In addition to speeches, the activities included the types of recreations that were common at such events: dancing, quoits, and football. A decade later announcements for similar excursions were sponsored by another Irish Republican organization called the *Clan na Gael*. Although the exact type of football played at these events is unknown, the Irish would continue to feature prominently in the development of soccer in the city.

The first documented soccer game in Cincinnati was not connected to Irish politics but was instead linked to a tragedy. On November 9, 1891, fire broke out at the Oscar Onken Picture Framing factory on West Second Street. According to later reports, a gilder named William Meyers and a boy went to the cellar to do some work. As soon as they reached the bottom of the stairs, flames shot out from among the barrels of alcohol, benzine, and varnish. An explosion rocked the building. The young man bolted up the stairs to safety and, as smoke filled the structure, another sixty or so workers escaped. Meyers was unable to reach the exit and was stuck below. Fire companies quickly arrived and began dousing the flames. One of their ladders broke, sending eight men crashing several stories to the ground. Six were injured and two died, one of them immediately on the scene and the other on the way to the hospital. The blaze was brought under control in just over thirty minutes, and they soon realized that Meyers was still trapped in the basement. Billowing smoke from underground slowed efforts at a rescue. When the air cleared, they found him standing in about four feet of water compulsively splashing it over his blackened skin. He was horribly burned, but he was alive. Meyers was taken to the hospital, where he lived in agony for two days before passing away, leaving a wife and three children. The city organized quickly in reaction to the calamity. Both major newspapers began subscription drives and entertainers organized benefit performances in the weeks that followed. One of these was a Thanksgiving Day soccer match between Keenan's West End and the Queen's City teams. Nothing is known of the two squads, and according to the *Enquirer*, the sport itself was "practically new to the Cincinnati public."[2] The game took place on November 26, 1891, and although no final score was given, the match did contribute $51.25 to the Meyers fund. Overall, fundraising efforts across the city raised at least $1,500, an amount worth nearly $50,000 today.[3]

The earliest permanent soccer club in the city was the Shamrock Football Club, organized by a magistrate court clerk named Dennis J. Ryan in late 1893. Ryan was local, born in Cincinnati in October 1868, but his parents had immigrated from Ireland. Ryan's father came from Castleyons in County Cork and his mother was born in Ballina, Tipperary. Although one newspaper reported that Ryan had "foot-ball fever," he may not have played much of a role with the team after its original founding.[4] One curious feature of soccer in Cincinnati is that until 1919, it was unusual for matches to be played in the spring. All formal competitions began in the autumn, usually October, and were completed by the turn of the new year. The first detailed report on the Shamrocks came in November 1894. The club took on the Caledonian team of Indianapolis, Indiana, on Thanksgiving Day for the self-proclaimed championship of Ohio and Indiana. The match was played on November 29 at East End Ball Park in Cincinnati. The site still exists today as part of the Schmidt Recreation Complex at 2944 Humbert Avenue. The game illustrates another unique aspect to newspaper coverage of the sport in the city. Matches were announced and lineups published, but often the results of the game never appeared in local papers. In the case of the Thanksgiving match versus the Caledonians, no account was published in the Cincinnati media, but the *Indianapolis Journal* reported the visitors won 1–0. The two sides met again on Christmas Day in Indiana, with the Caledonians again taking home the honors by the same score line.

The 1896 Shamrocks team, featuring Thomas Faragher, second row, second from left, and Daniel Faragher, bottom row, third from right. (Source: *Cincinnati Enquirer*, November 29, 1896.)

Dennis Ryan was not on the team sheet for the Shamrocks on Thanksgiving and no lineups were recorded for the second holiday match. Nevertheless, several important players did appear for the Cincinnati squad. The first was defender and team captain John Morrissey. Little is known of Morrissey's background except that he was described as an accomplished athlete and may have been part of a football team prior to the formation of the Shamrocks. He was of Irish descent, although it cannot be determined for certain whether he was born abroad or to immigrant parents in Ohio. He may have worked for the railroad, which could be where he met a group of brothers named Faragher. The family came from County Galway in the far west of Ireland and arrived in the United States in the 1880s. Almost all of the seven brothers had ties to the railroad and at least six of them—Patrick, Anthony, Daniel, Michael, Thomas, and Edward—played soccer. The name Faragher appeared on team sheets for city squads as late as 1902.

Morrissey may have supplemented his regular income with money derived from playing and managing soccer teams. In June 1894 the *Enquirer* reported that he had an undefined offer from New York but would remain in the city if the Shamrocks "desire his services for next season."[5] If they decided affirmatively, he would call off his proposed move to the East Coast. Presumably they agreed to keep him on, as he was again named captain of the team that fall. Later that year the same paper called the Thanksgiving 1894 match the first professional game in the region, although it is doubtful that they meant it in the way we do today. Instead, the newspaper's use of the term "professional" may have implied a certain level of organization that previous soccer matches in the city had lacked. It could also have meant that the players received some minor compensation, perhaps paid out of gate receipts or wagers on the outcome. A few months later, Morrissey advertised that the Shamrocks were seeking a manager. By January 1895 the club had a new gaffer named Sheehan and was preparing for another season of play. In a rare spring contest, the squad travelled to Glouster, Ohio, a small town about 170 miles east of Cincinnati. The match was played in a raging snowstorm on March 16, 1895, and was supposed to be the first of a three-game series for the championship of Ohio, Kentucky, and Indiana. Morrisey and at least one Faragher brother played in the 3–1 defeat. The team continued to practice throughout the spring and fall, yet newspapers did not report on any more matches for the rest of the season.

The following year the Shamrocks played an ill-tempered series of contests against the Unions of Muncie, Indiana. The visitors won the first match in Cincinnati on February 22, 1896. According to the *Muncie Daily Herald,* the Shamrocks played a very physical style designed to intimidate their opponents. The game also featured a great deal of trash talking between the teams. Two months later a few hundred Muncie supporters traveled to Cincinnati on a special train to see their side draw 3–3 with the Shamrocks. Scheduled for a perfect spring day with a sweet breeze coming off the Ohio River, the game almost didn't happen. At first the Shamrocks declined to pay the agreed-upon travel expenses for the visitors, who refused to kick off until the matter was settled. Once that situation was resolved, the game commenced and immediately the Unions felt the referee was unfairly favoring the home side. It is clear why the Muncie team had concerns. The Shamrocks had selected Archibald Jamieson, a twenty-five-year-old originally from Derry in Northern Ireland, to officiate the game. The issue was not with his age or his nationality but the fact that he was a member of the Shamrock Club and had played in the previous fixture between the two sides. Indiana newspapers reported that every decision went against them and that if Jamieson had not wrongly chalked off a Unions goal, they would have won the match. The series continued in November at Muncie, when the Shamrocks took advantage of a weakened home side to secure a 3–1 victory. As if to add insult to injury, Jamieson was in the lineup again and scored the insurance goal. The bubbling tension came to a boil when a November 29, 1896, game ended early after the Unions walked off the field in the second half. With the score 2–1 in their favor, the Shamrocks netted a third, but the visiting players disputed the call. When the referee stuck to his decision, they refused to play on.

Generally, Cincinnati teams held their own against relatively local squads from Indianapolis, Glouster, or Muncie, but they struggled when facing a higher level of competition. In early 1897 the Shamrocks issued a notice to teams in St. Louis declaring that, as champions of Ohio and Indiana, they wished to travel there to face a local side. The challenge was successful, and they were scheduled to face the St. Teresa Football Club on March 27 and 28. The *St. Louis Globe Democrat* hyped up the series, declaring, "The Shamrocks are rated as the equal of any team in the country, and their battles with the St. Teresas should be well worth seeing."[6] A week before the first match, the same newspaper praised the quality of the visitors, noting that some of the Shamrocks had previous success playing abroad. In the opening match, the two teams played to a first half draw before the Shamrock team fell apart in the second half, giving up four goals and scoring none. Local newspapers differed in their evaluation of the club. The *Post-Dispatch* described them as "plucky" and "determined," but the *Globe Democrat* called the team a disappointment, with only three players showing "more than ordinary ability."[7]

A crowd of over 2,500 people witnessed the second game, in which the home team prevailed by the lopsided score of 10–2. The Shamrocks had strengthened their side and even netted the first goal, but the Saints quickly tied it up and soon notched another to make the score a still respectable 2–1 at the half. Once again it all came undone for the visitors in the second half and the Saints ran out easy winners. The St. Louis media was even more critical in 1910, when a Cincinnati team called the Nationals visited to play the St. Teresas. The *Post-Dispatch* headline read "Cincinnati Soccer Men Stick in the Mud" after the visitors lost 10–1 on a waterlogged pitch.[8] The match report was especially contemptuous, noting that if this team was the champion of Ohio, then the level of play there must be on par with that of thirteen- and fourteen-year-olds.

In 1902 and 1903, teams from Cincinnati renewed the interstate rivalry with a Muncie squad now coached by familiar face James Morrissey. A few years later, the Shamrocks, by this time a team made up almost entirely of Scots, faced off against the Five Points side of Muncie. Like soccer communities in other cities, the visit of the English Corinthians squad in 1906 had Cincinnati buzzing. As was the case in places like Minneapolis and Denver, local kickers hoped that the famed visitors would play a match in Porkopolis. Unlike those other locations, Cincinnati was successful in luring them to town. The game was only possible because the Cincinnati Reds and New York Giants baseball teams agreed to cancel a game set for August 27 and instead play a doubleheader on the following day.

As match day approached, the excitement built; the vice mayor promised to welcome the visitors to the city and Reds manager Ned Hanlon recounted his time with the Baltimore squad of the ill-fated American League of Professional Football in 1894. In the end the game was not even close, as the Shamrocks, representing Cincinnati, fell to the Corinthians by the score of 19–0. In fairness, the English side was clearly better than most of its opponents in the United States and only a squad from Fall River, Massachusetts, managed to beat them. Still, the score line of the game was the worst of the entire trip, just edging out the All-New York side, who lost 18–0. Three years later another touring English side called the Pilgrims visited Cincinnati. This time the visitors faced what was dubbed a local all-star side but in truth the players came from just two teams. In some ways the media coverage ahead of the match was greater than before the Corinthians visit as articles appeared daily in newspapers in the week before kickoff. Some of the excitement was because the October 14 match would be the first soccer game in the city played under electric lights. Another interesting feature was that an intercollegiate football game took place immediately after the soccer contest. Unfortunately, most of the crowd, estimated at between 1,500 and 3,000 depending on the newspaper, came for the football and cared little about the soccer. The locals were competitive for the first forty-five minutes and the Pilgrims took a narrow 2–0 lead into the dressing room. After the break the superior skill of the visitors showed, and they galloped to a 9–0 victory. The *Enquirer* praised their talents, calling them "fast as a hare and as slippery as an eel."[9]

In addition to matches against opponents from outside the city, local teams eventually organized competitions within the region. The fall of 1897 saw the formation of the first soccer league in Cincinnati, called the Ohio and Kentucky Football League (OKFL). New clubs had formed over that summer and officials hoped that at least five teams would commence play in early October. One of the new squads was St. Patrick's, which had some familiar names on the team sheet, including a few of the Faragher brothers and James Morrissey. Local middleweight boxer Jim Franey was elected captain. He was a mediocre fighter who had only seventeen professional bouts before he died of injuries suffered in the ring on August 17, 1899. Ultimately, the teams that joined the competition included the Shamrocks, St. Patrick's, Indians, Bellevue Browns of Kentucky, and the Cincinnati Gym.

The Young Men's Gymnastic Association (YMGA), colloquially known as the Gym, formed in 1851. It was part of a broader national movement aimed at counteracting the negative effects of urban living and physical inactivity among middle- and upper-class white men. The YMGA, now known as the Cincinnati Athletic Club, remained segregated until 1977 and still does not allow women to join. The club has had a number of prominent members over the decades, including four US presidents: Rutherford B. Hayes, James A. Garfield, Benjamin Harrison, and William H. Taft. At first, activities focused on individual exercise and gymnastics, but the Gym formed an Athletic Club in 1879. Members began to compete in various sports, including running, walking, and cycling. The decade of the 1890s saw an increased emphasis on team sports, with intercollegiate football soon becoming the most popular. The Gym also formed a soccer team and during the period 1897–1902 were the dominant side in the city. The Gyms just managed to edge out the Shamrocks for the OKFL title in 1897. The two sides finished with five wins each, but the Shamrocks had three losses and the Gyms had two defeats and one draw. The tied match came against the league's weakest side, the Browns, on October 10, 1897. It was a hard-fought contest, and the Browns soon went ahead. On the ensuing kickoff, Gyms forward and captain Charles Iglauer shocked fans and players alike as he struck the ball from the center circle, launching it the length of the field, just off the keeper's fingertips and into the goal.

Charles and his brother Samuel were a key part of the Gym's title winning side. As was often the case in Cincinnati, these prominent early footballers were native sons, with Samuel born in the city in 1871 and Charles in 1875. In addition to being important parts of the soccer community, the Iglauer brothers embodied certain aspects of the Jewish experience in Cincinnati. Although not home to large numbers of Jews, Cincinnati was, according to historian Jonathan D. Sarna, "the oldest and most cultured Jewish community west of the Alleghenies, and had, many thought, a spirit of its own."[10] The first Jewish congregation in the city was founded in 1824, although individuals had been present in Cincinnati for much longer. The middle part of the nineteenth century featured growing immigration from Germany, especially from southern provinces such as Bavaria. Arnold Iglauer, the brothers' father, came from the town of Burgkundstadt in the district of Lichtenfels, northern Bavaria. Although their mother, Delia, was born in Ohio, she was part of the Fechheimer family, who had roots in the municipality of Mitwitz, located about ten miles north of Burgkundstadt. Like many Jewish immigrants the Fechheimer brothers began as itinerant peddlers until Delia's father, Solomon, opened a dry goods store. Eventually, they entered the clothing manufacturing business, supplying uniforms to both armies during the Civil War. By 1860 over 50 percent of Cincinnati's Jews worked in the garment sector and 65 percent of the city's wholesale clothing firms were Jewish owned. Arnold Iglauer worked for the Fechheimer Brothers, eventually becoming president of the company. His son Charles followed him into the business, rising to the position of vice president.

During much of this period Cincinnati's Jewish residents enjoyed good relationships with gentiles and were broadly accepted as members of important business and civic organizations. Such inclusion generally extended to social associations and German cultural activities. Charles began his athletic career playing intercollegiate football for Eden Park and Woodward High School. Another member of a prominent Jewish family made at least one appearance for the Gym's soccer club in the 1897 season. Max Fleischmann's father was famous for developing dry yeast and his brother Julius served as mayor of Cincinnati from 1900 to 1905. Despite general acceptance of Jews as full members of the community, the turn of the twentieth century saw a rise in anti-Semitism. Some organizations, including the Avondale Athletic Club, began to reject Jewish applicants. Nevertheless, Charles Iglauer remained an important figure within the soccer community and the broader sporting world of the Gym into the twentieth century. His brother Samuel, however, left the city around 1900 to study medicine in Vienna, Austria. An ear, nose, and throat specialist, he returned to Cincinnati and became a prominent and beloved part of the city's medical community.

Once again there seemed to be no matches in the spring of 1898 and the OKFL resumed that fall. The league elected new officers and there was genuine optimism that more players had taken up the game. The St. Patrick's team dissolved but the competition hoped to continue with four clubs: Gyms, Shamrocks, Browns, and Indians. The scattered nature of newspaper coverage makes it hard to tell exactly what happened over the course of the season. The league opener on October 9 featured the Shamrocks versus the Gyms. Tom Faragher had returned to the Shamrock lineup and formed a good partnership with fellow midfielder Tom Anderson. Presumably a slight man given his nicknames of "Dumpling" and "Midget," Anderson had reportedly played for the Wolverhampton Wanderers. The match ended up being a tight and slightly nervy affair that featured a Gyms missed penalty and a 4–4 score at the half. The Shamrocks just edged the second half to take the victory 6–5 with Tom Faragher assisting on the game winner. The same teams played to a 2–2 draw a few weeks later before what was described as the largest crowd in the history of the East End grounds. After a seemingly exciting start, the season quickly fizzled out. By November the Gyms and the Shamrocks were not facing league teams but instead were matched up against picked sides made up of various local players. The two clubs agreed to meet for the city title, but the results of this series went unreported. The situation remained much the same over the next three seasons, with the Shamrocks and the Gyms playing select teams and challenging each other for the city championship.

The formation of a team called the National Association Football Club in 1902 injected new life into the Cincinnati soccer community. The origins of the Nationals are not known, but they may have been linked to a baseball team of the same name. Soccer clubs sometimes emerged out of existing sporting clubs, such as baseball, cricket, and cycling, in part to provide members exercise and competition during the offseason. Within the next few years, the Nationals and the Shamrocks overtook the Gyms as the leading teams in the area. Other clubs also formed, including the Burns, Thistle, and Caledonians. Around this time, soccer matches began to be played as part of doubleheaders with intercollegiate football games also on the bill. The notion of having the two sports play on the same day, before the same crowd, was not common in other locations. The 1907 season featured something new for the region: a silver cup to be awarded to the winning side.

The trophy was donated and named for Theodore M. Foucar, a well-known sportsman and bar owner. Foucar's Café had several locations over the years but the last at 429 Walnut Street was the most luxurious. Patrons entered through a heavy wrought-iron and plate-glass doorway flanked by marble columns. Electric bulbs surrounded the opening to spell out the name of the establishment in lights. The interior featured decorations and fixtures of mahogany, glass, onyx, bronze, and various artworks. Foucar was something of a collector and owned pieces by well-known local artists such as Henry Sharpe and Henry Farny. The most notable work, placed above the bar at the center of the space, was a large pastel drawing called *Siesta* that featured a nude woman reclining on a bed. Her crossed legs and carefully placed arms preserved some modesty. The image was the work of Frank Duvenek, a local painter born in 1848 just across the Ohio river from Cincinnati in Covington, Kentucky. He began his career as an apprentice church decorator but moved to Munich, Germany, when he was twenty-two. Duvenek joined what was known as the Munich School, a genre of painting that favored a naturalistic style along with strong contrasts between light and dark. Art historian Mahonri Sharp Young called Duvenek "a bluff and hearty, no-nonsense man, a bit of a bully boy himself and every bit a man's man."[11] Upon his return to Cincinnati following the death of his wife, Duvenek withdrew from the wider art world and concentrated on working and teaching locally. He was a regular at Foucar's Café and would have felt comfortable in its atmosphere of masculine socializing and deal making. Theodore Foucar held on to *Siesta* after the

Frank Duvenek's pastel drawing *Siesta* hung over the main bar at Foucar's Café. (Courtesy of Cincinnati Museum of Art.)

closing of the bar and donated it to the Cincinnati Art Museum shortly after Duvenek's death in 1919.

The winner of the inaugural edition of the Foucar Cup was the Thistle squad. Foucar remained honorary president of the local competition in 1908 but inconsistent newspaper coverage again makes it difficult to know the results. The league continued over the next few years, with some teams joining and others dropping out. One of the most unusual squads was composed of Cincinnati police officers and was coached by an immigrant from Belgium. Perhaps the most important event of this period, apart from the visit of the Pilgrims, was the formation of a public-school soccer league. The driving force of the effort was longtime player and administrator Archibald Jamieson. Over the next few seasons, the schoolboy league developed a cadre of players who appreciated and enjoyed the game. By 1916, it was clear that these young men had no way to continue playing the sport because the high schools generally favored intercollegiate football. City park officials limited the number of places where gridiron football could be played but all facilities were open to soccer. As a result of these factors, a city-wide soccer league for adults emerged, with many of the clubs named for their old school associations. One of the most dominant squads in both the child and adult leagues was the Fourth Intermediate School. Over time some of these sides moved away from their schoolboy origins. The Sand School team for example, changed its name to the Buckeye Soccer Club. Eventually, works teams joined, including the Feather Valve Rangers, named for a product manufactured at the Laidlow Works, and another squad that was linked to the Procter & Gamble Company. The league eventually grew to include two divisions, with the winner of the senior circuit taking home a silver cup donated by Archie Jamieson.

Perhaps because many of the players grew up in Cincinnati, World War I did not prove as devastating to the sport as it did in other locations. By and large soccer officials in Cincinnati did not face the same challenges as in other regions after players enlisted and teams and competitions folded. In fact, John Ramsey, writing in *Spalding's Official Soccer Foot Ball Guide,* described the 1918–19 season as the most successful in history. Nevertheless, the city was not unaffected by the conflict and Ramsey also noted that it had been "one of the most trying years that athletics in this section has ever experienced."[12] Perhaps because it saw less disruption during the war, the Cincinnati soccer league continued being a small but active part of the city's sporting culture into the 1920s.

Notes

1. "Soldiers! And Rifles! For Ireland!" *Cincinnati Enquirer*, August 14, 1865.
2. "Football Benefit," *Cincinnati Post*, November 20, 1891.
3. MeasuringWorth.com.
4. "Seized the Scenery," *Cincinnati Enquirer*, December 7, 1893.
5. "Sporting Gossip," *Cincinnati Inquirer*, June 25, 1894.
6. "Racing Property to Be Sold," *St. Louis Globe Democrat*, March 19, 1897.
7. "St. Louis Takes First Game," *St. Louis Post Dispatch*, March 28, 1897; "St. Teresas' Easy Victory," *St. Louis Globe-Democrat*, March 28, 1897.
8. "Cincinnati Soccer Men Stick in Mud," *St. Louis Post-Dispatch*, January 3, 1910.
9. "Outclassed," *Cincinnati Enquirer*, October 15, 1909.
10. Sarna, "The Lofty Vision," 58.
11. Young, "The Two Worlds," 99.
12. Ramsey, "Soccer in Cincinnati," 117.

Sources

Bolsmann, Chris, and Dilwyn Porter. *English Gentlemen and World Soccer: Corinthians, Amateurism and the Global Game*. New York: Routledge, 2018.

Bunk, Brian D. *From Football to Soccer: The Early History of the Beautiful Games in the United States*. Champaign-Urbana: University of Illinois Press, 2021.

Cincinnati: A Guide to the Queen City and Its Neighbors. Cincinnati: Wiesen-Hart Press, 1943.

Dembo, Jonathan. *The History of the Cincinnati Athletic Club, 1853–1976*. Cincinnati: Cincinnati Historical Society and Cincinnati Athletic Club, 1995.

Fechheimer. "About Us." Accessed July 11, 2022. https://www.fechheimer.com/.

Hopson, Laura A. "Cincinnati Athletic Club: From 1853 to the Present." June 25, 2016. *AEQAI*. https://aeqai.com/main/2016/06/cincinnati-athletic-club-from-1853-to-the-present./

Ramsey, John. "Soccer in Cincinnati." In *Spalding's Official Soccer Football Guide,* edited by Thomas W. Cahill, 117. New York: American Sports Publishing Company, 1920.

Sarna, Jonathan D. "The Lofty Vision of Cincinnati Jews." In *Coming to Terms with America. Essay on Jewish History, Religion, and Culture,* 58–85. Lincoln: University of Nebraska Press, The Jewish Publication Society, 2021.

Stephen, Sarah. *Cincinnati's Brewing History*. Charleston, SC: Arcadia Publishing, 2010.

Whiteman, Maxwell. "Dry Goods, and Clothing: An Introduction to the Study of the Cincinnati Peddler." *Jewish Quarterly Review* 53, no. 4 (April, 1963): 306–321.

Young, Mahonri Sharp. "The Two Worlds of Frank Duveneck." *American Art Journal* 1, no. 1 (Spring, 1969): 92–103.

NEWSPAPERS

Cincinnati Enquirer
Cincinnati Post
Indianapolis Journal
Muncie Daily Herald
St. Louis Globe-Democrat
St. Louis Post Dispatch

WEBSITES

Ancestry.com
MeasuringWorth.com

7

Crossing Borders in Detroit

Detroit, Michigan

Hiram Walker was born in Massachusetts but made his fortune in Detroit. The family traced their lineage back to 1661, when his great-great-grandfather ran a school and later a tavern in Boston. Walker moved to the Midwest in 1838 because, like many New Englanders at the time, he felt the western region offered more opportunity. Working as a grocery clerk, he saved his pennies until he could buy a share in a tanning and leather business. Eventually, he opened a grocery store and obtained a liquor license in 1847. Within two years the firm was advertising the production of five hundred barrels of whisky per year. A stringent liquor law passed by the state legislature in 1855 spelled an end to the business and Walker again changed professions, becoming a grain merchant. Perhaps because of the prohibition on alcohol in Michigan, he began to look for economic opportunities across the border in Canada.

By 1856 he purchased his first properties, mostly agricultural and pastoral lands, near the city of Windsor, Ontario. Two years later he constructed a flour mill and a distillery and in 1859 moved his main residence to Canada, settling into a house known as The Cottage. Even after he returned to live in the United States four years later, Walker kept expanding his Canadian holdings. By 1869, the settlement of Walkerville had been founded and in 1890 it was incorporated as a town. In that same year, the whiskey business, now known as Hiram Walker and Sons Ltd., was capitalized at $5 million, roughly $154 million today.[1] The year 1890 proved important in other ways as well because the first soccer club in Detroit formed. Five years later Walker and Sons donated a cup to be played for by soccer teams in an international competition called the Peninsular Association Football League. The activities of Hiram Walker and his business anticipated the nature of soccer in Detroit. The sport had its highs and lows and throughout its early history maintained a distinct international character, with teams and competitions regularly crossing the border between the United States and Canada.

In the beginning football in Detroit was a loosely organized, rough and tumble version of the game mainly played as informal matches on holidays or by ethnic societies and other groups at summer picnics. Perhaps the earliest documented notice of such games came in the 1830s, when prominent Detroit merchants gathered to play on Saturday afternoons. By the 1870s and early 1880s, high schools, colleges, and independent clubs played a type of football that either followed the rugby rules or the version derived from them known as the intercollegiate game. The Detroit Association Foot Ball Club became the first documented soccer team in the city when it organized in September 1890. Throughout this era, soccer in Detroit remained underdeveloped and until the late 1890s there was only one major team in the city.

Although participants came and went, a few key figures, including Archibald W. Stewart and Frank E. Corbett, generally remained involved as players and managers throughout most of the early period. Stewart was born in 1866 in Linlithgow, Scotland, to a Scottish father and a Swiss mother. When he wasn't playing soccer, Stewart worked as an architect. Corbett was the same age as Stewart and arrived in the United States from his native Canada in 1887. Corbett's main occupation was a mechanic, but he was heavily involved in Detroit athletics. In addition to playing and later coaching soccer, Corbett served as secretary of the Michigan Athletic Association (MAA). As in some other locations, many of the soccer pioneers were Scots but others came from the United States, Canada, and Poland. The *Detroit Free Press* covered major games and at times tried to generate broader support for the sport, but it never really blossomed. Incomplete and inconsistent coverage make it difficult to accurately reconstruct the sport's history in the city. Nevertheless, the development of soccer in Detroit followed a similar path as other cities: it emerged around 1890, received some media attention, and grew steadily if not spectacularly over the next decade before tailing off as teams disappeared and competitions withered.

The influence of Scottish players on Detroit AFC is clear given many of the surnames on the first team sheet: Fleming, McEwan, Wilkie, McKay, Stewart, and Young. Stewart, who initially played as a center forward, was described by one newspaper as "an old Glasgow player."[2] The article singled him out for his excellent play in the team's first match, a 1–1 draw against a squad from Windsor, Canada, on September 20, 1890. It was an auspicious beginning for the newly formed club and marked the start of a long and sometimes contentious soccer rivalry between the two cities. After being reinforced by more Scots, including three McKendrick brothers and Duncan McMillan, the club won the Western Football Association (WFA) fall challenge cup series against Chatham, Windsor, and Essex. About a year after its founding, the press featured an extensive profile of the team along with an article on the history of soccer in the United States. The profiles of the players confirmed their immigrant origins, as nine of the regular eleven had been born in Scotland while the remaining two were from Canada.

In late summer 1891, Detroit took home the Michigan state championship along with eleven gold medals after beating Almont 4–0. Success buoyed the club, and they were confident of fielding a strong team as part the WFA fall schedule. The competition featured an all-Canadian lineup apart from the boys from Detroit. The club picked up where it left off the previous season, winning their opener 6–0 over Chatham. By the end of October, the US team had claimed the title following back-to-back wins over Preston, outscoring the Canadian side by a total of 8–0. The following month they lined up against the formidable Toronto Scots for the Championship of Canada. On a cold and blustery Halloween day, the Detroiters won the first leg 2–0, with Duncan McPherson scoring the opener on a rocket from thirty yards out. A week later the two teams met again in Toronto, with the home side wearing black and red and the visitors dressed in blue. The crowd of around one thousand supporters cheered their squad to a 1–0 win, but Detroit still captured the honors on aggregate. A few weeks later, Detroit faced off against a select squad of players drawn from WFA teams. The fast-paced match featured plenty of physical play, including a collision that resulted in the WFA team's goalkeeper being knocked unconscious. He was carried from the field, and it took ten minutes to revive him. The injury undoubtedly influenced the final score line as Detroit ran out easy 4–0 winners.

According to the *Detroit Free Press,* soccer was growing in popularity, but college-educated young men still refused to give it a chance. "For one reason or another there exists among the local athletic clubs a great deal of contempt for foot ball as played under the association rules." Many viewed the game as unscientific or a pastime solely for children. The author of the story acknowledged the difficulty in convincing "enemies of the Scotch game" to give soccer a chance and argued that the sport was a challenging and graceful one that had eliminated the "cultivated brute force" of rugby and intercollegiate football.[3] The notice included information on soccer's popularity overseas, a fact that had been cited since the sport first began to be played in the city. Efforts to expand soccer's reach outside of its core fanbase generally were not very successful. Almost six years after asking sports enthusiasts to give soccer a chance, the *Detroit Free Press* again felt the need to educate readers on the basic rules of association football, including the fact that a team won by scoring more goals than their opponents. The paper also testified to the attractions of the sport: "The long kicking, swift running, quick passing, dodging and hard body checking make the game very pretty and exciting."[4]

The newspaper claimed that association football had been introduced to the United States "some twenty years ago" by Scottish immigrants who had previously settled in Canada.[5] It named Fall River, Massachusetts, as the center of play in the United States, reporting that matches in the city attracted crowds of four to five thousand people. The article noted that leagues and cup competitions had emerged in other cities and that there was talk about forming a national championship series. Detroit's squad had already played at least one match with a team from outside its local area, defeating the visiting Chicago Thistles 2–1 on September 17, 1891. Such intercity clashes were not uncommon, although they usually took place only on special occasions and holidays. No interregional leagues of sustained competition developed even though soccer clubs had been founded in a number of nearby cities including Chicago, Cleveland, and Pittsburgh. One reason for this might be that visiting teams often required large guarantees to offset the cost of travel and lodging. Teams scheduled games on holidays because to break even, they needed to ensure that crowds could attend, otherwise intercity matchups were simply not financially viable.

One newspaper article provided insight into how these contests were organized and how expensive they could be. When a Chicago club visited Detroit in 1896, they demanded that local organizers wire them $110 for train tickets. The promoters "raised the amount after a great deal of effort" but ultimately lost a large sum of money on the contest.[6] The fact that it took quite a bit of work to come up with the travel expenses reveals just how thin the margins of profitability were for these organizations. Generally, tickets to games cost just twenty-five cents, later slashed to ten, and women were admitted for free. Sometimes the price for children was also reduced by half. In addition to transportation costs, the promoters had to rent the ground, advertise, and pay expenses for match officials and security. If the game day weather was poor or the match failed to attract a crowd, the association could very easily lose money. It may also have been difficult for most players to take several days off work to make such trips. Despite the challenges there was an attempt to organize an intercity association that would have included teams from Chicago, Detroit, Cleveland,

Cincinnati, Pittsburgh, and St. Louis. The impetus for the organization came from John C. Myers, president of the Western Football League of St. Louis, who also donated a cup for the winner. The competition would not be set up as a regular league but instead would have the winners of each district meet using a challenge cup format. Despite such reports, the association never got off the ground.

By 1892 Detroit AFC had become linked with the Michigan Athletic Association (MAA) and changed its name to reflect the new affiliation. The MAA club continued to play in the largely Canadian WFA but were soon involved in a dispute. After winning the spring western district championship, the team was scheduled to meet Galt for the WFA title. The first match took place on June 4, 1892, and resulted in 1–0 win for the Canadians. It was an entertaining game, with the only score coming as a result of a mix-up between the MAA goalkeeper and his defense. A week later Detroit triumphed by the same score line and the two squads were now tied. Competition rules stated that two fifteen-minute halves would decide the contest, and the referee soon called for extra time to kick off. Galt, however, refused to play, insisting that the tie be settled at a neutral ground. MAA lined up anyway, kicked the ball into the goal, and claimed the victory. Despite the result, the two sides met again at Essex on June 18. Galt dominated the first half and led 2–0 at the break. Shortly after the restart, Detroit netted two quick goals to draw level and the game remained tied after ninety minutes. MAA claimed the title on aggregate, thanks to the uncontested goal scored when Galt refused to line up for extra time.

A few months later, a similar argument erupted after a protested match was awarded to Essex. During the disputed game, the Detroit squad felt the referee had missed a foul in the buildup to an Essex goal. One newspaper report alleged that after MAA players surrounded the referee, one of them kicked him, and then the team left the field and refused to continue the match. The *Toronto Daily Mail* offered a slightly different version of events, with the referee stating that after the ball was knocked from his arm, he kicked the MAA player and one of the victim's teammates retaliated by kicking the official. MAA directors refused to give up the trophy, saying, "It will take a lawsuit before we let it go."[7] Eventually, they agreed to abide by the ruling, giving the match victory to Essex, but argued that they had won the tie on aggregate and should be allowed to compete for the WFA cup. The Association disagreed and after beating Essex in the final, Preston were champions.

During the earliest period of Detroit soccer, few teams seem to have been founded in the city itself. In the spring of 1895, however, the *Detroit Free Press* reported the formation of the Peninsular Association Football

League (PAFL). The competition planned to have six clubs, three from the United States and three from Canada. The announced teams included old stalwarts MAA along with two new squads from Detroit—Caledonians and Diamonds. A good number of Scots turned out for the Diamonds, but despite the claims made in the article, the Caledonians never organized. The Canadian entries came from Windsor, Walkerville, and Essex. The structure of play was that each team would face the others home and away during a spring and a fall season and that teams would be awarded two points for a win and one for a draw. In a savvy move, the organization deliberately scheduled matches during the spring season for dates that would not conflict with baseball games.

The players would not be paid and the McKendrick brothers, who had briefly left the city in 1894 to play for Baltimore in the American League of Professional Football, had their amateur status restored. Two years later, Chatham protested that Windsor had fielded a pro in a league match. Although an investigation into the matter failed to reach a conclusion, the club agreed to sit the player in the next match in case he later proved to be ineligible. These incidents reveal that despite the amateur nature of the league, at least some players received compensation for playing and could be considered professionals. Without more documentation it is hard to know how widespread the practice was, but it may explain the movement of players from one local team to another. Two players from Windsor moved to MAA in the summer of 1895, reportedly because they were offered free memberships in the athletic club. During the following season, center forward James Clennan, who had also played for Windsor, joined rivals MAA.

The formation of the PAFL was expected to help develop the game in Detroit, and this time soccer was going to be given "a thorough trial" because the establishment of new teams meant the league would be more challenging.[8] The name of the Caledonians and the presence of well-known local players including the McKendrick brothers on the Diamonds roster showed that the sport retained its Scottish flavor. The competition got off to a fine start and league earnings were solid. The figures were positive enough that the organization decided to purchase a trophy to be given to a new junior league formed in order to grow the game.

The league proved competitive and featured an exciting race in its inaugural campaign. A few games into the season, Windsor and Detroit renewed their rivalry, now possibly heightened by the defection of two players from the Canadian side to MAA. On a blazing hot day in early June, the two sides took to the field, with MAA dressed in white jerseys with a black sash. The first half was quite even, but Windsor dominated the second forty-five minutes. For much of the time, Detroit was hemmed into their own end, and Windsor's keeper watched the action from the halfway line. In the end the Canadians took home the honors 1–0 and went top of the table. MAA remained third, two points behind the leader, but with a game in hand. By the end of the month, the team from Detroit had made up the deficit and clinched the title with a 2–0 win over Essex on June 22. The success was built on a stingy defense, and they won the championship even though their forward line scored only six goals in five games.

The same clubs returned for the fall 1895 season, and they now battled for the Walker Cup, donated by the makers of Canadian Club whiskey. The *Windsor Star* described the Walker Cup as a "massive silver urn mounted on a large ebony pedestal."[9] One side of the jug featured an etching of a soccer game in progress while the other had space for an inscription. A soccer player with a ball at his feet topped the prize. Once again Windsor took an early lead in the standings but could not hold on as Essex captured the crown after a 2–1 win over MAA on November 28. The *Windsor Star* was gracious in defeat, acknowledging that Essex were deserving winners, calling them "an aggregation of pure grit leather hustlers."[10]

Although still very much a league filled with Scots and Canadians, the MAA did field two Polish-born players during the PAFL's fall season. Poles began to arrive in the city in the 1880s and by 1904, the community numbered at least thirteen thousand. Just over twenty years later, the population had grown to nearly one hundred and fifteen thousand. One of MAA's new recruits was twenty-one-year-old Aleksander J. Grudzinski, who arrived in the United States from Poland in 1891. He graduated from the Polish seminary and by 1918 had been appointed pastor of St. Casimir's Catholic Church. Founded in 1882, the parish was the first Polish congregation established in Detroit's West Side neighborhood. The church's grand basilica was modelled after St. Peter's in Rome and featured two square towers at the front with a large central dome. It was completed in 1890, just a year before Grudzinski's arrival in the city. Later he was assigned to lead the St. Francis D'Assisi parish. The congregation's large church at 4500 Wesson Avenue could seat 1,700 worshippers but was struggling under heavy debt when Father Grudzinski took over in 1919. Thanks in large part to his unceasing efforts, the parish was debt-free in less than a decade.

Despite the promising start to the PAFL, the organization of the game in Detroit entered a period of instability. MAA dominated the league in spring 1896, sweeping both Windsor and Essex while scoring eleven goals and giving up just two. By the fall of 1896, there were three organized teams in Detroit—MAA, Detroit College of Medicine, and St. Mary's College—but a newspaper article declared that interest in the sport was not as great has it had been in previous years. The MAA club had been reorganized and hoped to schedule matches against some of the leading teams not only from the region, but from places farther afield like Toronto, Cincinnati, Chicago, and St. Louis. The Thistle team from Chicago came to Detroit on November 26 to meet the championship MAA squad. Despite claims by the *Detroit Free Press* of waning interest in the sport, 1,500 people came out to see the two sides lock horns. Old heads A. W. Stewart and Fred Corbett were in the team, and the former even scored a goal in the first half. Although the home side led by three at the break, they were unable to hold on and Thistle managed a 6–6 draw after their poor start. Meanwhile, many of the players from the MAA club decided to break from the association and reform the old Detroit AFC squad. The team took the place of MAA in the PAFL, although that competition was little more than a three-game series between Windsor and Detroit. The Motor City squad again took home the honors, winning two out of the three matches.

By the spring of 1897, the *Detroit Free Press* reported that clubs from the city had founded a league consisting of five teams: Detroit College of Medicine, MAA, Tribune Team, West Ends, and Rouge. Despite the notice, it does not appear that any league games were played, and the only match reports linked to any of these clubs came from friendlies or exhibition games. Windsor finally captured the Walker Cup in the spring 1897 season, beating out Detroit, Essex, and Chatham. The *Windsor Star* was ecstatic, celebrating a 4–0 win over Detroit with a long story led by the headline "They Did Rub It In." According to the article, years of mostly ending up on the losing side of games versus Detroit made the victory all the better: "If revenge is sweet the members of the Windsor football team will not take sugar in their tea for a month."[11] They clinched the title after Chatham refused to play the final match, and the paper's headline read simply, "It's All Ours."[12]

In the fall of 1897, Detroit AFC disbanded because many of the players had reportedly left town. As a result, the city had no representative in the Peninsular League and only Canadian clubs fought for the trophy. Overall soccer activity in the city had diminished and the *Detroit Free Press* wrote that there was "a dearth of association football games in the city this fall."[13] In 1898, however, soccer activity in the city increased dramatically. First, in April the Columbia Association Football Club formed and its list of officers contained many names that had been active in previous clubs. The announcement noted that the team planned to represent the city in the Peninsular League. Despite the notice there is no evidence that the club played a game, and by August the newspaper was reporting that another attempt was being made to launch a soccer team in the city. Within a few weeks, the St. Andrew's Society announced their intention to organize, and two days later so did the Canadian American Club. The St. Andrew team's lineup included several veteran players, many of whom had been a part of the earliest Detroit AFC squads, including Stewart, McKendrick, Henderson, and Ramsey. Both teams declared their intentions to join the Peninsular League and compete for the Walker Cup.

After not having a representative in the competition in the year prior, Detroit began the 1898 fall season with three clubs in the PAFL: St. Andrews, the Canadian American Club, and Detroit Medical College. The league's winning team, nicknamed the Medics, came from Detroit's med school, although ten out of the eleven players had been born in Canada. Many of them, including Jack Gibson, Archibald Coutts, and P. H. Wilson, had previously played for some of the PAFL's Canadian clubs. Halfback Gibson had even served as captain for the Windsor team in the spring of 1898. Once again, a Detroit side broke Windsor fans' hearts as the title was settled when the Medics beat the previously undefeated Canadian club

The Detroit College of Medicine Team, Walker Cup champions, fall 1897. (Source: *Souvenir Annual*, Detroit College of Medicine, 1900.)

1–0 on November 5. Despite its success the medical college team declined to compete in the spring season and, apart from some friendly matches, seems to have disbanded.

It was not apparent at the time, but the Medics would be the last team from Detroit to capture the PAFL title. Motor City teams, including St. Andrews and the Canadian-Americans, or Can-Ams, as they were known, entered in 1899 but were generally unsuccessful. In March 1900 Detroit AFC announced the election of new officers, with A. W. Stewart chosen as president and manager. That spring the team competed for the Walker Cup against Windsor, Walkerville, Glencoe, Ridgetown, and eventual winners Chatham. By March, the club announced that it was going to travel to St. Louis for a two-match weekend series against the Cycling Club and West Ends. Although representing the Motor City, the travelling side was really a select or all-star team featuring players from Detroit, Windsor, Berlin, and Clinton. The captain was A. W. Stewart, who also played in goal. The St. Louis media praised the visitors and Stewart in particular, calling him "the best goal keeper in this country and Canada."[14] The *St. Louis Post-Dispatch* published a brief biography of him (no other players got such treatment), noting that although he had played every position, he was most comfortable between the posts, "where his coolness and judgement have met with success."[15] One wonders if it was Stewart himself who provided the information to the local newspapers. Even though Detroit was on the losing end of a lopsided 5–1 score line in the first match against Cycling Club, the paper still found time to praise Stewart, claiming that he had a good game despite letting in a handful of goals. The praise vanished abruptly after the second game finished 6–1 in favor of the home side. The *St. Louis Globe* called out Stewart for a poor performance and the *St. Louis Republic* judged the team "a faint-hearted lot of athletes." The *Post-Dispatch* did not single out the keeper but speculated that "perhaps it was the high living at the St. James Hotel" that contributed to Detroit's lackluster play.[16]

It was at the St. James Hotel where the trip went from a disappointing pair of losses for the visiting team to something even stranger. Troubling reports began to surface even before the team arrived in the city. According to one account, St. Louis soccer officials provided Stewart with train tickets for twelve players, but the manager sold one of them and brought an eleven-man squad instead. Perhaps the rest of the Detroit team heard of this because they became concerned even as they were headed to Missouri for the games. In addition to transportation costs, the travelling party was due ninety dollars for expenses. Eventually, the Detroit players requested that the local committee not pay this money to Stewart, as had been planned, but to instead give the funds to another player chosen by the team. Stewart had already asked for and received twenty dollars, but the rest of the money was given out to the designated representative.

After the weekend series had concluded, the Detroit squad gathered at Union Station on Monday evening for the trip home. Stewart never showed up with the return tickets. Infuriated, the team set out along with three delegates of the St. Louis Football Association to find the missing manager. They soon located him at another hotel near the St. James. Local association president R. M. Gillespie met privately with Stewart and asked him to give up the tickets. The Detroit man refused unless Gillespie handed over $12.50. Before things could be resolved, Stewart suddenly bolted for the door and ran down the street. President Gillespie gave chase but soon lost sight of him. The angry players organized search parties, vowing to bring Stewart back "dead or alive."[17] It was after midnight when Stewart placed a call to the St. James Hotel and spoke briefly with Gillespie. Other members of the party were able to trace the call, but Stewart had gone by the time they arrived at the location. At some point, the Detroit manager contacted a local lawyer and, with the attorney in tow, he now demanded twenty dollars for the train tickets. When the group refused his offer, Stewart drew a pistol and threatened to shoot them all. The players withdrew and although they resumed the search, they were unable to locate him before dawn. The train company invalidated the tickets still held by Stewart and provided the Detroit players with new ones at no cost. Finally, they could return home.

As might be expected, Stewart himself had a different version of events. He stated that the group's expenses were greater than anticipated and that he paid for some things out of his own pocket. When he requested the money from local officials, they told him that it had already been given to another player. He was angry about this and became even more upset when he discovered that his hotel bill had not been paid by the person who had received the funds. For these reasons he decided to keep the train tickets until he was reimbursed. Stewart claimed the other players threatened to take the tickets by force and he felt surrounded. In response, he drew his hotel key and shouted, "Stand back or I will kill you."[18] He denied that he had a revolver. Eventually, Stewart tried to leave town, but the train company refused to allow him to board. He vowed to stay in St. Louis and use the courts to get the money he felt that he was owed.

When news of the incident reached Windsor, one newspaper observed, perhaps a bit late, that Stewart had a poor reputation among local players. Less than a week later, Detroit AFC fired him as manager of the club. Surprisingly, the incident was not the first time that Stewart had been suspected of financial mismanagement. In 1894, he had been captain and de facto manager of the Baltimore squad of the American League of Professional Football. After the organization shut down, the English players brought in by the club complained that they had not been paid at all during the brief season. After reportedly wandering the city penniless, the baseball team eventually bought them tickets, the cheapest available, to return home. It is difficult to know how common such incidents were, but they did occur elsewhere. Perhaps the highest-profile case of the era came in 1921, when James Scholefield disappeared with $1,200 from the treasury of the United States Football Association, now known as US Soccer. Born in England, Scholefield came to the United States around 1911 and was prominent in state associations in New England. He was described as one of the best and most experienced referees in the country. He was located a few years later in South Carolina. In an interview with the *Columbia Record,* Scholefield claimed that he had fallen in with "fast company" in New York City and blacked out, eventually finding himself in Rhode Island.[19] He made his way south, raising money for religious organizations such as the Salvation Army and Red Cross. He settled in Greensboro, South Carolina, where he got married and worked as an accountant for an automobile firm. No charges were filed for embezzlement, but he did spend time in jail for bigamy.

It is unclear what happened to Stewart after the debacle in St. Louis. Did he return to Michigan or stay in Missouri? The next confirmed trace of him comes with his marriage in New Orleans, Louisiana, to Jessie McLeod on June 2, 1902. Someone named A. W. Stewart had arrived in the city from St. Louis on December 6, 1900, but it is not known for certain that this was the same man. The bride had been born and raised in the Big Easy and, except for a brief time in Florida, the couple spent the rest of their lives in Louisiana. Stewart continued to play soccer and was involved in efforts to create a league in New Orleans. After many years of inactivity, the soccer community in the city began organizing matches again in 1906. Stewart turned out for the Young Men's Gymnastic Club (YMGC) team, lining up in his familiar spot in goal. His—perhaps self-reported—reputation as a player followed him and his photograph appeared in the *New Orleans Item* on October 17, 1907. The caption noted that he had managed the successful Baltimore side in 1894 and claimed that he had been part of an all-American squad that defeated Canada in 1892. The latter match was either Detroit's victory over Toronto Scots from 1891 or when MAA captured the fall 1892 WFA title. A few weeks later, a newspaper announced the formation of the New Orleans Soccer Football League. It planned to begin play the following month, with up to six teams competing for the honors. Ironically, the organization selected Stewart to serve as secretary and treasurer! Ultimately, four teams contested the title, including Stewart's new team, St. Andrews, who finished third. A. W. Stewart died in 1944 and Jessie in 1953; they had two children. The farcical incident in St. Louis is perhaps a fitting end to the early history of soccer in Detroit. The city had no representative in the PAFL for the 1901, 1902, and 1903 seasons. Plans were made for a club to participate in spring 1904, but they had difficulties organizing. It appears that they played only one match and, appropriately enough, it was a 0–0 draw with old rivals Windsor.

Notes

1. MeasuringWorth.com.
2. "Foot Ball," *Detroit Free Press*, September 22, 1890.
3. Cooke, "Cornell Wins the Third," *Detroit Free Press*, November 22, 1891.
4. "Association Football," *Detroit Free Press*, May 16, 1896.
5. "Association Football," *Detroit Free Press*, November 22, 1891.
6. "Association Football," *Detroit Free Press*, December 2, 1898.
7. "Football," *Toronto Daily Mail*, October 19, 1892.
8. "Sporting Topics," *Detroit Free Press*, April 14, 1895.
9. "Sporting News," *Windsor Star*, September 20, 1895.
10. "We're Out of It," *Windsor Star*, November 29, 1895.
11. "They Did Rub It In," *Windsor Star*, June 5, 1897.
12. "It's All Ours," *Windsor Star*, June 28, 1897.
13. "Association Football," *Detroit Free Press*, November 26, 1897.
14. "Detroit's Best Team," *St. Louis Post-Dispatch*, March 22, 1900.
15. "Now the Ball Opens," *St. Louis Post-Dispatch*, March 25, 1900.
16. "Wolverines Flew the White Flag," *St. Louis Republic*, March 26, 1900; "Detroit's Football Players," *St. Louis Post-Dispatch*, March 26, 1900.
17. "A Missing Manager," *St. Louis Post-Dispatch*, March 27, 1900.
18. "Football Players Depart," *St. Louis Republic*, March 28, 1900.
19. "Bigamy Is Laid to Religious Worker," *Columbia Record*, March 27, 1924.

Sources

Brown, Paul. "Football Hustlers: The Doomed Attempt to Establish a Football League in the USA in the 19th Century." *The Blizzard*, no. 22 (September 2016).

Chauvin, Francis X. *Hiram Walker: His Life and His Work and the Development of the Walker Institutions in Walkerville, Ontario*. (1927). SWODA:Windsor and Region Publications, 12. https://scholar.uwindsor.ca/swoda-windsor-region/12.

Crawford, Scott. *A History of Soccer in Louisiana: 1858–2013*. N.p., LAPrepsoccer, 2013.

Farmer, Silas. *The History of Detroit and Michigan*. Detroit: S. Farmer Co., 1884.

"History of St. Francis D'Assisi Parish." *St. Francis D'Assisi Catholic Church*. Accessed October 29, 2022. http://stfrancis-sthedwig.org/StFrancis/History.htm.

"St. Casimir's Catholic Church (old)." *HistoricDetroit.org*. Accessed October 23, 2022. https://historicdetroit.org/buildings/st-casimir-s-catholic-church-old.

"St. Casimir Roman Catholic Church." *West Side Detroit Polish American Historical Society*. July 16, 2017. https://www.detroitpolonia.org/st-casimir-roman-catholic-church/.

NEWSPAPERS

Chatham Free Press
Chicago Tribune
Columbia Record
Detroit Free Press
The Inter Ocean (Chicago)
New Orleans Item
St. Louis Globe-Democrat
St. Louis Post-Dispatch
St. Louis Republic
Times-Picayune (New Orleans)
Toronto Daily Mail
Windsor Evening Record
Windsor Star

WEBSITES

Ancestry.com

8

The McKendrick Brothers: Scottish Professionals in the Motor City

Detroit, Michigan

The town of Greenock sits on the banks of the Clyde River in the west central lowlands of Scotland. The settlement initially thrived because of the abundant fishing nearby, and soon barrels of salted herring were being sent forty miles downriver to Glasgow. The town's access to the Firth of Clyde and the deep waters there meant that international commerce became an important part of Greenock's economy. Originally, the cargo was mostly tobacco brought over from the Americas, but later sugar became king of the imports. Thirteen vessels laden with raw sweetener arrived in 1813 and the next year there were ninety-two. The industry really took off after 1834; soon Greenock was one of the largest sugar processing centers in the United Kingdom. By mid-century the town generated fifty thousand tons a year and two decades later it produced almost five times as much. The city became so closely associated with the product that it was nicknamed Sugaropolis. Much of the raw sugar arrived on ships from plantations in Cuba, Indonesia, and Brazil. As a result, the wealth that Greenock's citizens derived from the sugar trade came in part from the labor of enslaved peoples.

The prosperity led to both economic and demographic growth in the town. To solve the chronic problem of a lack of housing in the 1860s, residents formed the Greenock Provident Investment Company. In 1867, the corporation finished construction on a housing development of four tenements called Morton Terrace. The site was named for builder and local notable James Morton, who served as provost, or mayor, of the town from 1868 to 1871. Groups of men began to kick a football about in an open field nearby and in 1874 they formed Morton Football Club. Questions remain about where the name came from, but it was likely drawn from the housing projects and ultimately the man who helped build them. Whatever the origins of the team's name, James Morton was an early supporter of the club. The direct connections between sugar processing revenue, investment in construction, and sponsorship of football clubs illustrate how communities, individuals, and even soccer teams benefited from the slave system, even if they were not directly involved in it. The prospect of employment in the construction industry along with the possibility of football drew people to Greenock. Among them was a young man from Glasgow named William McKendrick. A stonecutter by trade, McKendrick also played football for Morton FC. Eventually, his brothers followed him, first to Greenock and eventually on to Minneapolis, Detroit, Toronto, and Baltimore. Today we tend to think of the global movement of players as a relatively recent phenomenon. The McKendrick brothers, however, show that the peripatetic life of top-level professional soccer players had developed as early as the late nineteenth century.

William Dixon McKendrick was born in 1865 in Glasgow. Nothing is known of when or how he and his brothers learned to play, but he joined Morton FC in the summer of 1884. During his time at the club, match reports describe his play as inconsistent. His natural position was at center forward, but he also took on other roles, often to the detriment of his form. By the fall of 1884, he was lining up for the first team and soon showed his quality and an eye for goal by scoring a hat trick in a third round Scottish Cup tie against Southern on October 25. His fine form continued until early December, when the local newspaper called him out for poor play. Even though he was clearly a talented finisher, McKendrick was moved to center back despite standing 5 feet 8.5 inches tall and weighing just 148 pounds. The columnist for the *Greenock Telegraph* known as "Dribbler" seemed cautiously optimistic about the move. "I have no doubt he will make a good back, though at times he appeared to be a little timid when meeting an opponent."[1] After five games, however, the same writer declared it a failed experiment because the club had better defenders, and without McKendrick up front, the goals had dried up. Perhaps the manager read the paper because he restored McKendrick to the forward line and the scoring resumed. He netted two against Northern on January 17, 1885, and added a hat trick in a friendly against Ayr a week later. Once again, Dribbler praised his play, comparing McKendrick's shot to that of Queens Park striker George "Geordie" Ker. It was high praise indeed: Ker was a three-time Scottish Cup winner, had been capped five times for Scotland, and scored a hat trick versus England in 1880.

John McKendrick, born June 24, 1868, in Glasgow, joined the team in the spring of 1885 and in March the brothers played together in a charity match versus Abercorn. A month later, William was tried at another new position—goalkeeper. It seemed an odd decision given his goal scoring ability and his size. If anything, it would have made more sense for John to be tried in goal because he was almost three inches taller and nearly thirty pounds heavier than his brother. Instead, the younger McKendrick was consigned to the reserves and made only occasional first team appearances. Apart from a few miscues, the move looked to be successful, and William began the 1885–86 season in goal. The newspaper's evaluation of his play was positive: "He proved himself cool, ready, strong, and active, and consequently did his work judiciously and well."[2] Because the match reports often do not give a first initial, it can be difficult to say for sure which brother appeared in a particular match. Only rarely, usually when the two of them played together, would a first initial be added. What is clear is that both William and John had turns in goal, at central defender and in the midfield at various points in the 1886–87 season.

William had one of his better games at center back in January 1887 when Morton defeated Queen's Park in a friendly by the score of 4–1. The win was attributed to the team's stout defense, including the "steady play" of McKendrick as part of the back line. It was only an exhibition match, but the local press declared the win "will stand out in the history of football in Greenock as one of the grandest of victories."[3] A few months later, McKendrick had a shocker in a defeat at the hands of Abercorn FC in the semifinals of the county cup. The *Greenock Telegraph* warned the team: "A just criticism means the use of strong words of condemnation of certain members of the local team." Losing at home before seven thousand fans left the squad "discouraged as well as discomfited." One can imagine how the supporters felt about the match. The article called out several players by name and had some choice words for McKendrick's play, describing his performance as "an utter failure." It also suggested there was a reason for his poor form: "he represents a first-class man almost wasted by the round of positions he has been asked to take up."[4] By April 1887, the press had only words of praise for the team, especially after they notched a miraculous 5–3 comeback win over Queens Park. In a classic "game of two halves," Morton was losing 0–3 at the break but roared back, scoring five unanswered goals to seal the victory. McKendrick, however, did not play well and was a passenger in the side. The local paper remarked that "he was not altogether bad, but he was very indifferent."[5]

By the fall of 1887, William had cemented his place in defense, playing well in the season opener against Aston Villa. Such friendlies were common, and the newspaper noted that bigger clubs had realized the benefits of making the trip to Greenock, a challenging match combined with a lucrative payday. Big games at Morton's home pitch, Cappielow Park, regularly drew crowds of several thousand. Over the next few matches, he was moved back and forth, first going up front and later returning to the defensive line. Perhaps it was unclear what his best position was, but as a striker he always seemed to find a way to score goals even when not playing well. It may have been the case that he was a versatile talent and the immediate needs of the club determined where he might be best utilized. Even when he lined up at wing, never considered to be his best position, William managed to impress. After one match the "Football Gossip" section of the local paper cataloged his strengths as a player.

> There is a singular freedom about his style and action; some people think there is too much of it about the arms, but an eccentricity of that kind can be forgiven if the legs and feet do their work well. He is one of the very few who go straight ahead with the ball, he always makes up his mind, and that quickly, what he is going to do with it, and he parts with it at a good moment. His shots for goal and centres were particularly accurate.[6]

Even as William established himself as a top-class player for Morton, his brothers were also making sporting news. Adam McKendrick (born 1870) played in goal for the club, while John left Morton to go to the United States. It must have been a brief sojourn, as he was back in Greenock and back in the Morton team by mid-December 1887. John's return to the side did not last long and soon he made his first sporting move to Port Glasgow. The stop was temporary, however, and within a few weeks he returned to Morton for a game or two before signing on with Abercorn. He was part of the side that defeated Port Glasgow 4–1 in the semifinal of the Renfrewshire Cup. Despite the victory, the *Greenock Telegraph* savaged John for his rough play, calling it "reprehensibly forcible" and "bull-like." Due to his rough tactics, McKendrick "gained the disapprobation of every right-thinking person, and no doubt he at the same time must have lost somewhat of his own self-respect."[7] At one point the Port keeper dove to cover the ball and as he went to ground, it spilled loose. McKendrick aimed to kick the ball but instead missed and connected squarely with the keeper, who had to be helped off the field. John did not appear in the final, a loss to St. Mirren, probably because he had again left for the United States.

William continued to play for Morton in the 1888–89 season, although he seems to have lost favor or was injured and struggled to return to the first eleven. By this time James McKendrick (born 1872) was also playing soccer, winning the Greenock and District Junior Football Association Cup with Ladyburn. William regained his place on the team sheet by the fall of 1889 and once again was leading the line for Morton. He played well against Glasgow Rangers in a 3–3 draw at Ibrox on November 9 and scored a hat trick against Ayr a few months later. In what may have been one of his last games with Morton, William was one of the few in the squad to show in what was an otherwise forgettable 0–3 defeat to Sunderland.

The McKendrick brothers crossed the Atlantic and ultimately made their sporting reputations in Detroit. Yet the Motor City was not their first stop after leaving Scotland. They originally settled in the area around the cities of Minneapolis and St. Paul, Minnesota. Soccer began in the region, known collectively as the Twin Cities, when the St. Paul Football Club organized in September 1886. Scots emerged as important promoters of the game and the Thistle Cricket and Football Club formed a year later. The two teams played in the first documented association football match in the Twin Cities on August 2, 1887. By the summer of 1888, John McKendrick played for Thistle and scored two goals in a 7–0 rout of North Stars. Another player in the side was Duncan McMillan, a Scotsman born in 1866 at Largs in Ayrshire. Later described as a "well built" fellow, he stood 6 feet tall and weighed 173 pounds. He may have appeared in some matches for St. Bernard of Edinburgh before leaving for the United States. McMillan later served as captain of the Detroit AFC squad. One report labelled him as a player who covered a lot of ground and was "adept at heading and chesting the ball."[8] McMillan later wed Marion McKendrick, the sister of William, John, Adam, and James. The relationship demonstrated the close social bonds between the teammates. On August 3, 1888, John McKendrick scored a goal for Thistle in a 2–1 win over St. Paul FC. The two squads competed for the George K. Shaw Cup along with the North Stars and Tam O'Shanters Football Club. Thistle dominated the competition, winning two straight titles. John McKendrick banged in loads of goals and served as team captain. William and James joined their brother at Thistle in the summer of 1890. The two newcomers seem to have made only a handful of appearances for the club, and within a few weeks, the trio was on the move again.

In the fall of 1890, all three McKendricks relocated to the Motor City. It did not take long for them to resume playing soccer and they soon joined Detroit AFC. The brothers instantly transformed the team from a mediocre squad into a championship one. Although they lost the league opener with the brothers in the lineup, the team ultimately cruised to the title. Detroit easily won their second game, beating Essex 12–0, and followed that up with a 10–0 drubbing of Chatham, the team they had lost to a few weeks earlier. In an away match at Windsor on November 8, the McKendricks put on a master class. The home side had been strengthened with a few new players and a close game was expected. Detroit opened the scoring after two minutes and a short while later John McKendrick sent a long, defense splitting pass to his brother James, whose shot was just tipped around the post by the keeper. On the ensuing corner, John made good on the second chance, nodding it home and giving them a two-goal advantage. After another goal made the score 0–3 for the visitors, the Windsor side looked dejected. William took advantage of the home side's low morale and went on an amazing run, dribbling past two defenders before ripping a shot into the goal. Mercifully, the whistle blew for halftime, with the score 0–4 in favor of Detroit. They shut out Windsor in the second half and scored three more to all but capture the title after the 0–7 win. The final game of the season took place on November 15 against Chatham. William, playing up top in his old position at forward, notched a brace in the 4–1 win and Detroit were Western Football Association (WFA) challenge cup champions. The local paper praised the siblings. According to one article, William was a "strong, speedy forward and a hard worker," while James was "a star of the first magnitude." John might have been the most talented of the soccer-playing brothers. The *Detroit Free Press* called him "one of the finest players that ever stepped on a foot ball field."[9] The squad continued to take part in the WFA championship, which included Canadian teams from the cities of Windsor, Berlin (now Kitchener), and Seaforth. The league named two champions each season, one in the spring and one in the fall. Detroit had a strong squad, but their performance dipped in the spring of 1891 due in part to a labor dispute.

Strikes by stonecutters in Pennsylvania and Wisconsin had taken place in the first half of 1891. In late March or early April of that year, the Journeymen Stone Cutters Association of Detroit asked contractors for an increase in pay from $3.60 to $4.00 for eight hours work. Ownership, represented by the Cut Stone Contractor's Association, refused, citing the fact they had already signed contracts for jobs under the original rate and would lose money if they raised wages. They made a counteroffer—upping the eight-hour rate to $3.75—but this was rejected by the union, who set a strike date of June 1. The contractors remained intransigent, claiming they had already given in too much to the demands of workers. "We have not stood up for our rights, and are glad the break has come. The men must shift for themselves and we are certainly able to do the same thing."[10] They quickly began advertising for scabs in newspapers around the country at the current pay rate and felt certain that other related trades, such as bricklayers, would not support the walkout. In what was characterized by the *Detroit Free Press* as a contentious vote, the Stone Cutters Association confirmed the strike would indeed begin on June 1. The newspaper quoted individuals who blamed outside agitators, including some from Canada, for the labor strife in Detroit. These itinerant stonecutters supposedly travelled from town to town, stirring up trouble and then leaving just as quickly. On June 1 over one hundred and fifty

The Detroit Federal Building, also known as the Post Office Building, c. 1902. William McKendrick helped build the structure and claimed to have lost his soccer medals in its foundation. He lived long enough to see it torn down in 1931. (Courtesy of Library of Congress, Prints & Photographs Division, Detroit Publishing Company Collection, LC-DIG-det-4a09640.)

stonecutters walked out, resulting in work stoppages at major construction sites in the city, including the Union Depot and Federal Building. At least some of the general public backed the strikers. A letter published in the newspaper from "Non-Stonecutter" argued that people should support the action because the nature of the job meant they could work only six or seven months of the year and that conditions were unhealthy due to the dirt and dust.

As the strike entered its second week, the paper celebrated the fact that, despite the disagreement between workers and management, there was no bad blood or violence from either side. The Contractor's Association sought to import replacement workers but were thwarted by the actions of the strikers. Thirty-five Italians brought in by the group were met at the station by union members, who quickly convinced the newcomers to join the strike or paid train fares out of town for those who chose not to. By the end of June, the contractors even tried to organize a new union called the Progressive Association of Journeymen Stone Cutters of Detroit. They hired someone from Boston to run the group and presented it as an alternative to the existing association. Meanwhile, the local union was paying out strike funds to men off work, fifteen dollars to those who were married and ten to those who were single. Finally, after nearly a month, the two sides came to an agreement to end the strike. The settlement called for no immediate change in the eight-hour rate but would increase it to $3.76 in August. As for the Progressive Association, it understandably was not well-liked in the city; one labor leader said the group should leave town, "crawling back into its hole and taking the hole with it."[11] It was reported that several players, including the McKendricks, had left town due to the dispute. Where exactly they went is unknown, but it may have been somewhere in Canada. The brothers would have had connections there and could have continued working and maybe even playing soccer, without crossing the picket line.

Lacking a full roster and many of its best players during the labor action, Detroit forfeited two matches and the Seaforth Hurons won the 1891 spring WFA title. The end of the strike meant the return of the players, and the full-strength Detroit squad captured the Michigan state championship, beating Almont 4–0. The lineup included the McKendrick brothers and Duncan McMillan as well as two new players: Duncan McPherson and George Collie. The debutants would go on to play prominent roles in the squad. A right back, McPherson was born around 1870 and came from Inverness. On the small side at 5 feet 4 inches tall, one reporter called him "a jewel of a player."[12] George M. Collie was born in 1866 at Montrose, Forfarshire. He reportedly played for Morton FC, although that is difficult to confirm. A solid two-way player, he was an effective tackler and a strong header of the ball. The victory over Almont in the state cup showed the potential of the squad. The *Detroit Free Press* noted that, on the field, they showed "grand combined team play."[13]

In the fall of 1891, Detroit AFC added another Scottish forward named Alexander Ramsey. The twenty-seven-year-old stood 5 feet 8 inches tall and weighed 140 pounds. Some reports claimed he once played for Arbroath Juniors. Detroit again won the WFA competition, and five of its members played on the victorious Caledonian Cup winning side. Teams picked from the Western, Central, and Eastern Football Associations in Canada played for the Caledonian Cup. The Western Association's victory in 1891 was the first for the region in some time. By 1892, Detroit AFC became known as the Michigan Athletic Association (MAA) team. The squad captured the WFA spring 1892 championship to make it two titles in a row. In the spring season, Adam McKendrick made a rare appearance for the team, playing in the midfield alongside his three brothers in a match against Pullman of Chicago on November 24, 1892. Adam was only an occasional player, perhaps filling in when an extra hand was needed. His next confirmed match was in 1895, when the MAA side also fielded a pair of young Polish players. By the following year, some reports claimed that the MAA club had disbanded and faced expulsion from the WFA unless they returned the organization's challenge cup. During this period, the McKendricks seem to have bounced around a bit, playing matches here and there for a variety of teams.

The brothers kept in shape by practicing with the Windsor, Canada, squad. By May 1893, reports of the MAA club's demise seemed premature, as the team played a friendly with three McKendricks in the lineup against a picked WFA side. A few months later, John and James wore the colors of Toronto Scots in a 7–1 victory over the Jerseys of Buffalo, New York. The pair seemed to have spent the season with the team, featuring in matches throughout the spring and summer of 1894. By that fall, John, James, and William joined the Baltimore squad of the American League of Professional Football (ALPF). Baseball team owners formed the organization in the fall of that year. A rival group known as the American Association of Professional Football also began play at the same time. These competitions were the first professional football leagues organized outside of Great Britain. The ALPF consisted of six teams in Boston, Brooklyn, New York, Philadelphia, Washington DC, and Baltimore. Ned Hanlon, the manager of the Baltimore team, enlisted the aid of prominent Detroit footballer A. W. Stewart to recruit and train the team. Stewart named himself captain and played goalkeeper. He convinced the McKendrick brothers to join him in the new league. The team ran into trouble for signing players from England, several of whom had played for Ardwick Association Football Club (soon reformed as Manchester City) and one who came from Sheffield. Baltimore did well in the competition but only managed to play three games before the league shut down. James McKendrick started the season hot, notching a brace in each of Baltimore's first two matches. He may have scored in the final one as well, but no details have emerged about the 0–3 win over Washington. He ended the season as one of the league's top goal scorers. Despite the support of prominent baseball magnates, the ALPF collapsed after only a few weeks. For the McKendricks, the ALPF's lasting legacy was probably the ban handed out by the American Football Association (AFA) to players who had signed professional contracts. Other footballing organizations respected the ban and for a time it prevented the Detroit players from participating in local competitions.

The Peninsular Association Football League (PAFL) formed in Detroit in the spring of 1895. The sides included the MAA and a new team called the Diamonds. Many of the city's Scottish players, including the McKendrick brothers, McMillan, and Collie lined up for the Diamonds. The Canadian clubs were Windsor, Walkerville, and Essex. The league was an amateur one, and by this time, the AFA had rescinded the McKendrick brothers'

John McKendrick, second row, far right, lined up for Toronto Scots in 1897. (Courtesy of Hockey Hall of Fame/Library and Archives Canada/ PA-050695.)

ban for professionalism. Despite the ruling, the league later ordered an 1896 match between MAA and Essex be replayed because John McKendrick was a professional. The MAA club won the spring league, spoiling hopes for a more competitive association, but it did not seem to impact league finances, which were reported to be good. The Peninsular League contracted in 1896, with just four senior sides contesting the prize. By the fall of 1896, there were only three senior teams in Detroit. The MAA club had been reorganized and hoped to schedule matches against nearby teams as well as clubs from Toronto, Cincinnati, Chicago, and St. Louis. Meanwhile, many of the players from the MAA club decided to break from the association and reformed under the old Detroit AFC banner. In a match before a crowd of 800, the club played well despite losing 2–3 to reigning Peninsular League champs Seaforth Hurons. The reestablished Detroit squad took the place of MAA in the Peninsular League and went on to capture the Walker Cup.

The 1896 fall title proved to be the last hurrah for many of the original Scottish professionals in the city. By the time the club lifted the trophy, only Duncan McPherson had been playing regularly. William McKendrick helped build the city's iconic Romanesque revival-style Federal Building, the same one where construction had been paused during the stonecutters strike of 1891. He dug foundations, raised stones for its walls, and was appointed a building fireman with an annual salary of $720 in 1897. Eventually, he was promoted to building engineer and worked at the facility for the next three decades. Nobody knew the structure better than the Scotsman; he even claimed to have lost the medals he earned playing soccer in the foundation walls. He died in 1938. John McKendrick spent most of the rest of his days in Detroit although he lived for a time in Canada and played for the Toronto Scots in 1897. He remained a stonecutter until he died of pneumonia in 1911. He had a wife and six children. One newspaper reported that James McKendrick returned to Scotland, where he continued to play professional football. The McKendricks' brother-in-law Duncan McMillan stayed in Detroit and died in 1922 of acute alcoholism, leaving behind his wife and seven children. Alexander Ramsey settled in Detroit, working as a plasterer until he passed away due to an enlarged heart, also in 1922. The fates of the other players—Duncan McPherson and George Collie—are not known.

Notes

1. Dribbler, "Football Gossip," *Greenock Telegraph*, December 18, 1884.
2. "Football Gossip," *Greenock Telegraph*, August 27, 1885.
3. "Football," *Greenock Telegraph*, January 21, 1887.

4. All of the quotations in this section are from this same story. "Football Gossip," *Greenock Telegraph and Clyde Shipping Gazette*, March 25, 1887.
5. "Football Gossip," *Greenock Telegraph*, April 29, 1887.
6. "Football Gossip," *Greenock Telegraph*, November 25, 1887.
7. "Football Gossip," *Greenock Telegraph*, February 17, 1888.
8. "Association Foot Ball," *Detroit Free Press*, November 22, 1891.
9. "Association Foot Ball," *Detroit Free Press*, November 22, 1891.
10. "Another Strike On," *Detroit Free Press*, May 31, 1891.
11. "End of Stonecutters' Strike," *Detroit Free Press*, June 28, 1891.
12. "Association Foot Ball," *Detroit Free Press*, November 22, 1891.
13. "Football," *Detroit Free Press*, August 4, 1891.

Sources

Mullen, Stephen. *The Glasgow Sugar Aristocracy: Scotland and Caribbean Slavery, 1775–1838*. London: University of London Press, 2022.

Smith, Robert Murray. *The History of Greenock*. Greenock: Orr, Pollock and Co., 1921. Inverclyde Council. https://www.inverclyde.gov.uk/assets/attach/5139/r.m.-smith-the-history-of-greenock-complete-cc.pdf.

NEWSPAPERS

Buffalo Courier
Detroit Free Press
Greenock Telegraph
Greenock Telegraph and Clyde Shipping Gazette
The Scotsman (Midlothian, Scotland)
Windsor Star

WEBSITE

Ancestry.com

9

Raising Thistles in the Twin Cities

Minneapolis and St. Paul, Minnesota

In September 1918, Harry Smith of Minneapolis, Minnesota, received a letter from his brother Alec. Writing from France, where he was serving with the 14th Canadian Infantry Battalion, Alec described his experiences on the Amiens front. A few weeks earlier, he had participated in an attack on the German trenches: "We were ordered to go over the top and through a barrage that was considered impregnable. We lost half the battalion, but we got there." Although he was not wounded during that operation, Alec did have some close calls: "another fellow and I were lying side by side in a wheat field when a shell took his leg off and never touched me."[1] Other near misses included a piece of shrapnel that grazed his face and another that pierced the mess tin he carried on his back. For his actions during the encounter, Alec Smith was awarded the Military Medal, an honor given to enlisted men for bravery in combat.

It is unknown what conduct prompted the award, but in August and September, the battalion had been involved in several intense operations. On August 7, they attacked at dawn near the commune of Gentelles outside the city of Amiens. The unit's war diary reported that "all ranks showed great dash and the objective was finally captured and consolidated."[2] During the battle, the troops confiscated ten field guns, forty-six machine guns, and eight trench mortars. In September, the 14th took part in attacks designed to secure the Canal du Nord and took four hundred prisoners. Despite these successes, Alec's luck appeared to have run out and he was reported missing on October 1. Almost a fortnight later, news filtered back to Minnesota that Smith and another local man had been killed in action. The announcement appeared on the sports page because both soldiers had been soccer players. One reason why Alec Smith's wartime activities were so widely reported is that he was one of the most talented and popular figures ever to grace local pitches. He also lined up for one of the most storied names in the history of soccer in the Twin Cities: Thistle.

The Thistle Cricket and Football Club of Minneapolis organized on May 23, 1887. As one might expect given the name Thistle, many of the founders originally came from Scotland. Later, the team had players born in England and the United States, and many of them held middle-class jobs. Alec Smith, born in Derby, England, in 1892, played for the second incarnation of the Thistle team and was a bookkeeper by trade, working for a local department store. By the summer of 1887, the Thistle Club was scheduling matches against local sides like the Glass Block team. The latter squad must have been formed by employees of Donaldson's department store since the firm's nickname was Glass Block due to the large number of windows in the firm's building. The company was founded in 1884 by the brothers William and Lawrence Donaldson. They were born in the small town of Milnathort, Scotland, and worked in dry goods stores in Glasgow and Providence, Rhode Island, before establishing themselves in the Twin Cities. The store soon grew into one of Minneapolis's great shopping destinations, alongside other establishments such as Young-Quinlan and Dayton's. It is unclear if the brothers were fans of soccer, but they did honor their Scottish heritage in other ways. William was an avid fisherman, a skill he claimed to have learned in the country of his birth. Although William died in 1899, the same year the local St. Andrew's Society was formed, Lawrence became an active member of the group. A photo from 1917, labelled the Donaldson Company Marching Band, reveals the unit was a traditional Scottish pipe band, complete with full kilt and regalia.

Although the newspaper reported that games had been scheduled earlier, the first documented match report is for an August 2, 1887, game between Thistle and St. Paul FC. The St. Paul side may have been the area's earliest-known soccer team when they came together in 1886. The Thistles easily took home the honors with a 4–0 victory. Although no league or cup tournament existed that first year, the *Minneapolis Morning Tribune* declared that Thistle could rightfully claim the title of best club in the region. In 1888, teams organized the first formal soccer competition in the Twin Cities. Four squads, Thistle, St. Paul, North Stars, and the Tam O'Shanters Football Club, played for the George K. Shaw Challenge Cup. Shaw was the editor of the *Tribune* and undoubtedly donated the trophy awarded to the league champion. Once again Thistle proved to be the area's class outfit, winning the Shaw Cup during each of the first three seasons.

In addition to local players, Thistle was fortified by newcomers, including the McKendrick brothers, who arrived from Scotland. John

McKendrick was a skilled finisher who led the team to a dominant 1889 season, where they went unbeaten in eleven games while scoring seventy-four goals and conceding just eight. The three siblings, John, James, and William, relocated to Detroit in 1890, where they played a key role in the Motor City's footballing community. Four years later they lined up for Baltimore in the short-lived American League of Professional Football. In 1891 Minnesota's competition expanded and included teams from the Twin Cities, Duluth, Minnesota, and West Superior, Wisconsin. The newcomers quickly showed their quality as Duluth ended Thistle's championship winning streak by capturing the title. The Shaw Cup remained up North in 1892 when West Superior finished top of the table. Over the next decade, the competition ebbed and flowed as some teams joined and others dropped out. The Northern teams left after just a few seasons, although they continued to play the occasional friendly with squads from Minneapolis and St. Paul.

One of the struggles that soccer playing communities often faced in this period was locating suitable places to play. As cities grew, previously open spaces or empty lots filled up, forcing the squads to seek out new sporting fields. By 1889, several of the Twin Cities clubs had their own home grounds. No descriptions of the sites are available, and while they may have been fenced off, it is unlikely that stands or other lasting structures were built on them. Most of these fields are hard to locate precisely on historical maps and in the contemporary cityscape. One possible location for the Thistle Club grounds at E. Twenty-Sixth Street and Cedar Avenue was a large empty lot near the Chicago, Milwaukee, and St. Paul Railroad Company's shops and yards. The open space fits the general location given in newspapers and was serviced by a streetcar line running down Cedar Avenue. Currently the area is mainly residential blocks of houses, a Department of Public Works facility, and a large industrial building. In 1890, the Tam O'Shanters and other clubs played matches in the heart of downtown Minneapolis, possibly on one of several empty lots at Thirteenth Street North and Vine Place. The location was just a block or two east of Loring Park, but you won't find it on any contemporary map. The area was redeveloped in the 1970s and 1980s, and Vine Place no longer exists, replaced by a series of upscale housing developments, including Loring Way Condominiums and One Ten Grant.

In the early 1890s, many clubs played games at Kittsondale in St. Paul. Situated between Minneapolis and St. Paul off University Avenue, the area was established as a recreational center by wealthy entrepreneur Norman Kittson in the 1870s and 1880s. Kittson had a passion for horse racing and bought up land to construct a breeding farm and racecourse. After he died in 1888, the land continued to host races and other events before being slowly converted to industrial uses after 1900. Kittsondale was vast and it is hard to know exactly where on the grounds the soccer matches took place, but the site of the main racetrack was eventually taken over by a refrigerator manufacturer located along University Avenue between Pascal Street and Hamline Avenue. Today, Allianz Field, home of Major League Soccer's Minnesota United FC, is less than a ten-minute walk from the place where soccer matches were played more than a century earlier. In 1896, teams often competed at what were known as the Fourth Avenue grounds in Minneapolis. The park was situated at Thirty-Eighth Street South and Fourth Avenue. Once again it is difficult to identify where exactly the pitch was sited, but a decade earlier there was one empty lot in the area as well as another that had been platted but did not yet have any structures. The location was serviced by a railcar line on Fourth Avenue, making it easily accessible to players and fans.

Generally, there is little evidence that soccer clubs in the area regularly held matches at baseball stadiums. Two exceptions are in 1905, when teams played at Lexington Park in St. Paul and a year later at Nicollet Park in Minneapolis. Lexington Park housed the St. Paul Saints baseball team from 1897 to 1956. The earliest structure was destroyed by fire in 1915, and the

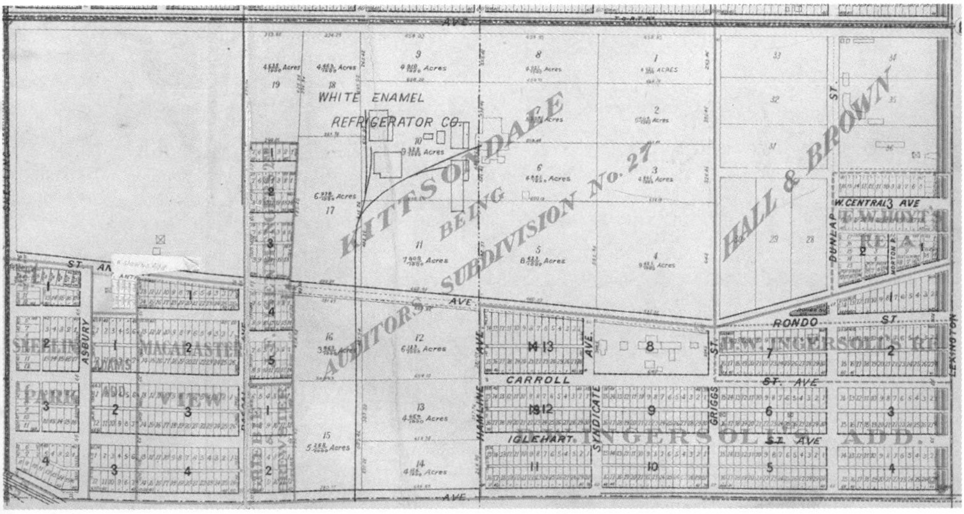

In the 1890s local teams held matches at Kittsondale, situated along University Avenue (running along the top of the image) in St. Paul. The site of the grounds was close to the place marked White Enamel Refrigerator Co. on the map. (Source: *Curtice's Revised Atlas of the City of St. Paul*. Courtesy of John R. Borchert Map Library at the University of Minnesota.)

orientation of the stadium was changed when it was rebuilt. The ballpark was located near Kittsondale, and the former site is just over a mile from Allianz Field. The Minneapolis Millers baseball team called Nicollet Park home from 1896 to 1955. It was situated on Nicollet Avenue between E. Lake Street and Thirty-First Street. As of 2024, the site mainly consists of a parking lot and open space. A Wells Fargo bank had been at the location, but it was damaged by fire during the protests following the killing of George Floyd in 2020 and was eventually torn down.

Local teams had long played on land owned by the Minneapolis Steel and Machinery Company. One site was likely a triangular piece of land along E. Twenty-Eighth Street, E. Twenty-Ninth Street, and Minnehaha Avenue. By the 1910s, the field was known as Thistle Park. It was located just a few blocks from the old Thistle Club grounds at E. Twenty-Sixth Street and Cedar Avenue. Eventually, the city of Minneapolis obtained the land, and it became known as Longfellow Field. A recent satellite photo of the area

Teams played matches on land near the Minneapolis Steel and Machinery Company at E. 29th and Minnehaha, Minneapolis. By the 1910s it was known as Thistle Park. (Courtesy of Minnesota Historical Society.)

around the former site of Thistle Park shows that the industrial buildings and railroad yard that existed nearby are long gone. The former soccer ground is now a grocery store and parking lot, just a block or two away from the police precinct building that burned in May 2020. In 1907–08, Clan Gordon played at Twenty-Fourth Street and Hennepin Avenue. In the mid-1910s, the Thistle Club moved its grounds down Minnehaha Avenue at Thirty-Eighth Street. The site was probably located kitty-corner to the Simmons School building (currently apartments) in the block that now houses an American Legion building and Howe Office Suites.

At some point around the turn of the twentieth century, the original Thistle team disbanded, and the sport largely disappeared from public view. The urge to crown a champion was still strong, however, and at times the title was decided by a winner-take-all match between two Scottish clans, the Gordons and the Campbells, during their annual summer picnic. The visits to North America of English sides the Pilgrims in 1905 and the Corinthians the following year revitalized the local soccer community. Fans and administrators hoped to lure one or both foreign squads to the area, but challenges in scheduling and weather made it impossible. One wonders if the Twin Cities' largely moribund soccer scene led tour organizers to doubt the profitability of a visit. The sport also received an unexpected boost as growing disillusionment with the violence of intercollegiate football led some to suggest soccer as a replacement on college campuses. Even Amos Alonzo Stagg, famed football coach at the University of Chicago, voiced his support for the sport and many schools organized soccer teams.

Although it seems odd to us now, some fans at the time genuinely feared that soccer would replace intercollegiate football. Critics railed against soccer, paradoxically declaring it to be a feminized version of football while at the same time accusing it of being equally as violent as the gridiron game. A newspaper column by "the Dutch Uncle" explained that he did not expect soccer to become very popular in Minneapolis. The main reason seemed to be that the sport did not produce the same sort of manly play that the intercollegiate game did. He wrote that in soccer, a player does not "rip up the opposing line and go fifteen or twenty yards with players hanging on him like a flock of cabdrivers after an intoxicated timber cruiser."[3] The next month, the *Minneapolis Journal* published a similar column called "Under the Sporting Spotlight," written by "O'Loughlin." Canadian efforts to support soccer made the author long "for the good old days of ping-pong when Genevieve MacGilcuddy was wont to smash the pampas plumes over the parlor mantle with a misplaced serve." He continued, "If we are to have docile sports and effeminate pastimes, why not organize tatting teams at the universities and feed only bale-o-hay biscuit and pink tea at the training tables?"[4]

A cartoon titled "When the Game of Football is Made Very, Very Gentle" appeared in the *Minneapolis Tribune* on February 11, 1906. It declared that one of the suggested football reforms was "that we change it to the dull English 'socker'." One section labelled "Football armor for next season" included a monocle, top hat, and corset. In another scene a man whose top hat and tails cover an almost feminine physique is shown wearing high-heeled boots. A panel declared that if a game lasted past 6 p.m., the players would be allowed to change into evening dress.[5] Overall, the imagery in the

Commemorative image of the Minneapolis Thistle Soccer Football Club, c. 1915. The portraits of several key players appear, including Dave Sharp, upper left corner; Alec Smith, below and to the left of Sharp; Pete McKenzie, below Smith; Wen Ping Pan and Jimmy Matthews, lower right. (Author's collection)

newspaper columns and the cartoon relied on the same clichés that have been leveled at soccer for decades and can still be heard today: soccer is a foreign, unmanly sport played by elitists. In February 1906 the *Tribune* published a short article describing a fistfight that broke out between a soccer player and a referee at a match in San Francisco. Such incidents were not uncommon during games in this era, but the attached headline trafficked in hyperbole or perhaps was meant as a snarky jab at those who touted soccer as a less dangerous form of football: "Horrible Brutality of Socker Football."[6]

Around this same time, a new outfit began playing under the revived name of Thistle. The league retained a British flavor with clubs such as the Sons of St. George, Wanderers, and Albions, but added new squads representing different nationalities including Danish AC, Vikings, Shamrocks, and Hibernians. Still more clubs included the Internationals and the Patriotic and Protective Order of the Stags of the World, usually abbreviated to just Stags. Not all teams competed each season, and some would participate one year and drop out the next. Eventually the campaign was split in two, with a fall season generally held in October and November followed by a spring one running between April and June. Sponsors offered new awards so that sides played for the Shaw Cup, the Burkhard Challenge Cup, the Spalding Pennant, the O'Hara Trophy, and the J. D. Olson Trophy. As in many other cities, competition prizes were often donated by sporting goods companies and the owners of eating or drinking establishments. William Burkhard, originally from Switzerland, owned a sporting goods shop in St. Paul, and the Spalding Pennant was presented by the internationally known company of the same name. James O'Hara was president of Thistle during this period and might have been the same man who ran a saloon located at 1840 East Franklin Avenue in downtown Minneapolis. John D. Olson co-owned the Unique Restaurant at 612 Hennepin Avenue, an eatery that served over 1,600 people per week. At least for the 1912 season, the league also offered an individual award, something unusual for the sport in this period. In that year James Tyre of the Albions earned the Burger Medal for scoring the most goals. Only two Burgers appeared in the 1912 city directory, a physician and a carpenter. Thistle was competitive most years and took home one or more honors in 1911–12, 1915–17, and 1919.

One of the players who lined up for Thistle during this period was Wen Ping Pan, the first Chinese student to attend the University of Minnesota. In 1914 he helped found the school's men's soccer team. Born in Beijing on October 30, 1894, he was a multi-sport athlete at St. John's University in Shanghai, an institution founded by Anglican missionaries. After graduating from UM, he took a job with a mining company and spent the rest of his life in the town of Hibbing before dying there in 1981. Around the same time that Wen Ping Pan played for Minnesota and Thistle, Chinese students in other parts of the country were also forming soccer teams. When students from the Massachusetts Institute of Technology organized a team, the news made headlines, including racist expressions, in papers around the country. The most prominent of these teams was the New York Chinese Students' Soccer Club. The players came from Columbia University and City College and were managed by United States Football Association (now called US Soccer) Secretary Thomas Cahill. Although a national tour was announced, the squad seems to have only played games in New York, New Jersey, Connecticut, and Pennsylvania. The team joined the southern New York State association and entered the National Challenge Cup in 1919 but forfeited their only scheduled match of the tournament.

Alec Smith led the line for Thistle during its years of glory, and in one season scored seventeen of his team's twenty-one total goals. After just two years in the Twin Cities, he traveled to Montreal before joining the Canadian army in 1917. Smith was not the only Thistle player to enlist in Canada's armed forces. Thomas Chalmers, the club's former trainer, joined the Princess Patricia's Canadian Light Infantry (PPCLI) shortly after the outbreak of war in 1914. The Scottish-born Chalmers was no stranger to military service, having spent seven years in the famed Black Watch. The PPCLI was one of the first Canadian units to see action in Europe. Chalmers was declared killed in action on May 5, 1915, during a part of the Second Battle of Ypres. The unit's war diary noted that the trenches near Bellewaarde Lake in Belgium had been heavily shelled on May 4, resulting in the deaths of twenty-eight men. Chalmers may have been one of them. At least four other local players died during the war: Kenneth McInnis, Thomas Scobbie, Alexander Sutherland, and Jimmy Robertson. Soldiers with connections to Thistle who survived the fighting included Dave Hamilton, Tom Harrison, Billy Johnstone, James Matthews, Pete McKenzie, Dave Sharp, and John Whelan.

Another Thistle player who eventually returned was none other than Alec Smith. It turns out that news of his death was premature. It soon emerged that he had been reported missing and presumed dead, but in fact had been wounded and taken prisoner by the Germans. A few months later, he was released and, after being discharged from the army on April 25, 1919, returned to Minneapolis. Smith played a few matches with Thistle during the 1919 spring season. Eventually, he relocated to Canada permanently and continued to play soccer. He helped Montréal Grand Trunk FC capture the Connaught Cup and Dominion of Canada Football Championship in the summer of 1919. Several newspapers picked him out as the star of the tie, helping to set up the winning goal in the first leg and assisting on the only tally of the second. The *Winnipeg Tribune* praised his skill, calling him "a wonderful dribbler of the ball as well as a sure goal shot."[7] He continued to play into the 1920s, becoming a two-time winner of the *Coupe de Québec*. Smith also represented Canada both informally and formally. First, as part of an all-Canada squad against a visiting Scottish team in 1921 and then, four years later, he earned his only international cap. He appeared in a 1–0 win over the United States in Montreal on June 27, 1925. After he was killed in a car accident in 1944, the *Montréal Star* called him "the best outside left to ever play for a local club."[8] He was mourned by a wife and two sons, both of whom were serving in the Canadian armed forces. In 2017, Smith was elected to the Canada Soccer Hall of Fame.

Notes

1. "Shot Hits His Mess Tin and Grazes His Face; He's Unhurt," *Minneapolis Morning Tribune*, September 29, 1918.
2. *War Diary, 14th Canadian Infantry Battalion*, entry for August 7, 1918.
3. Dutch Uncle, "Boosts and Boots," *Minneapolis Tribune*, October 22, 1905.
4. O'Loughlin, "Under the Sports Spotlight," *Minneapolis Journal*, November 8, 1905.
5. "When the Game of Football is Made Very, Very Gentle," *Minneapolis Journal*, February 11, 1906.
6. "Horrible Brutality of Socker [*sic*] Football," *Minneapolis Journal*, February 18, 1906.
7. Quoted in *The Connaught Series*, 99.
8. "Soccerdom Mourns the Death of Alec Smith," *Montréal Star*, October 16, 1944.

Sources

Bergerson, Roger. "Once Upon a Time in the Midway: Trotters Ruled at Kittsondale." *Park Bugle*, November 19, 2017. https://www.parkbugle.org/once-upon-a-time-in-the-midway-trotters-ruled-at-kittsondale/.

Cahill, Thomas, ed. *Spalding's Official "Soccer" Football Guide*. New York: American Sports Publishing, 1918.

Cahill, Thomas, ed. *Spalding's Official "Soccer" Football Guide*. New York: American Sports Publishing, 1919.

The Connaught Series. The Dominion of Canada Football Championship. Soccer Canada, 2019. https://issuu.com/canadasoccer/docs/2019_canada_soccer_connaught_series.

Cui, Jane. "Wen Ping Pan—The First Chinese Student at the University of Minnesota." *Hennepin History* 81, no. 2 (2022): 24–26.

Curtice's Revised Atlas of the City of St. Paul. H. M. Smyth Printing Co. St. Paul, Minnesota, 1908.

Davison's Minneapolis City Directory. Vol. 40. Minneapolis: Minneapolis Directory Co., 1912.

Davison's Minneapolis City Directory. Vol. 42. Minneapolis: Minneapolis Directory Co., 1914.

Files of the Canadian Expeditionary Force (CEF). Library and Archives Canada.

War Diary, 14th Canadian Infantry Battalion. Library and Archives Canada. http://central.bac-lac.gc.ca/.redirect?app=fonandcol&id=1883222&lang=eng.

War Diary, Princess Patricia's Canadian Light Infantry. Library and Archives Canada. http://central.bac-lac.gc.ca/.redirect?app=fonandcol&id=1883202&lang=eng; http://central.bac-lac.gc.ca/.redirect?app=fonandcol&id=2005880&lang=eng.

NEWSPAPERS

Boston Globe
Evening Herald
Minneapolis Journal
Minneapolis Morning Tribune
Montréal Star
St. Paul Daily Globe

WEBSITE

Ancestry.com

10

James Matthews: Minnesota's Canadian War Hero

Minneapolis, Minnesota

In the early morning darkness of September 26, 1918, members of the Canadian Army's 44th Infantry Battalion prepared for combat. A day earlier they had moved into position along the Drocourt-Quéant line, stopping at a small ridge facing a dry section of the Canal du Nord. Even though summer had just been left behind, the nights were cold, and their boots slid and squelched on the wet, slippery ground. The 44th was tasked with an assault on the canal as part of the Hundred Days campaign, an operation designed to smash the Hindenburg Line and hopefully end the war. Among the men waiting in the chill air was a young soldier from Minnesota named James Matthews.

Known as Jimmy to his friends, Matthews left home for Winnipeg in July 1917, so antsy to fight that he couldn't wait, even though the United States had declared war that April. He initially signed on with the 79th Cameron Highlanders of Canada and sent home a photograph of himself decked out in the unit's traditional kilt. He signed his attestation papers on July 26, 1917, listing his birthplace as Owen Sound, Ontario. In fact, Matthews was born in Minneapolis on March 11, 1894, but his family did have roots in Owen Sound. He attended South High School in Minneapolis, where he played basketball and ran track. The Tigers did not have a school-sponsored soccer team, but at some point, Jimmy developed an interest in the game and lined up for a few local clubs. Eventually, he began playing for Thistle, one of the most illustrious names in Twin Cities soccer.

The earliest matches in the region were played in 1887 and regular competition began a year later. Thistle soon emerged as the area's best team, winning the first three championships. Regular play continued until around the turn of the century, when interest in the sport waned and many of the original teams, including Thistle, disbanded. The 1905 and 1906 seasons saw a revival of the game and, due to the harsh winters, competition was soon divided into spring and fall seasons. A new squad took up the name of Thistle and, just like the original side, became one of the region's most successful clubs. When war broke out in Europe in 1914, some local players moved to enlist, with many choosing to go over the border to join Canadian units. Some of these volunteers never returned. At least four men connected to Thistle perished in the conflict, including the team's former trainer, Thomas Chalmers, and goalkeeper Jimmy Robertson. Thistle striker Alec Smith was reported missing and then as dead, but it turned out he had been taken prisoner and eventually returned to Minnesota.

Jimmy probably wasn't thinking very much about the risks when he enlisted in the Canadian Army in 1917. As part of the first British-American draft, he sailed from Halifax, Nova Scotia, on October 6, 1917, on board the *SS Metagama*. We don't know if they were aware of it at the time, but

A section of the Canal du Nord, 1918. (Source: Canada. Dept. of National Defence/ Library and Archives Canada.)

other Thistle players, including Alec Smith and Tom Scobbie, traveled to England on the same voyage. After disembarking at Liverpool on October 17, Jimmy spent the next few months training and waiting for an opportunity to join the fray. He was offered a job drawing maps but turned it down, explaining to his mother in a letter that "I enlisted to fight, so I'm going to stick with it."[1] One can only imagine what she thought of that decision. While in England he continued to play soccer and began training for a road race to be held in London. On March 12, 1918, he finally got his chance when he was drafted into the 44th Battalion and was soon sent across the channel to join his unit in France. Jimmy's first months on the continent were quiet, as the 44th spent much of its time on work details, periodic duty in the trenches, or as mobile reserves. They also trained, played baseball, and boxed. Members of the battalion also took up a game called "massed football." The rules called for fifty players a side, with multiple balls, usually four, in play at the same time. After twenty minutes each team was subbed off and a new set of a hundred men took the field. One point was awarded for a ball kicked over the end line and a goal earned the team four points. On Dominion Day (July 1) 1918, the 44th won the corps massed football championship, outscoring their rival 75–8.

We do not know if Jimmy played soccer for an organized team or if he just participated in pickup or intrasquad games. During the war, the sport was incredibly popular among soldiers of all nations and important matches attracted thousands of spectators. Canadian units played against each other and sometimes formed squads made up of wounded men recovering at English hospitals. In 1916, for example, a chaplain named W. H. Bayley organized a soccer team at the Canadian Convalescent Hospital in Bear Wood, Wokingham. The club played a variety of different opponents, including Reading Football Club. Several members of the team went on to compete in the Inter-Allied Games soccer tournament held at the conclusion of the war. The games were an Olympic-style event organized by the YMCA and the US military, held in Paris from June 22 to July 6, 1919. The soccer competition featured squads from the United States, Canada, Czechoslovakia, Belgium, France, Italy, Greece, and Romania. Bayley was responsible for recruiting the Canadian team, and all but one of the identified players in the squad were born in the United Kingdom. The most decorated member was William Alfred "Alf" Spouncer, who won the English Football Association Cup with Nottingham Forest in 1898. He made a single appearance for England's national team and after the war spent the 1923–24 season as coach of famed Spanish club F. C. Barcelona. Ultimately, Czechoslovakia defeated France in the final to take home the trophy. Jimmy did not compete in the games, although both the United

States and Canada could have used an experienced forward like him. The Canadians lost every match, and the US team ended the tournament with a minus-twelve goal differential and only a single win over Canada.

Although the summer of 1918 seemed to have been relatively calm for Jimmy and his mates, they still faced harassment from enemy trench mortars, artillery, and aircraft. In August, as they moved to positions in preparation for an assault near Amiens, they suffered through a harrowing night raid by German Gotha bombers. No one knows for sure what Jimmy experienced during the attack, but he did report a few close calls during the war. Once a piece of shrapnel hit his shoe, a bullet clipped the rim of his helmet, and a slug grazed his upper lip. Former Thistle player Tom Scobbie was not so lucky. In many ways, his experiences mirrored Jimmy's: both had been players for Thistle in Minneapolis, both enlisted at Winnipeg in July 1917, both sailed to England on the *Metagama,* and both were eventually drafted into the 44th. Scobbie was killed in action on September 2, 1918, and it was Jimmy who wrote back home to report that another Thistle man had died.

Jimmy's luck would be put to the test again as the 44th prepared for the assault on the Canal du Nord in September 1918. At the appointed hour, the artillery opened up with a barrage designed to wear down the German defenses. The men of the 44th quickly surged forward, some carrying ropes or ladders to scale the twenty-foot dikes enclosing the canal. A deadly problem developed as the advancing soldiers quickly overtook the barrage. Soon Canadian shells were raining down on Canadian soldiers as officers and NCOs struggled to recall the troops. All four company commanders were injured in these efforts and several officers and sergeants were killed. The speed and relentlessness of the attack surprised the German garrison, and it was quickly overrun. Despite facing sheets of machine gun fire, the men of the 44th soon captured their main objective, a sunken road about six hundred yards beyond the canal. By 7:30 a.m. the assault was over, and they quickly prepared defensive positions. A total of forty men were killed in the action and over one hundred fifty were wounded. Jimmy Matthews was not among them.

Two days later Jimmy and his unit prepared for another attack, this time assembling at a site northeast of a village called Bourlon. The shelling began at 6:00 a.m. and, due to shortages of ammunition on the German side, the advance was relatively smooth until they arrived near Raillencourt-Sainte-Olle. Here the 44th faced stiff resistance as fierce fighting broke out over control of the village. The Canadians soon gained the upper hand and the battle turned into a rout as the enemy fled. A few hours later, however, they returned, launching a series of ferocious counterattacks.

The situation of the 44th took a turn for the worse as they ran low on ammunition and a bomb landed a direct hit on a command post, killing three officers. At three that afternoon, the Germans once again threw themselves forward, and only brutal hand-to-hand fighting combined with artillery support prevented a total collapse. Hours later, around 10:00 p.m., the 44th was ordered to advance to occupy an area along the Cambrai-Douai Road, where finally they could rest. The casualty numbers climbed even higher on this second day of operations, with a total of seventy-six killed and one hundred and fifty-two wounded.

Later, when Jimmy Matthews was awarded the Military Medal for bravery in battle, it may have been for his actions during this stretch of fighting. After the war, his friends and family hounded him for details about what he did to earn such a prestigious honor. Perhaps out of modesty, a continuing sense of *esprit de corps* or a desire to forget the horrors of close combat, he refused to talk about himself and instead celebrated

The road into the village of Raillencourt-Sainte-Olle, 1919. (Courtesy of Canada, Dept. of National Defence/Library and Archives Canada.)

the actions of his comrades. One soldier Jimmy singled out for praise was Donald B. Martyn. He was a schoolteacher before the war and served as a major during the fighting near Cambrai. By the time Jimmy joined the 44th, Martyn had already seen plenty of action. In 1916 he was severely wounded, suffering gunshot wounds to his left wrist and thigh, his right foot and leg, and both buttocks. He also had a compound fracture of his left foot and a perforated eardrum. The army sent Martyn home to Canada to recuperate, and he only returned to action in the spring of 1918, about a month after Jimmy came into the unit. Jimmy and the other soldiers revered Martyn and felt that they would be OK if they had the major with them. Jimmy explained Martyn's actions during the fierce fighting of September 28. "At Cambrai, with men falling all around him and the rest of us seeking cover where it could be had, the major strolled up the road with the battalion, waving his little stick as if on boulevard parade."[2] For his heroic actions during the conflict, Martyn received the Distinguished Service Order, Military Cross with bar, and French *Croix de Guerre*. He survived the war and continued his military career, eventually obtaining the rank of colonel. Martyn died in 1958.

The combat at the Canal du Nord and Cambrai was some of the fiercest ever experienced by the soldiers of the 44th. The official history of the unit, written by Edward Stanford Russenholt, declared, "Morally and physically, Canal du Nord and its immediately succeeding operations are the severest ordeal the 44th men have ever undergone. Their achievements in these actions outshine all others in the history of the unit."[3] During the course of the fighting, the battalion recorded over four hundred men killed, wounded, or missing, and out of the hundreds who began the operation, only a few dozen men, two officers, and three sergeants remained. Jimmy Matthews was one of them.

After the signing of the Armistice in November 1918, Jimmy was granted a two-week leave in Paris. One wonders what the Midwestern boy thought of the war-weary French capital. In January 1919, he was promoted to lance corporal, although he reverted to private just a month later at his own request. He sailed for home on May 28, 1919, from Liverpool and disembarked at Quebec on June 6. By the next month, he was back in Minnesota and soon took up his prewar job as an artist with the *Minneapolis Morning Tribune* newspaper. For a time after his return, he remained connected to Thistle and may have also briefly played for another local side known as the Citizens Club Albions. He designed the Citizens Club Challenge Soccer trophy given to the winner of the local fall season—a plaque depicting a player with a soccer ball at his feet.

On the evening of February 19, 1921, Jimmy was out with friends in Minneapolis when he was hit by a streetcar. The collision mangled his body and dragged him a considerable distance. He was rushed to the hospital, where surgeons fought to save his life; his gas-damaged lungs did not help. Surrounded by his family, James Matthews died on February 20, 1921. His colleagues at the *Minneapolis Morning Tribune* published a moving eulogy to Jimmy that ended this way:

> Courage flames up on the battlefield to spectacular service. It impels men to great deeds where all the world may see its torch flare forth. But it shines no less splendidly in the common ways of life, to those who have eyes to see; it is a fire no less divine when it lights and warms the lives of those about it in humbler walks, as did James Matthews' fine steadfastness in peace as in war—steadfastness that arose from the faith and love and right living which lift men upward toward higher things.[4]

Soon after his death, members of the Citizens Club paid tribute to him at a meeting by silently standing and facing west. A few weeks later, they attached a notice to the challenge cup trophy he designed, proclaiming it the James Matthews Memorial Shield.

Notes

1. "Former Tribune Artist in Kilts," *Minneapolis Morning Tribune*, August 11, 1918.
2. "Jimmy Matthews; Home from France with British Medal," *Minneapolis Morning Tribune*, July 6, 1919.
3. Russenholt, *Six Thousand Canadian Men*, 200.
4. "A Modest Hero," *Minneapolis Morning Tribune*, February 22, 1921.

Sources

Bunk, Brian D. "Soccer at the Inter-Allied Games of 1919: Top Stars." *Society for American Soccer History*. March 6, 2020. https://www.ussoccerhistory.org/soccer-at-the-inter-allied-games-of-1919-top-stars/.

Christie, Norm. *The Canadians at Cambrai*. Ottawa, 2004.

"David Bruce Martyn." Personnel records of World War I. Files of the Canadian Expeditionary Force (CEF). Library and Archives Canada.

Hennepin County Yearbook Collection. Hennepin County Public Library. https://hclib.org/programs/genealogy-local-history/hennepin-county-yearbooks.

"James Joseph Matthews." Personnel records of World War I. Files of the Canadian Expeditionary Force (CEF). Library and Archives Canada.

Nicholson, G. W. L. *Canadian Expeditionary Force, 1914–1919*. Ottawa, 1962.
Russenholt, Edward Stanford. *Six Thousand Canadian Men: Being the History of the 44th Battalion Canadian Infantry, 1914–1919*. Montfort Press: Winnipeg, 1932.
"Thomas Scott Scobbie." Personnel records of World War I. Files of the Canadian Expeditionary Force (CEF). Library and Archives Canada.
War Diary, 44th Infantry Battalion. Library and Archives Canada. http://central.bac-lac.gc.ca/.redirect?app=fonandcol&id=1883256&lang=eng.

NEWSPAPER

Minneapolis Morning Tribune

WEBSITE

Ancestry.com

11

High Plains Kickers

Denver, Colorado

In 1865, Frances Clelland celebrated her fifth birthday along the Overland Trail, perched atop a covered wagon next to her mother. Travelers followed the Trail from the state of Kansas to areas in the far West, including California, Utah, and Colorado. For a short distance, it ran parallel to the more famous Oregon Trail. During the journey, Frances wore a gingham dress and bolero jacket, with a blue chambray quilted bonnet to keep the sun out of her eyes. Her wagon and others in the group were packed with a family's worth of possessions: carpets, feather beds, blankets, even a rocking chair. Dust filled the air, along with the sharp, musky scent of the oxen as they strained to keep the caravan moving. The gamey smell of the team competed with other, fresher scents, including the soft aroma of prairie grass and the sweet bouquet of wildflowers. Decades later she could still recall how the wagon creaked and jolted over the seemingly endless plains. Her father, a Scotsman named James, rode at the head of the group; a rifle set across his lap and a pistol strapped to his hip. He had made the six-week trek from Atchison, Kansas, to Denver, Colorado, many times, but this would be one of the last. James Clelland worked in freighting, moving goods across the region to supply the growing cities and mines of the West. He saw that the railroad would soon mean the end of traditional wagon trains and decided to resettle permanently in Colorado. He loved the natural beauty of the place and felt that it might have a favorable influence on his son George. The boy was just twelve years old and, according to his little sister at least, was "not very robust."[1]

After living in Denver for several years, the family eventually settled in Cañon City in 1871, where James became a prosperous merchant and real estate developer. Frances grew up and married James Hamilton Peabody, who twice served as governor of the state. George worked a variety of jobs, including writing humorous newspaper articles under the byline "Dicer Swift." In one of his missives, he recounted how he played a foundational role in bringing football to Denver. Long before the development of soccer, young men played a series of games that more closely resembled kick-abouts than organized contests. Generally lumped together under the name football, these activities were common across the country. In most places it is impossible to pinpoint when such games began. Denver, however, is different. In 1890, the *Rocky Mountain News* published a letter written by Dicer Swift. According to Clelland, the sport began in Colorado when he and a group of schoolboy friends pitched in to buy a six-dollar football and have it shipped out West. Once it arrived in the spring of 1867, the lads kicked it around a bit but never formed a proper club or held an organized match. Although that was not much of a beginning, soccer eventually took hold in the Mile High City. Over the next half-century, the game in the region had its successes and its failures, reflecting in some sense the lives of those who played it.

A decade after Clelland and his friends did their kicking, a high school team played against various clubs, including the Quicksteps and Denver Stars. These games were likely closer to traditional football or intercollegiate rules than they were to soccer. A newspaper report from 1883 confirmed that by that date, the high school squad was playing by the "national rules" but would be better served in taking up rugby. In 1887, the earliest mention of soccer appeared in the *Rocky Mountain News*. A short notice on Christmas Day informed readers that the Denver Rangers would play the opening game of the season that morning at Riverfront Park. The club had formed about a week earlier, and since there were no other teams in the city, they held an intra-squad game. Although most of them had never played soccer before, the match ended in an entertaining 1–1 draw. The club was ongoing, as the same paper reported in January and February 1888 that the Rangers continued to meet and practice.

By the fall of 1888, interest in soccer was growing in Denver. On November 18, two sides, both made up of members from the Arapahoe Football Club, played a practice match. A few days later, a notice in the newspaper, signed by "Collegiate Football Player," declared that the Five Points baseball club was planning to organize a football team. They might challenge Arapahoe FC but preferred to play using the intercollegiate code rather than the association rules. The writer felt that the Five Points squad would be better able to utilize their superior pace under the gridiron rules. In response, the newspaper published a note from "Lover of True Sport" declaring that the association rules are "the only proper ones which bring out all the points of the game of football." He chastised "Collegiate Football Player" for thinking that speed did not matter in soccer and declared the intercollegiate game to be "tiresome."[2] Finally, "Lover of True Sport" noted that soccer was much more appealing to spectators. Presumably made up of men from the city neighborhood of the same name, the novice Five Points squad eventually came up against the Arapahoe club. The match report noted that although the Five Points team was indeed quicker, the Arapahoe side was more skilled and the 4–0 score line confirmed the judgement.

In 1889 Denver was home to several football clubs, although many of them played only sporadically. The Five Points team likely returned to baseball, and the Arapahoe, Rangers, and Thistle squads were generally inactive. Things changed in the fall as a new team formed and the foundations of regular competition took shape in the city. The *Rocky Mountain News* printed a letter from "Lover of Sport" on August 19, 1889. The note declared that it was now a good time for football, but not of the intercollegiate kind. Middle-class men with white collar jobs would be wise to choose soccer because the possibility of injury was much lower. On November 6, 1889, twenty-three men met at Foreman's photography studio on Larimer Street to organize a soccer club called the Swifts. Walter H. Foreman, proprietor of the studio, was elected president and his uncle, Walter E. Freeman, served as vice president. An Englishman by birth, Foreman immigrated to the United States in 1884. Over the next decade or so, the photography studio emerged as the center of Denver's footballing community. Just two days after forming, the Swifts joined Denver Football Club and Denver Athletics in launching the Western Association Football League (WAFL). A week after that, the league elected officers, received a trophy donated by a team manager, and added a fourth club called Rangers. It is unclear if the latest Rangers side had any connection with the one that had existed a few years earlier.

In addition to the metropolitan competition, teams from Denver prepared to face off against squads from the rest of the state. In late 1889, John White, secretary of a club known as Mountaineers FC, offered to play any team in the city, with Rangers or Denver FC the preferred opponents. A month later Denver FC met to consider a challenge from the Rocky Mountain Rangers of Crested Butte. Although it was later canceled, the Swifts agreed to meet a team from Colorado Springs and scheduled a match versus Louisville. The earliest confirmed interstate clash in Colorado took place in July 1890 when the Starkville Athletic Club from Trinidad lost to a visiting side from Blossburg, New Mexico. At the time both towns were coal mining centers and later experienced periods of labor unrest as workers struck for improved wages and safety conditions. Blossburg was eventually abandoned, and the site of the town now sits on private property owned by media mogul Ted Turner.

Detailed results from the first season of the WAFL are unavailable, although in December 1891 the *Rocky Mountain News* declared that Denver FC could rightfully claim to be champions. In what was probably the most anticipated match in the city's soccer history, Denver FC and the Swifts put up one hundred dollars each on a contest to determine who would take home the cup. The winning squad would retain possession until a proper series of matches could be scheduled. On December 28, 1890, the Swifts lined up in maroon and blue, while Denver FC wore scarlet and white. A crowd of around six hundred watched as Denver FC captured the trophy with a resounding 4–1 victory. A few months later, the soccer community experienced its first controversy. After Denver FC reportedly ignored the Swifts' calls for a rematch, the spurned team began to claim the championship due to their opponent's inaction. On February 15, 1891, the *Rocky Mountain News* published a response from Denver FC club secretary Alec Duthie. He stated that it was categorically false that his club had refused to play the Swifts, or that they would only agree if stakes were involved. Instead, they had informed the Swifts that they had a full schedule after arranging a series of matches with Rangers. Duthie also noted that Denver FC had offered to participate in a benefit match for "Eastern Colorado sufferers" but the Swifts had refused.[3]

The tussle did little to dampen enthusiasm for the game in the city. By the fall of 1891, membership in the Swifts club had doubled, not just because of the soccer, but also due to the popularity of the smoking concerts, receptions, and dances the club put on. Joining the association provided an opportunity for leisure activities as well as access to a whole series of social events. Information on the backgrounds of the men involved in the early soccer community in Denver is sparse, although reportedly many players came from the building trades. Alec Duthie, who was connected to both the Denver FC and Rangers squads, was a general contractor who had been born in Scotland. Others, like photographer Walter Foreman, held middle-class professions while some labored in less refined circumstances. Several Ballentynes, a Scotch-Irish family of stonecutters, also played soccer in these years. Despite the growth of the Swifts as an organization, they still could not compete with Denver FC on the pitch. In November 1891, the two sides met before a crowd of over five hundred. The newspaper called them the state's leading clubs. Denver FC took a 2–0 lead after forty-five minutes before scoring three more in the second half to capture a 5–2 victory. The match signaled the end of the first great period of early soccer in Denver. Over the next decade, both clubs continued to meet and reorganize almost every season, but whatever on-field activities took place received little attention from the press.

It was not until the turn of the twentieth century that match reports and other articles about Denver soccer begin to appear once again in newspapers. Despite renewed attention, an article from the *Denver Post* in 1900 may explain why so few stories about soccer had been published in previous years. The headline read "Association Game at City Park," and the story described a match featuring just fifteen players unevenly divided between two teams: "The game, of course, was very slow compared to the Rugby game of today and did not attract much interest."[4] Despite the negative attitude of some members of the press, a reorganized Denver FC took to the field for practice games and played against teams from outside the area. Christmas Day 1900 began a tradition that became one of the most anticipated matches of the season—a contest between teams of local players representing England and Scotland. In October 1901 the *Rocky Mountain News* announced that fans of "the great Scotch game" were discussing the possibility of forming a state soccer league.[5] The article also reported that the Denver Cricket Club and the Caledonian Club may combine to form a team to represent the city. Rekindled interest in the sport also brought a new generation of players and administrators to the fore.

One of them was a young man from Manchester, England, named Sydney Foden. Standing five feet, eight inches tall, Foden had blue eyes and light brown hair. He came to the United States as a child and was still only a teenager when his name began appearing in match reports, including the Christmas Day contest in 1900 where he lined up at forward on the victorious English side. For many years Foden worked as a clerk at the Great Western grocery store, and another market clerk named Stephen Bamber also played a key role in organizing soccer competitions. Slightly older than Foden, Bamber was also born in England. In November 1901, both Foden and Bamber were tasked with running practice sessions designed to prepare a team to play in the upcoming state competition. The nascent organization also chose Bamber to be secretary. Although the state-wide competition never materialized, the lads played together on the forward line for Denver FC in various matches over the next two years.

Foden's time as a soccer player seems to have been cut short by a terrible personal tragedy that unfolded in the summer of 1903. Ever since they had been kids, Sydney Foden had been in love with a girl named Bessie Schrontz. By the time she was eighteen years old, she worked as an operator with the Denver telephone company. At some point in 1903, she became infatuated with a streetcar driver and conductor named Thomas

Kayne. Described by one newspaper as a "sport" and heavy drinker, the well-dressed Kayne "had that easy, reckless air that so often appeals to girls of youth and inexperience."[6] Kayne responded positively to her affections and the two began going out, even though her mother disapproved of the match. The affair caused her to lose focus at work and she was eventually fired. After a time Kayne and Schrontz traveled to Golden, Colorado, where they were supposedly married. Upon returning to Denver, Schrontz's mother demanded to see the marriage license, but the pair continually put her off, making excuses for their inability to produce the document. Meanwhile, they had "assumed the relations of husband and wife," presumably a euphemism meaning that they slept together. One day Schrontz arrived at her mother's workplace, saying that she and Kayne had an argument and he had struck her. Bessie explained that she had left him and confessed that they had never been married. Friends of the young woman later accused Kayne of orchestrating a sham ceremony designed to trick her into believing they had wed. At some point, however, she found out the truth.

All the while, Foden's love for Bessie remained strong, even after everyone believed she had married another man. Following the revelations that her union with Kayne was never real, Foden "stepped into the breach and offered his love and his name that her name might not be degraded." Eventually, the two were married on June 15, 1903, at the Champa Street grocery store where he worked. Three days later, apparently after learning that Kayne had left Denver for New York, Bessie became despondent and swallowed poison pills. After lingering for almost a week, Bessie Schrontz Foden died on June 24, 1903. Publicly, at least, Foden never expressed regret for his decision to marry her, and he shared a house with his mother-in-law until her death in 1924. Foden eventually remarried at some point in the 1930s and lived on South University Boulevard until his death in 1944. Despite his relative prominence in the soccer community, he seems to have stopped playing entirely after 1903.

If Sydney Foden and Stephen Bamber were enthusiastic supporters of a new soccer competition in Denver, they nevertheless remained junior figures. The real force behind the organizational efforts was Archibald "Archie" P. Gibson. Until his untimely death in 1911, Gibson played a key role in administering and promoting soccer in Denver. He was born in Kilmarnock, Scotland, around 1878 to a family involved in the wool-trading business. Gibson arrived in Denver in 1895 and worked as an agent for wholesale woolen merchants Robert Gibson Campbell and Co. He was also heavily involved in the associational and sporting culture of the city. At one time or another, he served as vice president of the Denver Athletic

Club, was elected chief of the Caledonian Club, and was a member of the Denver Golf Club. It is hard to determine if he played much soccer himself, but the community appreciated his efforts and thought of him as one of the most important figures in the early history of the sport in the city. In 1901 he was elected president of Denver FC. Over the next decade, he was the leading evangelist for the game in the state.

As in other locations around the country, the visit of the English club Pilgrims to North America in 1905, along with questions over the safety of the intercollegiate game, sparked a revival of soccer in Denver. Gibson remained at the forefront, continuing as president of Denver FC while also serving as a referee and linesman. In a published photograph from 1907, he looks every inch the middle-class sportsman. Dressed in a natty suit and checked-wool tweed, flat cap, he is seated at a desk or table, holding open a small book with one hand while a pipe rests comfortably in the other. In the columns of the same newspaper, he made a passionate case that a player from the west of the country be included on a planned All-American team that would travel to England. Gibson felt that his own team captain, Donald MacKay, fit the bill and offered to pay the player's train fare to New York City, where the selection was set to take place. MacKay had supposedly played professionally abroad before coming to the United States and believed that at their best, Denver FC would be a match for any second division club in England. Ultimately, the trip never materialized, and MacKay remained in the Mile High City. On October 26, 1907, Gibson wrote an article defending the sport headlined "Soccer Football is not a 'Sissy Game.'" The motivation for the article came after Gibson heard a high school boy disparage the sport. He urged students to play soccer, as it "requires strength, will power, judgement and a good disposition." He also challenged readers to "try the game of soccer and you will find it a game for manly men."[7]

Despite the long history of the sport in Denver, it was only in 1910 that the first truly competitive league formed. The Colorado League of Association Football (CLAF) began play late in the year with six teams: Clan Gordon, Denver FC, Crescents, Annunciations, Golden, and Sacred Heart College (now Regis University). Archie Gibson led a group of donors, who purchased a cup for the league winner, and the Spalding sporting goods company donated a trophy to be given to any side that captured the title three years in a row. In addition to league games, teams participated in friendlies and in stake matches for as much as two hundred dollars a side. Players and administrators also planned social events and smokers, appointing committees to "arrange for jollification."[8] Socializing off the pitch was a common activity in most soccer playing communities, but in

Denver such activities often proved equally important—if not more so—as the play on the field. After a fast start in the league, the Gordons were pegged back by Denver FC and the two ended the season tied at the top of the table. The championship match, played on March 5, 1911, ended in a 4–2 victory for Denver.

The captain of the winning squad was a six-foot, brown-haired, blue-eyed auto mechanic from England named James Oswald Heathcote. Born January 1, 1890, in Melbourne, Derbyshire, Heathcote anchored the back line for the champions. In a team photograph taken before a match, he stands up straight, shoulders back, chest out, easily the tallest figure in the frame. His arms are crossed in front of his body, and although some of the other players are smiling, Heathcote practically glares at the camera, his face set with a look of stern determination. In another image of the team, this time a studio portrait taken after they had won the league, he stands in the back row, still upright but with a more placid expression. The squad poses with their hardware as well as two bekilted musicians, one holding a bagpipe, the other a drum. The postcard originally belonged to an enthusiastic supporter who carefully decorated the back. Written in pencil

Denver FC in 1911. James Heathcoate stands in uniform on the far right. (Author's collection)

at the top is "Denver Soccer Football Team." Underneath in large, thickly drawn decorative letters is "1911 Champs." The names of the captain and manager follow, and in smaller script below that are the players and their positions. Numerous erasures and pencil lines reveal the care that went into creating the memento.

Just as the league began to plan a follow-up season, the sudden death of Archie Gibson shocked the soccer community. Sometime in late September 1911, Gibson fell ill with pneumonia. Doctors visited the newly

Studio portrait of Denver FC, 1911. (Author's collection)

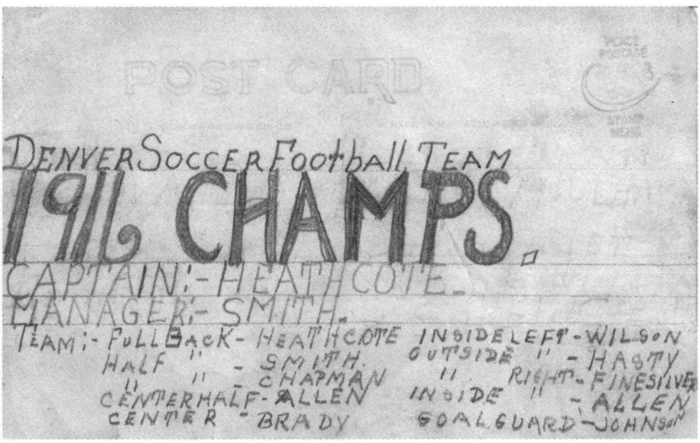

The back of Denver FC's studio portrait postcard reveals the decoration added by a fan of the club. (Author's collection)

built house he shared with his wife and son at 444 Gilpin Street, treating him with medicinal waters, tincture of digitalis, and strychnine tablets. All these efforts were unsuccessful, and Gibson died at home at 10:45 p.m. on October 7. The local papers eulogized him for his contributions to the city's sporting culture and praised him for his unwavering support of soccer. A few years later, William Halyburton emphasized Gibson's contributions to the sport in his brief history of soccer in Denver published in *Spalding's Official Soccer Foot Ball Guide*. His last will and testament provides a snapshot of the life of one of the city's most prominent sporting fellows. The document includes a list of outstanding creditors, tradespeople, and businesses that Gibson owed money to upon his death. The most heartbreaking expenses are the ones associated with his illness and death, doctor's bills, medication costs, and money for a memorial service. Several are related to what must have been the finishing touches on the family's new home: $5 for a light fixture and $115 to Thomas H. Miller for wallpapering, painting, and floor finishing. Others tell the story of a prosperous middle-class professional—monies owed to the Denver Omnibus and Cab Co., the Auto Livery Company, and Carl F. Erickson and the Nathan Brothers, both tailors. Still more reflect his interest in associational activities, including settling his account with the Denver Athletic Club for $8 in dues and $46.05 in other expenses and a subscription to the *Scottish American* newspaper published out of New York. Gibson's brother, who had been on his way to visit Denver before Archie's untimely death, took the body back home to be buried in Scotland.

Despite the loss of Archie Gibson, Denver's soccer community continued to grow in the fall of 1911. The CLAF discussed adding a second division, schools began playing the sport, and all city parks were supplied with a soccer ball. The momentum continued into the next year as the earliest report of a woman playing soccer appeared in the newspaper. Anna Belle Holland was an instructor who ran an afterschool program at the Sherman School grounds. More than three hundred children took part, and they appreciated Holland's hands-on approach: "she gets right out and plays soccer football and rugby football with the older boys."[9] In 1913, both the *Denver Post* and *Rocky Mountain News* ran long stories with photographs about a soccer demonstration staged by local teachers. The five female instructors gave an exhibition of the sport "as women may play it" at the North Side High School Gym.[10] Only five players took part, and they used a set of rules described as less strenuous than the men's version. Despite such advances and the ongoing hopes of league officials, the CLAF struggled to expand outside of the city. Although teams formed in communities around Colorado, the challenge of developing a state-wide league remained too difficult to overcome. Even in the city itself, teams such as the Welsh Rovers, Pansy Cycle, White Sox, and even another iteration of the Five Points squad often played a few games or even a season or two before disappearing.

In 1915–16, a group of teams formed a breakaway competition called the Rocky Mountain League, but few if any games were played and the upstart organization soon dissolved. Newspapers failed to report on the exact causes of the schism but often published teasing stories that all was not well within the soccer community. Many of these hints appeared in a new column called "Soccer Notes" (sometimes called "High Kicks" and "Soccer Shots") that began to appear in the *Denver Post* in 1916. The *Rocky Mountain News* added a similar section, also called "Soccer Notes," written by an anonymous author known as "The Secret Agent." The articles featured match reports and other traditional material but also contained inside jokes, rumors, and gossip. In January, "Soccer Notes" reported that Sacred Heart, one of the CLAF's longest-serving teams, had dropped out. A week later, the columnist wrote indirectly about the tensions within the community: "Early in the season when the league was starting someone suggested that harmony prevail. All agreed, but nevertheless that was the last of harmony."[11]

As in many communities around the country, Denver soccerites struggled to deal with the impact of World War I. In October 1917 the *Denver Post* reported that the league was optimistic about the new season and would soon begin play featuring a mixture of established teams such as the Gordons and Denver FC along with new ones, including Cadillac Motor, White Walker (another car dealership), and Hibernians. By December, teams began canceling matches due to lack of interest. Much of the player base, and many of the sport's most ardent fans, had enlisted. Newspapers reported that almost the entire Gordons team had gone overseas, and league president J. R. Taylor's four sons were in military service, including one who perished at the Battle of the Marne. In addition to the difficulties brought on by the war, the soccer community also suffered repeated blows at the hands of "Kid Weather."[12] Snow and other climate-related issues had happened in the past but seemed particularly severe during the war years. As a result of these challenges, the soccer community in Denver virtually disappeared by 1919. The return of soldiers by the end of the year, however, sparked renewed interest in the game. The impetus to form a new competition came from men who had previously been involved in the sport, as well as those who learned to play in Europe. By early 1920 a league had formed, and Denver embarked on the next era in its long history with the game.

Notes

1. Peabody, "Across the Plains DeLuxe," 72.

2. Lover of True Sport, "For Association Rules," *Rocky Mountain News*, November 22, 1888.

3. "The Swifts and Denver," *Rocky Mountain News*, February 15, 1891.

4. "Association Game at City Park," *Denver Post*, October 22, 1900.

5. "May Form State League," *Rocky Mountain News*, October 29, 1901.

6. "Vain Struggle Against Fate," *Rocky Mountain News*, June 26, 1903. All quotations in this section are from this same story.

7. A. P. Gibson, "Soccer Football is not a 'Sissy Game'," *Rocky Mountain News*, October 26, 1907.

8. "Soccer Players Plan Big Smoker for January 21," *Rocky Mountain News*, January 4, 1911.

9. "Girl Athletic Instructor Makes Sherman School Yard Favorite Resort for Children After Hours," *Denver Post*, November 16, 1912.

10. "Girls Play Soccer," *Rocky Mountain News*, May 2, 1913.

11. "Soccer Notes," *Denver Post*, February 16, 1916.

12. "Soccer Again," *Denver Post*, February 10, 1918.

Sources

Cannon, Helen. "First Ladies of Colorado: Frances Clelland Peabody." *Colorado Magazine* 52, no. 3 (Summer 1975): 244–56.

Ferrie, R. A. "Soccer Football in Colorado." *Spalding's Official Association "Soccer" Foot Ball Guide*, 185–89. New York: American Sports Publishing, 1912.

Ferrie, R. A. "Soccer Football in Colorado." *Spalding's Official "Soccer" Football Guide*, 85. New York: American Sports Publishing, 1917.

Halyburton, William. "Soccer Foot Ball in Colorado." *Spalding's Official Association "Soccer" Foot Ball Guide*, 217–19. New York: American Sports Publishing, 1913.

"In the Far West." *Spalding's Official Association "Soccer" Foot Ball Guide*. New York: American Sports Publishing, 1907.

Peabody, Frances Clelland. "Across the Plains DeLuxe in 1865." *The Colorado Magazine* 18, no. 2 (March 1941): 71–76.

NEWSPAPERS

Colorado Springs Gazette
Denver Post
Denver Tribune
Rocky Mountain News

WEBSITE

Ancestry.com

12

Soccer in the City of Roses

Portland, Oregon

On the morning of June 5, 1873, hundreds of people streamed down Pine, Ash, and Oak Streets to the Oregon Steam Navigation Company's wharf in downtown Portland, Oregon. Nestled along the Willamette River, the building was an immense rectangular structure constructed of wood, about half a city block long. From the riverside, the two levels of the dock looked like they were put together with Lincoln Logs from a child's play set. The large building had skylights, but on this day, they provided only gentle illumination, as the forecast said storms were possible. Despite the chance of poor weather, there was excitement in the air. Today was the day of the Portland Hibernian Benevolent Society's summer excursion.

The group sponsored social events to help raise money to fulfill its primary mission: "to relieve the distressed, support the afflicted, attend upon the sick, bury the dead, and locate a fund out of which such kindly and humane services may be performed."[1] Anticipation had been building over the past few weeks as the group advertised the trip in newspapers. The notices loudly proclaimed that it would be the "Grand Picnic of the Season," featuring a specially built dance platform adorned with pine boughs and flowers to create "FAIRY-LIKE ENCHANTMENT."[2] Couples and families handed over their one-dollar tickets and boarded a sidewheel steamship called the *Oneonta*. Built in 1863, the boat featured two funnels forward of the pilot house and two sidewheels near the stern. The ship was a stark white, with its name painted in large black letters over the enclosed sidewheels. As the ship got underway, passengers heard the metronome-like splash—splash—splash of the wheels starting up and the long, whooshing hoot of the steam whistle. For this trip the *Oneonta* was also towing a platform barge and dancing started there almost as soon as they shoved off. The two-hour, thirty-minute cruise took them about six miles north of the city of Vancouver, Washington, to a place known as Harmony Grove. After more dancing to the music of the East Portland Brass Band and a luncheon, games and other activities took place in the afternoon. Like many of these events around the country, they featured a variety of happenings, including foot races, shooting contests, and climbing a greased pole. A football match was also on the schedule. To be clear, it was almost certainly not soccer. Instead, it was a version of the game that had been played in Great Britain and the United States for decades. The football was not the most notable sporting event at the picnic, however; that honor went to the fat man race. Three husky gentlemen competed for the prize, but sadly the winner's name is lost to history. The lack of attention given to football in this period would come back to haunt proponents of soccer in the Rose City. While fat man races did not offer much of an alternative, games like baseball and intercollegiate football had more staying power. Despite slow development, by the mid-twentieth century Portland had embraced the sport and now hosts one of the most devoted soccer communities in the country.

The earliest recorded games of football in Portland took place in the 1860s. Around the same time as the Hibernian picnic, local sporting goods shop William Beck and Son regularly sold footballs alongside other recreational items such as rifles and fishing tackle. A decade later, notices for the first organized football teams began to appear in newspapers, with the Portland Football and Cricket Club and the Columbia Foot Ball Club announcing what seemed to be intra-squad games. The rules these sides used cannot be known for certain, but there is reason to believe they may have been playing rugby. In the fall of 1882, teams of US and British players met on at least two occasions, and the lineups included fifteen players a side.

By the second half of 1890, football players in Portland seemed to be experimenting with different codes, scheduling games using the intercollegiate, rugby, and association or soccer rules. A meeting at the end of August drew over forty men interested in starting a football team. Soon afterward, the Portland Football Club held two practice games using the rugby rules. A few months later, the team, now christened the Portland Amateur Athletic Club (PAAC), scheduled a Thanksgiving Day doubleheader, with the first match to kick off at 12:30 p.m. and the second at 8:30 p.m. The early game was against the Bishop Scott Academy team using the intercollegiate rules, while the second came against a side called the Wanderers under the association code. Three men, Mills, Jones, and Sparks, were listed in the lineups for both games, although it is possible they were different family members or distinct players that shared the same, fairly common surnames. In what was called the first game in Oregon played "under Eastern college rules," PAAC won the midday match handily by a score of 8–0 in front of 1,500 spectators.[3] The results of the second, evening game were not reported. In January 1891 the PAAC met to determine the roster for another game against Wanderers to be held on January 25.

In addition to facing off against other city teams, the Portland squad competed with a side from Astoria, Oregon, a small city just over ninety miles to the northwest. Situated on the Columbia River, Astoria was known as a trading center for various products, including furs, timber, and salmon. Although the 0–1 score of the intercity clash held on December 6, 1890, seemed to indicate that visiting Portland had won a soccer game, later reporting suggested the teams had played using a version of the rugby code. At some point in 1892 or 1893, soccer clubs began to form in both Portland and Astoria. One of the earliest squads in Astoria was organized by employees of the Pacific Can Company. By the end of the decade, the town had become one of the leading soccer playing areas in the state. Matches between Portland and Astoria football clubs were not regular occurrences, with only a handful played in 1893. Wearing dark blue and black uniforms, the Portland squad won every time, including an October 21, 1893, clash that the *Oregonian* newspaper deemed the first soccer game played in the city. The rivalry between the two communities continued into 1894, with several games taking place. On May 30 the Astoria Football Club, kitted out in blue and white, defeated Portland for the first time, taking home the victory 3–2 in front of six hundred local supporters. A few months later, on July 4, the home side once again proved too much for a picked eleven from Portland as Astoria cruised to a 4–0 victory. In some ways these wins signaled the changing fortunes of the sport in both Portland and Astoria. Interest in soccer declined in Portland, even as it increased in Astoria and in communities just across the border in Washington state.

On July 2, 1896, delegates met to form the Oregon-Washington Association Football League (OWAFL). Representatives from the following clubs attended the first meeting: Ilwaco, South Bend, and Chinook from Washington; Astoria, Oregon City, and Thistle FC of Portland from Oregon. Astoria High School was also affiliated with the league, and the final team listed the Wallacott Rangers, which hailed from parts unknown. Unusually for a soccer league in the United States at the time, the schedule called for a total of forty-six games to be played over the course of the summer. Several of the clubs originally listed, such as the Thistles and Rangers, proved to be paper teams and no record of them ever taking the field has been found.

Within a week of organizing, the *Oregonian* reported only six clubs in the competition, none of them from Portland: Ilwaco, Stringtown, Chinook, South Bend, Astoria, and Long Beach. Eventually, the Portland Football Club began the season in the league but soon withdrew following a dispute over the postponement of a match. The most active teams consisted of Astoria, Ilwaco, South Bend, and Long Beach, communities separated by only about fifty miles. The towns, clustered around the Columbia River and Pacific Ocean, served as a summer holiday area, and the soccer matches were deemed part of the seasonal attractions. By August the league had a trophy to award to the winning side. Donated by George Bartley, the prize was an eighteen-inch silver cup made in Boston, topped by the figure of a player kicking a ball. Engraved on one side was a scene of a field with players scoring a goal, and on the other was an inscription: "Astoria Challenge Cup / Presented by George Bartley / Association Football."[4] Bartley was the proprietor of the National Resort, located on Commercial Street in Astoria. The establishment sold National beer, "the thing to drink when you are hot and thirsty," in two varieties: "Old Oceans foam" and "National foam." Later, the National described itself as the "Mariner's resort" and touted its expanded beer list, now including Bavarian and Kopp's beers.[5]

The Ilwaco team captured the 1896 league title and with it the Bartley cup. The club had been the favorites going into the season and were said to have five of the best players in the state. They also travelled with "two colored mascots."[6] It was not uncommon for young children to play this role for soccer clubs during this era, although no ages were given for those with the Ilwaco squad. No other example of a soccer team in the United States with people of color as mascots has been found. It was more common in baseball, when male children took on the job beginning in the 1870s. Perhaps the earliest example of an African American mascot was in 1877, when George Wright, manager of the Boston Red Stockings, hired a young man to serve in the role. Many of these African American boys began working around eight or nine years old and were aged out as teenagers. In the beginning some newspapers refused to publish their true names, only referring to them using racist nicknames. No other information about the Ilwaco mascots has been found, beyond the passing reference in a single newspaper article. African American communities in the area were small, with population numbers in Portland and Tacoma, the nearest large cities to Ilwaco, being just 775 and 307, respectively, in 1900. The federal census of that year counted just two Black residents in the whole of Pacific County, neither of them in Ilwaco. Elsie Dickison lived in Long Beach and Harry Gorman in South Bend; both were employed as servants. Dickison would have been about eight or nine in 1896 and Gorman a teenager, but it is extremely unlikely that one or both were the mascots mentioned in the newspaper.

The OWAFL continued into 1897 with seven teams: Astoria FC, Chinook, Fort Canby, Ilwaco, Nahcotta, South Bend, and Royal Fats, the latter based out of Ilwaco and so called because all the players weighed over 200 pounds. Once again Ilwaco proved the class of the competition and took home the cup. After the conclusion of its second season, the OWAFL seems to have disbanded. Soccer in Oregon entered a period of inactivity, with few reported games taking place. In Portland, the sport was only revived following the turn of the twentieth century. The renewed interest in soccer was largely driven by matches played between crews from visiting British ships and the local Seaman's Institute. Historian Zachary R. Bigalke calls the Institute "a catalyst for the rebirth of soccer in Portland in the first decade of the twentieth century."[7] Nevertheless, progress was slow, and even the resurrection of Portland FC in 1901 did little to spur anything more than modest growth. A key figure in the newly revived soccer scene was George J. Cameron, a Scottish-born immigrant, who eventually became a local judge. Cameron had been involved with Portland's soccer community almost since its founding and continued to play a major role until his death in 1921. He had represented the Portland Club at the first meeting of the OWAFL and in 1901 was elected president of Portland FC. He would continue as a player, referee, and administrator well into his forties. Despite the herculean efforts of Cameron and the presence of English-, Scottish-, and Canadian-born residents, soccer once again failed to launch. Aficionados of the sport in Portland hit upon the idea that the 1905 centennial celebration of the Lewis and Clark expedition would be the key to the game's expansion in the area.

The locals based their optimism on the fact that soccer had been a feature of fairs and other gatherings since the 1893 World's Columbian Exposition in Chicago. The organizers of that event hoped to host an international soccer competition as part of the fair's attractions. Teams from Ontario, Canada, and Philadelphia pledged to make the trip, and the planning committee even went so far as to invite additional clubs from Europe and South America. Historian Gabe Logan notes that "Chicago soccer organizers clearly envisioned an international-soccer-championship, decades before the World Cup and eleven years prior to the first Olympic soccer matches."[8] Despite these grandiose ambitions, the tournament soon fell apart, mainly because the famed Corinthians squad of England canceled their visit and other squads quickly backed out as well. Eventually, the scaled-down soccer competition was organized by the local Caledonian Society and featured six teams playing nine-a-side games. The squads involved came from Chicago except for two entries from the nearby mining community of Braidwood, Illinois. The local Thistles team captured the honors, with the Braidwood B squad coming second. A year later, in 1894, teams played soccer on the grounds of the California Midwinter International Exposition in San Francisco. Unlike Chicago, however, these matches were part of the local league schedule and did not seem to have any official connection with the Exposition.

The soccer community in Oregon may have found greater inspiration in the tournament held at the Pan-American Exposition of 1901 in Buffalo. The format was a cross-border clash between teams from the United States and Canada. The clubs first competed against their countrymen, and the top squads from the United States and Canada played in the final. The announcement of the soccer tournament on September 2, 1901, listed the

One half of a stereoscope image of the champion Fall River team at the 1901 Pan-American Exposition in Buffalo, New York. (Author's collection)

US teams as coming from Paterson and Trenton, New Jersey; St. Louis; Fall River, Massachusetts; and Pawtucket, Rhode Island. The two Canadian entries came from Toronto: Scots and Gore Vale. The day after the notice appeared, however, the *Buffalo Inquirer* informed readers that the teams from Trenton and Pawtucket had withdrawn. In the end only four sides played for the championship: Fall River, Christian Brothers College of St. Louis, Toronto Scots, and Gore Vale. In the preliminary round, Fall River dispatched the Christian Brothers, while the Scots defeated Gore Vale. The final took place on September 5, 1901, and ended with Fall River taking home the honors after a 5–1 win.

Although generally successful, the Pan-American soccer tournament showcased the challenges facing event organizers, challenges that the men of Portland were unable to overcome. As in Chicago seven years earlier, the planners of the Pan-American soccer tournament were forced to put on a much smaller event than they had hoped for. One reason for this is that, while the winning teams earned prizes, they were not given any financial support to attend. The teams that chose to compete needed to cover their own expenses. Such costs included transportation and lodging for a travelling party that could number anywhere between fifteen and twenty people. Because clubs during this period often had trouble raising enough funds to maintain their position in local leagues and cup competitions, the money required to participate in a distant tournament proved to be too much. One St. Louis paper reported that, originally, they were told that the winning side would receive a $1,500 prize, but this was later dropped in favor of medals and banners for the winner. Even a soccer-mad city like Fall River found it a challenge to come up with the required funding. Immediately upon receiving the invitation to the tournament, soccer officials in the city inquired about possible subventions that might help two Fall River teams travel to Buffalo. Within a month organizers wrote back saying that no money was available to help defray expenses, and since admission to the Exposition was free, there would be no gate receipts to split. As a result the soccer community in Fall River spent most of the summer raising money for just a single club to attend the competition. A prominent businessman agreed to pay the train fares; furniture store owner W. W. Coolidge provided kits and caps, and William Low, shoe dealer, offered the boots for cost, including a pair, size 3, that had to be special ordered for "Little" Willy McNeil. The Enterprise Brewing Company donated $150 in cash, the Shay Brothers kicked in $25, and even the town's mayor pledged $5. Practice games brought in additional funds, as did a raffle that was won by Ellison R. Fuller, who instantly donated the $20 prize back to the team. All in all the club raised a total of $364.75, enough to compete and win the tournament. For the Spindle City, the money was well spent, as the community basked in the glow of the international championship. A parade of over fifty athletic clubs and a reception featuring local politicians and dignitaries celebrated the victorious team.

Although perhaps better known today than the other competitions, the 1904 Olympic soccer tournament generally attracted less attention than the 1901 Pan-American contest. Rather than issuing direct invitations to teams, the organizing committee accepted entry applications during a narrow window about two weeks before the scheduled start date. Up to eight teams expressed interest and were at some point included on the list of competitors: Christian Brothers College (CBC), St. Ann, St. Alloysius, and St. Rose, all from St. Louis; Thistles of Edgemont, Illinois; and the University of Toronto, Berlin Rangers, and Galt of Canada. By the time the games kicked off on November 16, just three teams remained: CBC, St. Rose, and Galt. According to the *Windsor Star*, one reason why teams withdrew was that the Amateur Athletic Union decreed that all players had to be registered with the organization before competing. The article believed this was a deliberate attempt to exclude the Canadian teams, since they would have difficulties in obtaining cards so near to the start of the games. This may explain why Berlin Rangers and Thistles withdrew, and it was also reported that the University of Toronto squad canceled because the school would not pay for the trip. In the end the experienced Galt squad easily defeated the St. Louis school teams, winning both matches by a combined score of 11–0.

A year after the Olympics, the soccer tournament of the Lewis and Clark Centennial Exposition in Portland followed essentially the same script as these other competitions. In March 1905 the Portland Association Football Club formed. Almost immediately they began discussing plans to hold matches at the Exposition grounds versus teams from South Bend and Ilwaco. They also contemplated the possibility of creating a regional competition featuring a circuit of teams from Tacoma, Portland, Seattle, Ilwaco, and South Bend. Less than a week after organizing, the Portland team held its first intra-squad practice game. Despite the lack of regular soccer in the area, the crowd seemed to believe that Portland AFC was as good as any team in the Pacific Northwest. By April the *Oregonian* reported that, in addition to the nearby sides of Ilwaco and South Bend, invitations to play at the Exposition would be sent to more distant teams in Seattle, San Francisco, Vancouver, and Victoria, British Columbia. Another story made clear that no cash prizes would be awarded at the tournament and that teams would be responsible for paying their own way to Portland.

Organizers felt that players might want to visit the Exposition and that the possibility of winning a medal playing soccer would be a bonus.

In the months leading up to the Exposition, Portland AFC hoped to schedule friendlies with squads from nearby towns and sailors from visiting ships, but it is unclear if any of these matches took place. Days before the start of the competition in September, a newspaper reported that, in addition to Portland AFC, several squads from outside the city would challenge for the title: Ilwaco, South Bend, Ladysmith from British Columbia, and other, unnamed Canadian squads. Despite the fact that soccer had been "in a somewhat dead condition in this city for the past two years" and that Portland AFC had played only twice in the three weeks leading up to the games, local boosters still felt their team had a good chance at winning the title.[9] In the end only Ladysmith showed up to play at the Exposition, and in three games versus the Canadians, Portland AFC lost by scores of 1–6, 0–4, and 0–4. The results showed that the quality of play in the city was poor, and by the third match Portland scrambled to field a makeshift lineup composed mainly of British sailors and players from other towns. The score line of the final contest could have been much worse had the game not lasted just two twenty-minute halves. To make matters worse, only "18 young men and one 'yallar' dog" had attended the first game of the series.[10] In fairness to the organizers, the match was played in a driving rain, but the fiasco of the Exposition tournament did not bode well for the future of soccer in the city.

Despite the failures of 1905, Portland's soccer boosters remained determined and within two years had formed a city league. The competition was unique in that it consisted of players from the Portland Association

Pop Bennett's Camerons, named in honor of one of the major figures in Portland's early soccer history, George J. Cameron. The club won the Portland soccer league in fall 1924 and spring 1925. (Author's collection)

Football Club divided into three distinct sides: Columbias, Crescents, and Hornets. In 1908 the organization had a more traditional structure, with six independent squads: Multnomah Amateur Athletic Club (MAAC), Oregon Railroad and Navigation Company, Columbias, Crescents, Caledonians, and the Portland Cricket Club. The MAAC proved the class of the league and ran away with the title, ending the season with a perfect 8-0-0 record. As in some other locations, soccer remained a sport whose appeal was generally limited to the British expatriate community. Longtime booster Cameron remained involved, and other immigrants, such as the architect Phillip Chappell-Browne, took on leadership positions. Chappell-Browne was born in England in 1865 and arrived in Portland in 1888 after living for a time in Auckland, New Zealand. He was an avid cricketer and served as president of the British Benevolent Society. Over the next decade or so, before briefly shutting down during World War I, Portland's soccer league continued playing but never managed to attract more than six teams. Although the sport was revived after the conflict, it would only be in the 1970s that soccer achieved popular recognition in the Rose City.

Notes

1. "Articles of Incorporation," *Oregonian*, May 6, 1873.
2. "The Grand Picnic of the Season," *Oregonian*, June 4, 1873.
3. "Won by a Score of 8 to 0," *Oregonian*, November 28, 1890.
4. "A Handsome Trophy," *Daily Astorian*, August 8, 1896.
5. "The National Resort," *Daily Astorian*, August 18, 1896; "Mariner's . . . Resort," *Daily Astorian*, July 25, 1897.
6. "Football," *Daily Astorian*, July 18, 1896.
7. Bigalke, "Soccer in the Heart of Cascadia," 211.
8. Logan, *The Early Years of Chicago Soccer*, 35.
9. "Association Football at the Exposition," *Oregonian*, September 25, 1905.
10. "Ladysmith Wins Game," *Oregonian*, September 29, 1905.

Sources

Bigalke, Zachary R. "Soccer in the Heart of Cascadia: Portland, Astoria, and the Growth of the Sport from 1890 to the Advent of World War." In *Soccer Frontiers: The Global Game in the United States, 1863–1913*, edited by Chris Bolsmann and George Kioussis, 201–20. Knoxville: University of Tennessee Press, 2021.

Blalock, Barney. "The Oregon Steam Navigation Company Dock." *Portland's Lost Waterfront*, January 9, 2012. https://portlandwaterfront.blogspot.com/2012/01/oregon-steam-navigation-company-dock.html.

Godfrey, Louise. *A History of the Multnomah Amateur Athletic Club 1891 to 1966*. Portland, OR: Multnomah Athletic Club, 1966. https://issuu.com/thewingedm/docs/a_history_of_the_multnomah_amateur_.

Logan, Gabe. *The Early Years of Chicago Soccer, 1887–1939*. Lanham, MD: Lexington Books, 2019.

Orr, Michael A. "Portland's Early Soccer History: Part I." *Stumptown Footy*, August 18, 2014. https://www.stumptownfooty.com/2014/8/18/6031011/portlands-early-soccer-history-part-i.

Orr, Michael A. "Portland's Early Soccer History: Part II." *Stumptown Footy*, August 19, 2014. https://www.stumptownfooty.com/2014/8/19/6031283/portlands-early-soccer-history-part-ii.

Stewart, J. W. "The Bat Boy or Whatever You Wish to Call Him." In *Baseball 11: New Research on the Early Game*, edited by Don Jensen, 67–89. Jefferson, NC: McFarland, 2020.

Taylor, Quintard. "The Emergence of Black Communities in the Pacific Northwest: 1865–1910." *Journal of Negro History* 64, no. 4 (1979): 343–54.

NEWSPAPERS

Buffalo Commercial
Buffalo Courier
Buffalo Inquirer
Buffalo Review
Chicago Tribune
Daily Astorian
Daily Intelligencer
Fall River Daily Globe
Fall River Daily Herald
Fall River Evening Globe
Fall River Evening News
Inter-Ocean (Chicago)
Nanaimo Daily News
Oregonian (Portland)
Oregon Journal (Portland)
Ottawa Journal
St. Louis Globe Democrat
St. Louis Post-Dispatch
St. Louis Republic
Windsor Star

WEBSITE

Ancestry.com

13

Soccer in Central Park

San Francisco, California

Match days were special in San Francisco. Central Park, a downtown stadium complex originally built in 1884, was the primary location for Pacific Coast Football Association (PCFA) matches when the competition began play in 1892. The park did not stand out from nearby buildings like today's stadiums because it was not surrounded by parking lots. Most people walked or caught a trolley car up Eighth to Market Street. While the field blended in with the surrounding cityscape, fans would know they were getting close when they saw the tower of City Hall located just across the street. That structure looked like a three-tiered wedding cake topped with a dome. The entrance to Central Park was on Market Street, and crowds of men and women gathered there in anticipation. In some ways the sensory experience was close to our own: the low buzz of excited conversation, the throbbing drone of music, and the garish colors of advertisements. While a band played, waiting spectators could gape at the two-story-high billboards that fronted the grounds, hawking coming attractions at the park as well as amusements held elsewhere in the city. In the fall of 1896, for example, one sign urged viewers to see a play called *The Ugly Duckling* while another announced a "Spanish Carnival" at Mechanics Hall. As they headed for the entrance, supporters passed by shops where they might have caught a whiff of cigar smoke mingled with the sugary aroma of candy. The site was large, 550 feet long and 270 feet wide. It was bigger than most soccer stadiums in the country. The Dexter Street grounds in Pawtucket, Rhode Island, opened about three years after Central Park and was about a third smaller. One reason for the difference may have been that in Pawtucket, the field only hosted baseball and soccer games. Central Park, however, was more than just a sports stadium. In addition to hosting athletic events, the facility was the site of various other happenings, including dramatic reenactments of historical events and balloon ascensions. Sometimes sport and other entertainments combined, as when a moonlight soccer game took place at the same time as dancers moved to the sound of a hand-cranked organ. The grounds also included a saloon, restaurant, barbershop, cigar store, and confectionary shop.

Like many areas of contemporary sport, things that seem new and innovative often have long roots in the game. Stadium redevelopment projects are no exception. When clubs build (or rebuild) arenas today, the undertaking is not just about where the games are played. Instead, teams speak about the field as the centerpiece, anchor, or magnet for a constellation of revenue-generating properties. In 2015, for example, the Green Bay Packers announced plans for the Titletown District development. The moniker was derived from the city's nickname, earned because the club has won more National Football League championships—thirteen—than any other team. The franchise's storied home, Lambeau Field, remained the central attraction, but the area also included residential, commercial,

Central Park as seen from City Hall, 1897. (Courtesy of San Francisco History Center, San Francisco Public Library.)

and "destination retail" properties.[1] Likewise, when English soccer club Tottenham Hotspur FC opened the new White Hart Lane stadium in 2019, it was not a stand-alone venture but instead was part of something called the Northumberland Development Project. Once you passed through the entrance to Central Park, or Lambeau Field or White Hart Lane, all those distractions melted away. There is something awe-inspiring about entering a large stadium for the first time, perhaps because of that slightly unnerving feeling of being both inside and outside at the same time. At Central Park folks could see the field stretch out before them, ending at yet more advertisements, for men's shirts, candidates for mayor, and the Lurline Baths. After they took their seats, however, fans in San Francisco were like those everywhere else: they cheered their team to victory.

Beginning in 1892, the progress of soccer in San Francisco generally followed a boom-and-bust cycle until after the turn of the twentieth century. Two years of rapid growth were followed by a collapse triggered in part by a broader economic depression in the city. A new side called the Vampire Association Football Club organized in 1897 and a handful of matches took place each year, but there was little formal organization. Such vacillations in the fortunes of a sport in the city were not unusual and not confined to soccer. Baseball had also experienced its own growing pains after the first documented game in the city took place on February 22, 1860. A post—Civil War boom fueled the development of the Pacific Coast Base Ball convention in 1866, and within a year the organization counted some twenty-five clubs as members. By 1878 a professional league had formed, but poor organization and infighting dogged the group for much of its existence. Owners sought to discipline the behavior of players to help burnish the sport's public image, and for a time multiple competitions existed as different stadium owners backed rival leagues. By 1887 one association had folded while the other limped on a few years into the next decade before collapsing in 1893. Eventually, the baseball league reappeared by 1898 and would remain stable well into the twentieth century. Soccer followed a similar trajectory. The first league organized in 1892 but collapsed a few years later. A new competition emerged in 1902 and has continued playing into the twenty-first century.

The earliest documented soccer match in San Francisco took place on March 25, 1888, when the California Rangers beat a Stanford University team 4–0. In a Christmas Day match that same year, a team of Scottish stonecutters recently employed by Stanford called the Mayfields defeated Rangers by a score of 5–4. A later account from 1905 claimed that the first regular team playing soccer in the region was the Oakland Football Club, who adopted the association rules in 1890. Since the club's fixtures were limited exclusively to the occasional game against informal teams made up of visiting British sailors, the development of the sport remained limited. The first significant soccer organization in San Francisco formed in August 1892 and was called the Pacific Coast Football Association (PCFA). A few weeks later, a group met on August 27 at St. Ann's building to form the Pacific Wanderers. Reports indicate that the new side's first match would take place in October versus Scottish Thistle. By that time San Francisco was home to at least four organized soccer clubs: Pacific Wanderers, Scottish Thistle, Oakland Athletic Club, and Alert Athletic Club. The formation of the PCFA and its clubs represented the start of the first truly organized soccer community in California.

Scottish Thistle and the Wanderers played several matches during the fall of 1892, and the *San Francisco Call* newspaper enthusiastically covered this "strange and astonishing game."[2] By the turn of the new year, the paper had declared a "football craze" in the city that saw large crowds of both men and women attending matches.[3] New clubs rapidly formed in the city, and the PCFA organized a youth league. In some cases, men joined clubs with coworkers, although it is unknown if these had any backing from the company. The Rovers Association Football Club, for example, had at least three Levi-Strauss employees, while the Richmond side featured several workers from publisher and bookseller Bancroft Whitney. Four players from Scottish Thistle labored at the Union Iron Works, at the time one of the largest concerns in the city. By 1891 the firm employed 1,300 people and its owners believed that it would soon be as big as Bethlehem Steel—an interesting comparison given the Pennsylvania company's later association with soccer. Newspaper match reports were extensive and detailed, showing that reporters had some knowledge of tactics and player roles.

Less than a year after forming, the PCFA included six junior squads and nine senior teams, although not all of them played regularly or competed for the local championship. The organization rebranded as the Pacific Association Football League (PAFL). The "football craze" ignited in the fall of 1892 led to large crowds and an increasing competitiveness among the clubs. A December 26 game between Thistle and Wanderers was seen by a "good gathering" of men and women, who blew horns to celebrate goals.[4] After losing the match 3–2, the Thistle captain declared a willingness to strengthen his squad. Over the next few weeks, reports in the newspaper revealed how the clubs sought to add quality athletes, many of whom had experience playing soccer abroad or had competed locally in other sports. By January 1893, Wanderers had signed a Canadian fullback as well as a pacey forward originally from Liverpool named J. W. Longbottom. Not to be outdone, Thistle added an English player who had reportedly played at Oxford. In February the league felt it necessary to affirm that players could only suit up for their own team in league matches. Later, at a well-attended PAFL meeting, one of the topics sparking "hot discussion" concerned a player named Marsh, who had already appeared for multiple teams. The former captain of a Portland, Oregon, squad had lined up for the Granites on February 5 and then for Thistles on February 9 and 22. These actions prompted Oakland to lodge a protest with the league, thereby sparking an "exciting and acrimonious debate" at the organization's next meeting.[5]

To solve the crisis, league officials docked Thistle two points and called a special session to diffuse what had become an increasingly "stormy" situation.[6] If the hope was to calm tensions, the decision of the league at the meeting only stoked the flames of discontent. League officials decided to throw out the result of the February 22 match, in which Thistle fielded the ineligible player. The verdict increased tensions because Thistle had lost that game to Wanderers, and by nullifying the result, the league effectively penalized Wanderers by denying them the two points. According to the *San Francisco Call,* many in the organization felt this was one of the "rankest" decisions ever made by the PAFL and Wanderers threatened to withdraw from the organization in protest.[7] In addition to punishing the team for Thistles' infractions, the league determined that Thistles and Oakland would be selected as the PAFL clubs scheduled to visit San Jose, despite the fact that Wanderers had supposedly introduced the game to that city. Within a few weeks, however, the league reconsidered its decision to subtract points from Wanderers and announced that Thistle and Wanderers would be the teams to play in San Jose, thus restoring peace within the organization.

The PAFL sought to forge links beyond the Bay Area by publishing the rules of soccer and giving them away for free. They sent players and other representatives to encourage the development of the game and the formation of clubs in nearby communities. Aficionados believed that intercity matches would help increase the popularity of the sport across the region. They also sought out opportunities to play clubs beyond the state of California. The initial success of the game in the city and the size of the crowds attracted the attention of Central Park promoter Daniel R. McNeill. Declaring that the "Association rules are the best for attracting public interest," McNeill praised the game's continuous action, speed, and combativeness.[8] A newspaper report indicated that he considered sponsoring an international soccer tournament, although there is no record of such an event being played. An exhibition game in Petaluma, California, on December 10, 1893, however, was billed as a match between England and

America, with the Wanderers representing England and the Fort Mason army team the United States. Central Park also hosted the earliest recorded women's soccer match in the United States on December 3, 1893. Two teams, named the Coleen Bawns and Bonnie Lassies, played before a good crowd, with the Bawns winning by the final score of 2–0.

Earlier in 1893, wine and liquor merchants Frederick and Christian Hilbert donated a solid silver punch bowl worth $100 (around $3,400 today) to be given to the winner of the PCFA.[9] Historians Tony Collins and Wray Vamplew argue that in Great Britain, soccer's relationship with alcohol was initially on the level of patronage. Brewers and distillers sponsored prizes for competitions, usually as a gesture of community involvement and goodwill. As the sport's popularity increased in the 1890s, brand identity grew more important and alcohol merchants saw the game as an opportunity for profit. A similar pattern seems to have been evident in the United States, although the links between soccer clubs and saloons or specific alcohol brands were never as developed as those in England. The newspaper reported that the Hilbert brothers donated the trophy due to their long-standing love for the game. They were born in Altona, a town that today is a borough of the German city of Hamburg. At the time of their births, however, Altona remained under the control of Denmark and only became a part of the Kingdom of Prussia in 1867. Interestingly, the city was an early center of soccer playing in the area and Altona FC von 1893 is one of Germany's oldest clubs. It is possible that they had experience with some football code during their younger years, before they arrived in the United States in 1882. The Hilbert brothers may have donated the prize out of community pride and a desire to maintain good relations with the largely middle-class soccer community.

For soccer clubs in San Francisco, socialization was an important aspect of the sport and perhaps the Hilbert brothers thought their generosity would drive sales from individuals, clubs, and associations. If they were counting on big profits thanks to the sponsorship, they were probably disappointed. By 1893, the pair had put their grocery store and bar up for sale, declaring that it must be sold at once. Financial difficulties were not the only problems facing the Hilberts. Months after listing the property for sale, a fire broke out, causing an estimated $200 (almost $7,000 today) worth of damage. A few years later, they again sought to rid themselves of the business, proclaiming that the need for a sale was urgent. In 1903 they incorporated as the Hilbert Mercantile Company, but another blaze a year later caused over $100,000 worth of damage, a figure that equals nearly $3.5 million today. It was by far the costliest fire in the city during 1904, as no other blaze resulted in a loss of more than $40,000.[10]

The men who organized the teams and the PAFL viewed the game as an opportunity to extend their camaraderie beyond the confines of the pitch. The evening before a match between Thistles and Oakland in early 1893, the teams gathered for a banquet at the Scottish side's clubhouse. In February 1893, the league floated the idea of initiating a monthly series of "smokers" that would include various types of vocal and musical performances. Following the conclusion of the inaugural season, many of the athletes seemed to regret that they would no longer be able to meet in competition. Some players called for one last match to be held, featuring one team made up of newly married men, called benedicts, and the other composed of unmarried bachelors. In addition to league-wide events, the regular meetings of individual clubs became a time for socializing. After members of Wanderers voted in 1893 to reelect the club secretary for another term, "the boys were treated to a fine spread and the liquid refreshments disappeared with astonishing rapidity."[11] Following the conclusion of the 1893–94 season, the Thistle club held its annual social at the Scottish Hall. The highly anticipated program included speeches and the presentation of gold badges to the organization's champion soccer team. The *San Francisco Call* wrote that many tickets had been sold and the event "will no doubt prove as big a success socially as the team has done on the football field."[12]

If part of the reason for the clubs and leagues was socialization, what can be known about the men who played the game? Because newspaper reports often only listed surnames and can be inaccurate, it is difficult to identify with certainty all the players involved in the sport. In addition, the most prominent athletes and those with a higher social, political, or economic profile outside the sport may have been overrepresented in newspaper coverage. The most detailed information comes from individual player profiles appearing in the *San Francisco Call*. In total the newspaper published sixteen short biographies of PAFL players and administrators. Eight of these men had been born in Scotland, and most reportedly had some previous experience playing the game, usually at a junior or scholastic level. Claims that a certain individual had played high-level football elsewhere, however, must be taken with a grain of salt. David Ferguson, vice president and forward for the Thistle squad, was born in Blantyre, Scotland, in 1862. According to the profile, he had lined up for Renton, one of the early powerhouses of Scottish football and winners of the Scottish Cup in 1884–85 and 1887–88. The paper wrote that Frank Reynolds had played in the Scottish Cup final for Thornliebank in 1878 and 1879. However, the club only reached the final in the 1879–80 season and Reynolds was not on the match team sheet. Among the rest of the Scots were

Archibald MacKillop, secretary of the PCFL, who hailed from Glasgow and Forfarians J. S. Orchison and A. Proctor.

The other men listed were from England, Australia, Canada, New Zealand, and the United States. The birthplace of two players was not given. J. W. Longbottom from Liverpool was known for his speed, while the other Englishman profiled, C. P. Morse, was called "an exceptionally brilliant dribbler."[13] Ernest G. Stoman was born in Melbourne, Australia, and played both cricket and soccer before coming to the United States. The Canadian, A. M. Thomson, hailed from Toronto, but the achievements listed in his profile are those of his brother. William Proudfoot Thomson had toured Great Britain in 1888 and 1891, appeared in several international friendlies in the United States, and was eventually inducted into the Canada Soccer Hall of Fame. Frank Gray was born in Canterbury, New Zealand, and perhaps due to his rugby background, played in goal. He was called one of the best keepers on the West Coast. Patrick H. Farrell came from Brooklyn, New York, and was the son of Irish immigrants. He was raised in California and seems to have been interested in all the major football codes, playing the intercollegiate game in high school and for the Union rugby team before taking up soccer.

Examining team rosters confirms the notion that most soccer players had names of Scottish or English origin. Such demographics served to differentiate the game from baseball, where most of the players had Irish or German roots. In addition, some baseball clubs were formed by, or included, African Americans and Latinos, something that, based on the names at least, was not the case for soccer. Only a few Spanish names appear in early newspaper reports. One was a halfback from Honolulu, Hawai'i, called Fernández, who was likely of Filipino origin. Another possible Latino player had the surname Leal and spent at least some time in Mexico.

Adherents of soccer favorably compared their game to what they characterized as the much rougher and more violent sports of rugby and intercollegiate football. One newspaper article claimed that increasing numbers of people, including male college students, had been attending soccer matches and that these spectators soon concluded "that for science and pure football the association game puts the intercollegiate or Gaelic games in the chase."[14] According to another report, football players of other codes should take soccer as model since the sport featured little "rough play or ungentlemanly conduct."[15] In late 1893 Edgar Pomeroy, one of the founders of the Oakland Athletic Club, penned an article for the *San Francisco Call* titled "Football. The True Way to Play it." Pomeroy argued that the "English-speaking race" was interested in two things above all else—money and football—although he professed not to know which was considered the most important. He explicitly linked the playing of the sport with national and perhaps racial power: "Football is the great game of the century. It is the great outlet and at the same time originator of the hardihood and energy of the nations now leading in the van of civilizations." Declaring that there existed five types of football—rugby, Australian, intercollegiate, Gaelic, and association—he concluded that soccer was the best. Fans and players were no longer interested in death and blood, he wrote, and instead wished to see "exhibitions of strength, endurance, strategy and manly self-control." Such desires ruled out sports such as boxing and bullfighting as well as intercollegiate football, which Pomeroy dismissed as "a lot of schoolboys scrambling in the mud." Instead, fans would flock to witness the speed and nonstop action of a sport where "there is nothing namby-pamby" in the game.[16]

An exchange of letters published in the *San Francisco Call* in the spring of 1894 reveals just how contentious the debate over football rules had become. The dispute kicked off when a newspaper article characterized rugby as "that relic of English barbarism." The story also reproduced a letter from a "prominent association player" that invoked Darwin's theory of evolution to argue that football was in the process of moving away from both rugby and the "gladiatorial and bullying exhibitions" of the intercollegiate game toward "the perfect . . . game" of soccer.[17] The letter prompted an angry response from E. D. Carpmall, former secretary of the California Rugby Union. In defending his favored game, Carpmall attacked soccer for its turn toward professionalism in England, claiming that "every true sportsman deplores this debasing of sport." Class bias was evident as he argued that, while both rugby and soccer were sports of English private schools, the association game also had roots on the "village green" and this connection ultimately led to professionalism. He also invoked visions of masculine honor typically associated with upper class sport, declaring that when the danger of injury was removed from competition, "sportsmen will have to return to that friend of their early youth, the milkman, for their succor and refreshment of their flaccid persons."[18]

Even as Thistle and other clubs celebrated the end of the 1893–94 season, plans were being made for the next one. Although early reports were optimistic, there were also troubling signs regarding the league's future. Initially, the 1894–95 season was scheduled for two rounds, the first running from November to January and the second from January to March. The number of clubs also seemed to be on the rise, with five teams listed as committed to playing and another handful as possibilities. The league had a new trophy donated and named for City and County Assessor John

D. Siebe to award to the winning side. Finally, contact had been made with soccer teams in Utah and Colorado about the possibility of arranging interstate matches, and there was even talk of forming a national organization that would consolidate the various leagues from around the country and even in Canada.

Despite enthusiastic reports on these developments, the plans quickly fell apart. One problem that traced back to the second half of the previous campaign was the lack of suitable playing fields. During the final stretch of the 1893–94 season, games were held on the grounds of the Midwinter Exposition at Golden Gate Park. Conditions at the site were often not ideal and transportation to and from the park was neither reliable nor convenient for both players and spectators. Without adequate facilities the league faced difficult challenges, such as the time when two teams arrived only to find that the field had been recently plowed, making it impossible to play. One story hinted at what might have been a deliberate attempt by a baseball team owner to sabotage the soccer games. The tension may have developed in part because, despite baseball's traditional summer season, games were also being played during the winter months as part of the Exposition. On March 25, 1894, the Wanderers and Pastimes were scheduled to play a match at the Exposition site but upon arriving were told by guards that only players and managers would be allowed inside. As a result of the decision, fans and members of the press were forced to watch the game from the hills surrounding the ground, a spot quickly dubbed Poverty Flat.

Although problems with access to playing fields was an issue, it was the inability or unwillingness of clubs to turn up for matches that became the most significant problem for the league. The reasons why teams failed to appear varied according to media reports. A brief story in the *San Francisco Call* illustrated the potential challenges teams faced when filling out the team sheet. According to the paper, the player named Leal would appear in a match only if his steamer ship arrived from Mexico on time. At the end of the 1892–93 season, the Granites' club reportedly disbanded because five of its players had been called away from the city. When they failed to appear for a match against Rangers a week later, one newspaper claimed it was because the remaining members were discouraged at losing their teammates. After an insufficient number of Pastimes arrived to face the Wanderers in February 1894, the *San Francisco Call* implied it was due to the distant location of the Expo grounds. Wanderers neglected to turn up for a late-season contest with Thistle, and the paper speculated it was because they knew they were going to lose the match. For a March tilt against Thistle, the Fort Mason side was without five key players; another two were present but claimed to be unfit to play because they had "been up nearly all night."[19] Despite these issues, the game went ahead as scheduled and the Thistles easily ran out 5–1 winners.

The lack of reliable fixtures did little to encourage interest in the sport. Why would spectators attend matches if teams failed to appear or were forced to play without a full squad of players? In a game to determine the club that would go on a visit to western Canada, Thistle appeared without a complete squad and the teams were forced to play with only ten on each side. An article about the match warned that disappointing the crowd in such a way was not helping to grow the game. Perhaps more alarmingly for supporters of the sport was the possibility that the repeated absences indicated a waning enthusiasm for soccer. In the case of Wanderers mentioned above, for example, the *San Francisco Call* later clarified that the team had not deliberately skipped the match but instead were absent due to "their inability to scare up a team strong enough to make a showing against the Scots."[20]

As the 1894 season wore on, the situation continued to deteriorate. In November, after Thistle again failed to show for a match, one newspaper blasted the club, writing that such behavior "showed a total disregard of sportsmanship which will tend to bring association football into contempt."[21] By January 1895 the *Call* reported that the Pastimes and Thistles had disbanded and some of the former players had joined a new club, but there is no evidence it ever played a game. The final match report for a PAFL game, a contest between Wanderers and Oakland, showed how far the competition had descended into farce. The Wanderers club came to the match with only nine men and so two players from Oakland were picked to complete the numbers. During the match, one of the Oakland players lining up for Wanderers performed "listlessly" and scored an own goal for his home club.[22] The debacle seems to have dealt a death blow to the league and it soon dissolved. By the late spring, some of its officers had moved on to other sporting endeavors, including Archibald MacKillop who was named vice president of the newly organized California Swimming and Water Polo Club. The internal problems of the league were compounded by a national economic collapse that occurred in 1893. Occasional games against British sailors continued for a time, but a truly organized competition would not reappear in the city for almost a decade.

Notes

1. Hammes Real Estate Consulting.
2. "Association Football," *San Francisco Call*, October 22, 1892.

3. "Football," *San Francisco Call,* January 1, 1893.
4. "One Goal Short," *San Francisco Call,* December 27, 1892.
5. "The Kickers," *San Francisco Call,* February 25, 1893.
6. "Football," *San Francisco Call,* March 5, 1893.
7. "Football," *San Francisco Call,* March 19, 1893.
8. "The Football Boom," *San Francisco Call,* November 24, 1892.
9. MeasuringWorth.com.
10. MeasuringWorth.com.
11. "Football," *San Francisco Call,* February 19, 1893.
12. "Sporting News," *San Francisco Call,* June 8, 1894.
13. "Football," *San Francisco Call,* March 12, 1893.
14. "Football," *San Francisco Call,* February 26, 1893.
15. "Football," *San Francisco Call,* February 22, 1893.
16. Edgar Pomeroy, "Football: The True Way to Play it," *San Francisco Call,* December 10, 1893.
17. "Football," *San Francisco Call,* March 24, 1894.
18. "Football," *San Francisco Call,* April 1, 1894.
19. "Thistles Ahead," *San Francisco Call,* March 19, 1894.
20. "Football," *San Francisco Call,* April 29, 1894.
21. "Football Season," *San Francisco Call,* November 12, 1894.
22. "Football across the Bay," *San Francisco Call,* February 23, 1895.

Sources

Brechin, Gray. *Imperial San Francisco: Urban Power, Earthly Ruin.* Berkeley: University of California Press, 1999.

Bueltmann, Tanja. *Clubbing Together: Ethnicity, Civility and Formal Sociability in the Scottish Diaspora to 1930.* Liverpool: Liverpool University Press, 2014.

Bunk, Brian D. "Colleen Bawns and Bonnie Lassies: Women's Soccer and Sporting Culture in Late Nineteenth-Century San Francisco." In *Soccer Frontiers: The Global Game in the United States, 1863–1913,* edited by Chris Bolsmann and George Kioussis, 243–64. Knoxville: University of Tennessee Press, 2021.

Bunk, Brian D. *From Football to Soccer: The Early History of the Beautiful Game in the United States.* Champaign: University of Illinois Press, 2021.

Franks, Joel. "The California League of 1886–1893: The Last Refuge of Disorganized Baseball." *The Californians* (May/June 1998): 50–56.

Franks, Joel S. *Whose Baseball? The National Pastime and Cultural Diversity in California, 1859–1941.* Lanham, MD: Scarecrow Press, 2001.

Hammes Real Estate Consulting. "Green Bay Packers Lambeau Field and Titletown District." Accessed May 9, 2022. https://www.hammes.com/commercial/projects/green-bay-packers-lambeau-field-titletown-district.

Holmes, Robin. *Forgotten: Scotland's Former Football League Clubs.* Self-published, 2020.

Macfarlane, Angus. "Baseball Goes East, the 1876 San Francisco Centennials' Magical Mystery Tour." *Base Ball: A Journal of the Early Game* 7, no. 1 (2013): 185–224.

McCabe, Thomas A. "Cooper's Block: America's First Soccer Neighborhood." *Soccer and Society* 18, nos. 2–3 (2016): 320–29.

Nelson, Kevin. *The Golden Game: The Story of Baseball in California*. Lincoln: University of Nebraska Press, 2004.

Park, Roberta J. "British Sports and Pastimes in San Francisco, 1848–1900." *British Journal of Sport History* 1, 3 (1984): 300–17.

Pomeroy, Edgar. "Oakland Hornets." In *Spalding's Athletic Library Association Foot Ball Guide,* edited by Jerome Flannery, 144–47. New York: American Sports Publishing, 1905.

San Francisco Historical Photograph Collection. San Francisco History Center, San Francisco Public Library.

NEWSPAPERS

Daily Alta California (San Francisco)
Los Angeles Herald
San Francisco Call
San Francisco Chronicle

WEBSITE

Ancestry.com

14

Bay Area Vampires

Alameda, California

On December 10, 1897, a group of men gathered at the Mills Building in San Francisco, California. The conversation flowed with an easy familiarity, as most of them had shared experiences as British immigrants to the United States. They worked in similar occupations as bank clerks, bookkeepers, and agents. Almost all had played cricket together. On this night, however, they were not there to reminisce about the old country or talk shop or cricket, but instead to form a soccer club. Teams had played organized soccer in the city since 1892, but after the collapse of the first league a few years later, the sport became less structured, and by 1897 matches were intermittent. Every club must have a name and traditionally it was based on the team's neighborhood, city, or region. Alternatively, it could be chosen to honor the backer of the squad, a church, club, or company. They could have stuck with tried-and-true names taken from across the Atlantic. Variations on Wanderers, Rangers, Rovers, and Thistles were commonplace in soccer communities around the United States. Instead of all these options, the bankers and clerks picked an unconventional name: Vampire Association Football Club (VAFC).

No explanation for the name was ever publicly disclosed, but at first glance a few possibilities present themselves. One is that it was a reference to the title character of Bram Stoker's novel *Dracula*. The book was first published in England in May 1897, and the earliest mention in San Francisco newspapers came in July of that year. The notice was small, even though Stoker had traveled to the city in the past as personal assistant to the actor Henry Irving. The first US edition of the work came out in 1899, two years into the team's existence. Given the close connections that most Vampires had with Great Britain, it may have been possible for one of them to obtain a copy of the book soon after it was published. It would not have been the first time that an English novel had an important impact on sports in the United States. A few decades earlier, the publication of *Tom Brown's School Days*, a fictionalized account of life at an English boarding school, inspired generations of boys and young men to take up rugby. Still, the general lack of publicity given to *Dracula* at the time makes it unlikely that it made a tremendous impact on the founders of VAFC.

Another possibility comes from a Rudyard Kipling poem called "The Vampire" that appeared in the spring of 1897. The verses were inspired by a painting done by the poet's cousin Philip Burne-Jones. In the picture, the vampire is a woman who has physically assaulted a man, but in the poem the damage is more emotional. A fool is smitten by "a rag and a bone and a hank of hair." Soon he loses both his money and his dignity.

> Oh, the toil we lost and the spoil we lost
> And the excellent things we planned
> Belong to the woman who didn't know why
> (And now we know that she never knew why)
> And did not understand!
>
> The fool was stripped to his foolish hide,
> (Even as you or I!)
> Which she might have seen when she threw him aside—
> (But it isn't on record the lady tried)
> So some of him lived but the most of him died—
> (Even as you or I!)[1]

The work was first published in a London newspaper on April 22, 1897, and the following day it appeared on the front page of the *Chicago Tribune*. Within a month of its debut in England, the poem had already been printed in newspapers around the United States. The *Chronicle* was the first paper in San Francisco to reproduce the poem on May 23, 1897. A few days later, the *Call* published a spoof of it, gently mocking Kipling and the original poem's popularity. On August 1 the *Examiner* ran a parody version that had a sporting connection. Instead of a woman being the cause of the man's suffering, it was a bicycle. The concluding verse summed up the rider's frustration:

> Oh, the spills we take and the bikes we break,
> And the terror that we feel,
> Belong to us all until we knew—
> And some of us know that we will never know—
> The way to straddle a wheel.[2]

The poem continued to draw attention from the press and the public in the months and years that followed its initial publication. During the nineteenth century, the United States and United Kingdom shared what literary scholar John Lee called a “transatlantic literary culture,” meaning that written links between the two regions were timely and strong.[3] Kipling was adept at exploiting this connectedness, using newspapers to promote both his work and, later, his political views. One reason why “The Vampire” received such attention in the United States is that he was already quite popular thanks to the success of his *Jungle Books*. Caroline Starr Balestier, the writer’s spouse, came from Vermont and the couple lived there between 1892 and 1896. According to Lee, Kipling targeted US readers, and he “self-consciously took care to produce, or allow to be produced, an American persona, . . . who wrote in a transatlantic idiom, inflected to an American taste.”[4] It seems that even after he returned to England, he was still creating work designed to appeal to his US audience. As a result, the poem and the painting were much talked about during the summer and fall of 1897, precisely the time when the idea of forming a soccer club took hold.

Despite all these factors, and as enticing as it may be to think they were inspired by a novel, poem, or painting, the reality is probably much more ordinary. I believe that VAFC named itself after an English soccer club called the Crouch End Vampires. The original Vampires team had been based in the Norbury area of South London before it merged with Crouch End in 1897. Although the nickname had been used for racing boats in England since the 1850s, the earliest documented football teams named Vampires were founded in 1875. The first was based in Surrey and had as many as seventy members within a year of forming. In the same year, a notice in the *Sporting Gazette* announced that a group of Oxford University students visiting London had formed a Rugby Union side and named it Vampires. This was a short-lived club that may have played a few games but did not seem to last much longer. Another rugby club with the same name appeared in 1879 and played games into the 1880s. It is unclear when a Vampires soccer club first organized, but by 1888 a team by that name was a member of the London Football Association. During the 1890s, the Vampires played in the London League and against clubs that are still well known today. One of the competition’s stronger teams, the Thames Iron Works, later became West Ham United. The Vampires suffered a 4–0 defeat at the hands of Tottenham Hotspur on Boxing Day 1896. The result was perhaps indicative of the squad’s fortunes during the 1896–97 season, and they consistently found themselves near the bottom of the league table. In late spring 1897, the Vampire junior club folded, and on May 29 the Football Association announced that a merger between the team and Crouch End had been approved. The club continues to compete as the Crouch End Vampires today.

Why would a team in California choose a relatively obscure, unexceptional English club to name themselves after? The answer has to do with the general attitudes of the San Francisco soccer community and the social status of the Vampires themselves. Unlike the socioeconomic profiles of soccer players in some other parts of the country, many of those identified in San Francisco held white-collar jobs as accountants, clerks, and salesmen. The relative economic security that such employment provided motivated the clubs to maintain a commitment to amateurism. Perhaps due to their middle-class status or as part of larger trends within San Francisco's British community, soccer aficionados were determined to emulate the lives of the bourgeoisie from back home. They did so by forming organizations, including social clubs and schools, while participating in a variety of recreational activities. Such attitudes permeated discussions over the values associated with soccer, especially compared to other popular football codes. A booklet published in the city in 1894 describing the sport invoked traditional upper-class values of good sportsmanship and honest striving:

> Always "play up" until the last moment, even if the game and luck are against you. Never feel dejected when a goal is lost; rather go in with the determination to make the next one yours. Never pay the slightest heed to the exclamations from excited spectators. Avoid wrangling about the decisions of the referee. Obey your captain in every way and success will often be yours.[5]

Upholding amateurism in soccer was in keeping with the desire to emulate traditional notions of British sporting activity that idolized the gentleman athlete. It may also have been part of an effort to distance the sport from baseball, which had been organized in the city on a professional basis since 1878. Critics of the national pastime often condemned the pernicious influence of gambling along with the unruliness and indiscipline of some of the players. Indeed, Edgar Pomeroy, one of the leading figures in the Bay Area soccer community, promoted the benefits of association football and dismissed the popularity of baseball by declaring that the public had lost interest in the "paid hirelings on the baseball fields."[6]

The original English Vampires squad and the Crouch End team were composed of "gentleman amateurs," many of whom did business in the City of London.[7] Home to both the Stock Exchange and the Bank of England, the City was the economic heart of the British Empire. Although situated on opposite sides of the City, the areas of Norbury and Crouch End are each less than ten miles from the financial district. Both clubs were steadfast opponents of professionalism in soccer, a notion first legalized in England in 1885. Crouch End refused an invitation to join a proposed Southern League because it would have meant turning professional. After the merger of the two sides in 1897, the new squad continued to defend amateurism in the sport. The Crouch End Vampires were deeply involved in the formation of the Amateur Football Association (AFA). The AFA broke from the Football Association (FA) in 1907 after the FA required local organizations to accept professional clubs. Most of the associations that rejected pro teams came from areas within and surrounding London. Eventually, the rift was patched up and the AFA rejoined the FA in 1914. The social makeup of the clubs along with their dedication to amateurism must have resonated with those who gathered at the Mills Building on that December night in 1897.

Sports historian Dilwyn Porter calls the players on teams like the Crouch End Vampires "gentlemanly capitalists," a phrase that could equally be applied to the men from San Francisco.[8] Not only did they hold similar positions in banks and insurance companies, many of them worked for firms that had strong links to the City of London. Team vice president George Theobald was a cashier for the Liverpool and London and Globe insurance company. Club captain G. H. N. Sexton had a position with the Hong Kong and Shanghai Banking Corporation. Founded in British Hong Kong in 1865, the firm, now known as HSBC, is still in business today. They even maintain a sporting connection as official banking partner of Tottenham Hotspur and sponsors of the KeyBank Arena in Buffalo, New York, home of the Sabres ice hockey team. VAFC vice-captain Charles P. Coles was a clerk for a local firm that served as an agent for the Indemnity Mutual Marine Insurance Company Limited of London. George T. S. White and John McGaw were bookkeepers at the London and San Francisco Bank and the Bank of British North America, respectively. In addition to professional ties to London, at least two members of VAFC had more personal connections. George Theobald was born in Shacklewell, a hamlet within greater London located about three miles from Crouch End, and John McGaw was also reportedly from the city.

Not all the Vampires had such close ties to London, but many were employed in positions that had a similar social standing. VAFC president Thomas Turner, born in Barrhead, Scotland, worked as an accountant, and Robert Hogue, a second-generation Scot born in Australia, was a colliery agent. No occupation was given for A. F. Chambers, but his business address was the Mills Building and it seems probable that VAFC's organizational meeting took place in his office. Built in 1892, the structure was an important city landmark. Designed by the Chicago firm of Burnham and Root, perhaps the most famous architectural company of the period, it was an early example of skyscraper design and one of only three steel-framed buildings in San Francisco. The Mills Building survived the 1906 earthquake with only minor damage and is now listed on the National Register of Historic Places.

The Vampires played their first match on December 19, 1897, against a picked group of mariners from British ships visiting the city. The game took place at the Alameda Cricket Grounds and ended in a 2–0 win for VAFC. Chambers and Coles scored early for the home side, and team president and goalkeeper Thomas Turner kept the sailors off the score sheet. Soccer historian Andy Mitchell calls Turner a classic "one-club man" who played for his local team, Arthurlie, for more than a decade.[9] Turner appeared regularly for Renfrewshire and the Scotch Counties sides and earned a single cap for Scotland in a 4–1 victory over Wales at Cathkin Park, Glasgow, on March 29, 1884.

By the summer of 1898, VAFC had become an established sporting club, playing regular fixtures against local and visiting sides. The team wore a kit that was as distinctive as their name. It consisted of a white shirt with a small black bat on the left breast, a black sash going from the right shoulder to the left hip, black shorts, and stockings. The choice of design may be another nod to the Crouch End Vampires, as a photograph published in the London-based *Penny Illustrated Paper* on October 2, 1897, showed a match between West Norwood and the English Vampires. Although it is difficult to tell for sure, it appears as though one team is wearing black shirts with white sleeves and a white bat on the left breast. In later seasons VAFC adopted a similar color scheme featuring all black tops with a white bat across the chest.

Newspaper headline writers had great fun with the team's name, penning lines such as "Sailors Beaten by Lusty Vampires" and "Vampires Wanted Blood and got Shasta Water."[10] A full schedule meant that line-ups changed constantly, and the club soon aimed to recruit new talent. Several veterans of the Pacific Association Football League (PAFL), San Francisco's first soccer competition, returned to the pitch. David Hunter, who appeared in a few games for the Vampires, had previously lined up for the Wanderers, one of the city's earliest soccer teams. Experienced players Douglas Erskine and C. P. Morse anchored a revived Wanderers squad, while former Thistle man David Pollock also made an appearance. Although clearly out of shape, Pollock showed that he still had a nose for goal, scoring a hat trick in a 3–0 win over VAFC on February 22, 1898.

Overall, in their first season the Vampires won seven, lost three, and drew two matches. They scored thirty goals and gave up only ten.

Over the next few years, VAFC continued to play games against sailors and other loosely organized clubs until the formation of a new league in 1902. By that time, many of the original members had moved on and a new roster of players took to the field. The social position of the team members had also changed. Instead of a club made up of bankers, bookkeepers, and agents, the Vampires now were carpenters, surveyors, and even a physical trainer. "Professor" George Hufferdine was born in England, attended the University of California School of Dentistry, and worked as a trainer for some of the college's athletic teams. He became known as a skilled athlete, primarily as a swimmer. In 1897 he swam against the current from a ferry slip at Sausalito, California, to Belvedere Point in eighty minutes, an accomplishment the *Call* heralded as "A Wonderful Aquatic Feat."[11] A year later he set a record swimming from Lime Point to Fort Point, essentially the same route as the Golden Gate Bridge, in just forty-eight minutes. Within a few league seasons, other clubs had surpassed the Vampires in social prestige and in results on the field. One of the highest-profile clubs in the early days of the competition was the Independents. The 1911–12 edition of the *Spalding Soccer Football Guide* included an extended profile of the team. It was one of the California Association Football League's founding members and one of the most successful, winning both the league and the state cup in 1904–05 and 1905–06. Perhaps it was not a coincidence that the Independents were also the richest club in the league, as wealthy backers hoped to use the team to promote the sport.

Efforts to create a new competition in the Bay Area began in November 1902, when the *San Francisco Call* announced the formation of the Pacific Coast Football Association (PCFA) with a handful of clubs including VAFC. A few weeks later, the organization launched the California Association Football League (CAFL). Membership included five teams: VAFC, the American-British Rifles, Independents, Seamen's Institute, and San Francisco. Sometime before kickoff, the Albions, a club affiliated with the Sons of St. George, replaced the Institute. The group elected Taliesin Evans president, and newspaper columnist Henry "Bobs" Roberts served as secretary and treasurer. Edgar Pomeroy, who seems to have been the driving force behind the association, was named as an official of the league competition.

The inaugural CAFL season ran from January to March 1903, and each club paid a two-dollar membership fee. Previous attitudes regarding professionalism remained, and as one newspaper reported, "the league is strictly amateur and charges no admission to its games which are played from real love of the sport."[12] Unusually for these early leagues, each club completed all their scheduled fixtures. The Vampires flew out of the gates, winning their opener against San Francisco 5–0. They were victors in the next four, outscoring opponents 13–2, and seemed to be cruising to the title. The club did suffer through some injuries, playing without number one goalkeeper W. Jamieson for much of the season and losing key defender Edward Petersen to broken ribs. After the Vampires closed out the schedule with a draw and a surprising loss to the Albions, the American-British Rifles pipped them at the wire to capture the honors. The season was undoubtedly successful, but later accounts highlighted the achievements of the CAFL while minimizing the importance of the earlier league from 1892.

In other parts of the country, knowledge of previous competitions was sometimes lost due to the movement of people, inconsistent recordkeeping, and the passage of time. In San Francisco, however, attitudes toward previous competitions and clubs were characterized less by a lack of knowledge and more by a deliberate strategy to downplay their importance. Writing in the 1904–05 *Spalding's Association Foot Ball Guide*, Taliesin Evans celebrated the third year of the CAFL, calling it "an intelligent effort" to create "a systematically organized field sport" in the city. He dismissed earlier attempts as being done "perfunctorily" and claimed that the city's first league collapsed due to "the absence of organization, the lack of discipline and an imperfect understanding of the rules of the game by a majority of the players."[13] While the PAFL had its share of challenges, Evans's judgement seems harsh and self-serving because he held the office of league president from the CAFL's founding in 1902. The CAFL also experienced some of the same issues that plagued the PAFL, namely difficulties in finding adequate facilities and problems with clubs not showing up with the correct number of players. In that same issue of the guide, Henry Roberts, another newspaperman and honorary secretary of the CAFL, praised the work of Edgar Pomeroy while diminishing the role the Vampires played in reviving the game in the region. Roberts declined to even name VAFC, noting that before 1902, "there had been only one regularly organized club, and their fixtures were composed of two games with the sailors each year." Roberts also made no mention of the previous Hilbert Cup competition despite the historical bent of his essay, "Ante-date Notes of the Game on the Coast."[14]

Over the next few seasons, the Vampires emerged as one of the more competitive sides in the league. The club earned its first trophy in 1906–07 when they took home the California State Cup. A record crowd of two thousand spectators witnessed the final played at Freeman's Park on April

21, 1907. It pitted the Vampires against their fierce rivals and league champions, Oakland Hornets. It was a tight affair, but Vampire keeper and captain Neil McFarlane played lights out, making at least two extraordinary saves to keep the score level. The Vampires' forwards had been lively all match and were rewarded in the sixty-fifth minute, scoring the game's only goal. It was a true team effort, with nearly all the frontline players touching the ball before David Hunter delivered a perfect pass for Lee to tap in. The Hornets buzzed around the Vampire goal as the minutes ticked away, but they were unable to find the back of the net. The *San Francisco Examiner* called it "the best exhibition of the association game given this season" and named McFarlane man of the match.[15] When he was handed the trophy, McFarlane's teammates and the crowd erupted in a loud ovation.

Two years later, McFarlane and Hunter were named to a league all-star team that visited British Columbia, Canada. The squad had a glorious kit: navy blue shirts with California poppies embroidered in gold thread across the chest, white shorts, and gold and blue stockings. Overall, the team finished the tour with a record of two wins, three defeats, and one draw. Hard travel played a role in what was viewed as a disappointing performance. The trek began with a voyage through rough seas and trips between cities

The California All-Star team that toured Western Canada in 1909. Goalkeeper Neil McFarlane stands in the center of the top row wearing a flat cap. (Author's collection)

often took place at night, preventing the players from getting enough rest. The social schedule that accompanied the games, including such events as excursions, smoking concerts, and banquets, may also have contributed to their fatigue. After they returned from Canada, the all-star team accepted a challenge from a picked side of players from Southern California. Once again McFarlane starred, keeping a clean sheet in the 6–0 win.

Another player on the Canadian jaunt was outside right Harry Walters, who played his club football for Albion Rovers. He was a speedy winger known for his wicked crosses into the box. In the first match of the trip, he collided with an opposing defender and fractured his arm. After a brief stay in the hospital, he was deemed fit, although he did not participate in any more of the squad's matches. He did find time to pen a postcard to someone, who may have been a family member, writing that "We are having a great time up here" before noting that he had broken a bone.[16] Despite reports that he had recovered, Walters missed the Albions' California Cup final win over Thistle that spring. Some newspapers wrote that he was more seriously injured than initially thought, and the fracture would have hindered his return to work as a carpenter. At the end of May, the local soccer community held a benefit match in his honor featuring his mates from the All-California team lining up against a picked squad of league players. Led by the indomitable McFarlane, the All-Stars took home the honors 3–0 before what was described as a "monster crowd."[17] By fall Walters was contemplating retirement from soccer due to a knee injury, but eventually he returned to the field.

Despite the success of the league, tensions remained beneath the surface. The problems exploded in 1910 as the region experienced its own version of a "soccer war." The dispute centered on the location and economic arrangements of cup matches. Three clubs, Albion Rovers, Thistle, and Vampires were based in Alameda, California, a city across the bay from San Francisco proper. The California Football Association (CFA) had scheduled all cup matches for the Presidio grounds, located in the northwestern corner of San Francisco. Even today in the age of interstate highways, the nearly twenty-mile trek across the bay would take at least forty minutes to drive under the best of circumstances. In 1910 the transportation challenges that clubs and supporters faced would have been even greater. As a result, the rebels asked that half of the cup ties be played closer to home in Alameda County. The teams also demanded that the gate receipts, minus expenses, for such games be evenly split between the two competing squads. Finally, they refused to pay rental fees for the pitch based on a percentage of the gate and instead offered a flat rate. If the CFA did not agree to these terms, the three clubs threatened to withdraw from the cup competition. A week later, the Vampires narrowly voted to abandon the insurrection and made peace with the association. The other teams, however, persisted with the protest. A cup match-up between Burns and Rovers initially looked like it would be played as scheduled. At the last moment, however, the Rovers' executive committee held a meeting on the pitch and declared they would not contest the match. Opinion was not unanimous within the organization, and longtime club secretary Jesse Moore immediately resigned.

Veteran soccer player and administrator Douglas Erskine wrote that it was the worst possible time for such a fight. The CAFL had recently completed a lively and exciting season, with the Thistles capturing the title just ahead of the Rovers, Vampires, and Burns clubs. He felt that, while Rovers had some legitimate grievances, their actions in forfeiting the match had done more harm than good: "They have laid themselves open to every punishment which the association can inflict on an insurgent member, and the original issue is likely to be overshadowed by the more serious exhibition of mutiny."[18] As the dispute dragged on, rumors circulated that financial problems at the club were the real reason behind Rovers' intransigence. In response to the club refusing to play, the CFA expelled the rebellious Rovers. Meanwhile, Vampires and Thistle pledged to support the original organization, even as Rovers formed a breakaway group called the Bay Counties Soccer League (BCSL). Local businesses soon pledged funding to back the new competition, and a four-team league looked to begin play by the end of March 1910. As the California state cup tournament ended with the Vampires taking home their second trophy, and the league season drew to a close, it looked as though the area might soon be home to rival competitions.

The long summer break did little to ease tensions. As teams began organizing for the 1911–12 season, the BCSL showed little willingness to compromise. In fact, the organization formed a committee with the express purpose of poaching both players and teams from the CAFL. The outlaws approached the Independents and Thistle clubs, but they ultimately refused to move. The BSCL announced it would play a split season, with the winner of the first round earning a silver cup and the champion of the second half taking home gold medals and a silver shield. On September 18, 1910, the *Chronicle* reported that a "bombshell" had landed in soccer circles.[19] Longtime referee Jimmy Askham organized an all-star team of sorts, with most of the players taken from Albion Rovers, the club that had initiated and maintained the soccer war. Askham christened his new side Pastimes and claimed to have signed Vampire stars Neil McFarlane and David Hunter. Although it turned out to be untrue and the two remained at VAFC, it nevertheless showed the ambition of the new club. One of the players who did switch sides was right winger Harry Walters, now fully recovered from his arm and leg injuries. Since the league continued to be strictly amateur, one wonders what inducements had been offered to secure player services. Another question that remains unanswered is what role the CFA played in the formation of the new club. Newspapers quickly announced that the loss of players would result in the destruction of the Rovers and the collapse of the BCSL. It turned out that none of these predictions came true, as the Rovers persevered, and the outlaw league began play just a week after the CAFL. Four teams lined up for the first full BCSL season: Rovers, Oaklands, Burns, and Alamedas. The organization also applied for membership in the Pacific Athletic Association, but after conditionally accepting the league, the group ultimately rejected the BCSL and pointedly suggested that the soccer organizations make peace.

Ultimately the two leagues played out their seasons independently of one another. The larger and more prestigious CAFL received the lion's share of press coverage, but the BCSL was not ignored. Oakland took home the Lancaster Cup as champions of the first half of the season, while the Albion Rovers captured the shield in the second half. Tentative movement toward peace between the two organizations finally began in July 1911. Officials of the BCSL invited representatives of the PCFA to a meeting, but at the same time the state association announced it had accepted a new club called Rangers FC, which was based in Alameda. Nothing seemed to come of the planned conference, but association leaders called for another meeting in August. The veteran organization held all the cards and decreed that past grievances were not open for debate. Instead, the CFA hoped they would find a way to move forward together to grow the game. On August 15, 1911, fifteen representatives of the BCSL met with thirty delegates of the CFA. The insurrectionists wanted to scrap the current association and start from scratch; the CFA rejected this but said it was open to revising the organization's bylaws. By the end of negotiations, the CFA emerged as the clear winner by keeping the existing structure intact and agreeing that, while BCSL clubs could apply for membership in the league, entry was not guaranteed.

Despite the seemingly unbalanced arrangement, the rebels managed to elect several of their chosen candidates to powerful leadership positions in the CFA, including chairman of the executive committee and secretary. The decision of the CAFL a week later to reject three BCFL clubs, Albion Rovers, Alameda Rangers, and Corinthians, raised fears that the battle was still not over. The peace held, however, and the BCFL continued as a subordinate league to the larger CAFL. Several major clubs, including the Independents and Barbarians, fielded second elevens in the BCFL, and the Corinthians competed in the California State Cup competition. The situation remained unchanged into the fall of 1912, although two BCFL teams, Alamedas and Rangers, were accepted into the senior circuit. The BCFL seems to have completed the first half of its second season and then disappeared. The Bay Area soccer war ended with a whimper.

The CAFL continued and, for a time, the Vampires remained competitive, winning the league in 1908–09 and 1910–11 and taking home another state cup in 1913–14. Although they kept playing into the 1920s, it was clear that the best days of the squad were behind them. They finished bottom of the league in 1923 and failed to rise for the following season, ending an adventure that had begun twenty-six years earlier. While not exactly immortal, it was still a remarkable run for a soccer club to survive for more than two decades during this period.

Notes

1. Kipling, "The Vampire."
2. W.W.N., "After the Vampire and Kipling," *San Francisco Examiner*, August 1, 1897.
3. Lee, "King Demos and His Laureate," 58.
4. Lee, "King Demos and His Laureate," 60.
5. "Football," *San Francisco Call*, July 1, 1894.
6. Pomeroy, "Football: The True Way to Play it," *San Francisco Call*, December 10, 1893.
7. "History," *Crouch End Vampires F.C.*
8. Porter, "Revenge of the Crouch End Vampires," 419.
9. Mitchell, *Men Who Made Scotland*, 205.
10. *San Francisco Examiner*, January 23, 1898; *San Francisco Chronicle*, January 30, 1898.
11. "A Wonderful Aquatic Feat," *San Francisco Call*, August 2, 1897.
12. "Will Association Football Replace Intercollegiate?" *San Francisco Chronicle*, February 8, 1903.
13. Evans, "The Game in California," 109.
14. Roberts, "Ante-date Notes of the Game on the Coast," 117.
15. "Vampires Outplay Hornets and Win Cup," *San Francisco Examiner*, April 22, 1907.
16. "California's Soccer Team at Vancouver, B.C. April 3 by Broadbridge, Bullen Photos," Real photo postcard, April 12, 1909.
17. "All-California Soccer Team Win Game 3–0," *Oakland Tribune*, May 31, 1909.

18. Erskine, "Albion Rovers Balk and Refuse to Play Cup Tie," *San Francisco Examiner*, March 7, 1910.

19. "Strong Soccer Team is Formed to Go into Association," *San Francisco Chronicle*, September 18, 1910.

Sources

"The Building." *The Mills Building*. Accessed May 25, 2022. https://www.themillsbuilding.com/about-the-building/facts-and-features.

"California's Soccer Team at Vancouver, B.C. April 3 by Broadbridge, Bullen Photos." Real photo postcard, April 12, 1909.

Crocker-Langley San Francisco City Directory. San Francisco: H. S. Crocker, 1897–1904.

Crouch End Vampires F.C. "History." *Crouch End Vampires F.C.* Accessed May 19, 2022. http://www.crouchendvampires.co.uk/history.html.

Duder, Josh. "VAFC: Vampires in The City." *The Protagonist Soccer*, October 7, 2020. https://www.protagonistsoccer.com/coverage-blog/vafc.

Evans, Taliesin. "The Game in California." "Soccer Foot Ball in California." In *Spalding's Official Association "Soccer" Foot Ball Guide,* edited by Jerome Flannery, 109–15. New York: American Sports Publishing, 1905.

Goodman, Sam. "Association Foot Ball in California." In *Spalding's Official Association "Soccer" Foot Ball Guide,* 93–108. New York: American Sports Publishing, 1909.

Hasbeen, A. "Soccer Foot Ball in California." In *Spalding's Official Association "Soccer" Foot Ball Guide*, edited by George Orton, 203–7. New York: American Sports Publishing, 1911.

Husted's Oakland, Alameda, and Berkeley Directory. San Francisco: F. M. Husted, 1907.

Kipling, Rudyard. "The Vampire." *Academy of American Poets*. Accessed May 30, 2022. https://poets.org/poem/vampire-0.

Lee, John. "King Demos and His Laureate: Rudyard Kipling's 'The White Man's Burden,' Transatlanticism, and the Newspaper Poem." *Media History* 20, no. 1 (2014): 51–66.

McGeever, Sean. "100th Anniversary: San Francisco Soccer Football League." June 8, 2002.

Mitchell, Andy. *The Men Who Made Scotland: The Definitive Who's Who of Scottish Football Internationalists, 1872–1939*. Dunblane, Scotland: Andy Mitchell Media, 2021.

Park, Roberta J. "British Sports and Pastimes in San Francisco, 1848–1900." *British Journal of Sport History* 1, no. 3 (1984): 300–17.

Pomeroy, Edgar. "Oakland Hornets." In *Spalding's Official Association "Soccer" Foot Ball Guide,* edited by Jerome Flannery, 144–47. New York: American Sports Publishing, 1905.

Pomeroy, Edgar. "Soccer Foot Ball in California." In *Spalding's Official Association "Soccer" Foot Ball Guide,* edited by Thomas Cahill, 237–55. New York: American Sports Publishing, 1912.

Porter, Dilwyn. "Revenge of the Crouch End Vampires: The AFA, the FA and English Football's 'Great Split,' 1907–14." *Sport in History* 26, no. 3 (December 2006): 406–28.

Roberts, Henry. "Ante-date Notes of the Game on the Coast." In *Spalding's Official Association "Soccer" Foot Ball Guide,* edited by Jerome Flannery, 117–29. New York: American Sports Publishing, 1905.

Van Rheenen, Derek. "Soccer in San Francisco: The Emergence and Endurance of the Ethnic and Amateur Game." In *Soccer Frontiers: The Global Game in the United States, 1863–1913*, edited by Chris Bolsmann and George Kioussis, 221–42. Knoxville: University of Tennessee Press, 2021.

Westby, Martin. *England's Oldest Football Clubs 1815–1889*. Self-published, 2019.

NEWSPAPERS

The Londoner
Oakland Tribune
Penny Illustrated Paper (London)
San Francisco Call
San Francisco Chronicle
San Francisco Examiner
Sporting Gazette (London)
Sporting Life (London)

15

Soccer in Surf and Sand

Honolulu, Hawai'i

Leopold G. Blackman was a twentieth-century renaissance man of sorts. He was an educator, poet, soldier, and, briefly, a convicted felon. He also played soccer. After moving to Hawai'i from his native England, Blackman became one of the earliest promoters of the sport on the islands. He was instrumental in creating Hawai'i's first soccer community, but he did not do it alone. Other Scottish, English, and Hawaiian-born players also took part. Blackman arrived in Hawai'i just after a period of tumultuous change. Non-native business and political leaders overthrew the reigning monarch, Queen Lili'uokalani, in 1893. Afterwards, these men formed the Republic of Hawaii, which governed the islands until they were annexed by the United States in 1898. Hawai'i remained a territory of the United States, led by an appointed governor, until granted statehood in 1959. Although the history of Hawai'i's soccer community shares some characteristics with those on the mainland, it was also distinctive in several ways. The process of creating a sustained, organized competition began later in the islands than in most other areas. The earliest soccer league did not form until December 1900, and the organization's first matches took place a month later, in January 1901. Unlike some other areas of the United States, many of the most prominent players came from established families and held white-collar jobs as accountants, clerks, and managers. Another unusual characteristic was that, although dominated by whites of British descent, there was some ethnic diversity, with Chinese, Filipino, and native Hawaiian players also taking part.

Born on the fourth of July 1874 at Cheltenham, England, Blackman was the son of a pharmacist. He attended St. Nicolas College (now Lancing College) and after graduation taught at a boarding school called Ardingly

College. His motivations for leaving Britain are not known, but he arrived in Hawai'i on January 24, 1900. He likely had arranged an appointment before coming to the islands and was soon named principal of 'Iolani College, one of several local academies. Blackman immediately became active in the recreational activities of the British expatriate community. By late spring he was a member of the Honolulu Cricket Club, and one local paper noted that he was a good athlete and "has shown promise of distinguishing himself in the near future."[1]

It is not known when the first football game of any code was played in Hawai'i. The earliest mention of the sport was a match between boys from Oahu College in 1877. The contest was probably a version of rugby or the intercollegiate game. In 1881 students played a match using the Rugby Union code on Christmas Eve. Talk of introducing soccer began in the fall of 1899, but there is no evidence that any games were played. The first documented soccer match in Hawai'i took place on April 28, 1900, when two teams named "Scotland" and "The World" played to a 0–0 draw. The match report noted that, while some had doubts about the sport, the large crowd showed that it could attract spectators. As one might expect, the quality of play was poor, and perhaps due to a lack of fitness, the teams played only two twenty-minute halves plus an additional ten minutes of extra time. The *Honolulu Advertiser* picked out Blackman, who lined up for the Worlders, as one of the game's best players. Occasional matches took place over the summer, including contests against crews from visiting ships, but no formal organization existed.

A newspaper reported in August 1900 that 'Iolani College would take up soccer, with Blackman serving as coach. Missionaries had established a Western-style school system in Hawai'i during the nineteenth century, although unlike on the mainland, the structure was much more centralized. One of only a handful of high schools in the territory, 'Iolani had fewer restrictions on racial makeup and as a result was more diverse than other academies. By the end of the nineteenth century, the main goal of educators was to assimilate non-white students, especially Native Hawaiians, into Western and, more particularly, US culture. According to education history scholar Kalani Beyer, the goal was "to convert Hawai'i into a tropical New England."[2] Perhaps Blackman thought soccer would fit this model, echoing the importance of student sports not only in Great Britain but also the Northeastern United States. It may also have been that he enjoyed playing the game and wished to create conditions that allowed him to compete on a regular basis.

Blackman wrote to the sports editor of the *Honolulu Advertiser* in September 1900 suggesting the formation of a four-team soccer league. Since the cricket club did not play during the winter, he felt members would appreciate some form of active recreation. Progress was slow, even after a newspaper published the association rules. Although Blackman hoped for a four-team league, by October only two squads were playing regular fixtures. The first was ʻIolani College and the second was called Scotland. Initially, the schoolboys, along with Blackman, who lined up as a midfielder, were vastly outclassed by the Scots. On one occasion he played forward and was sharply criticized after a poor performance: "[Blackman] would be more use to his team if he would combine with the other forwards" and not play such a "selfish game."[3] The younger players improved over time but generally failed to offer much resistance to Scotland.

By the end of November 1900, the Thistle Club had decided to formally organize a soccer team, with the squad's colors being light blue and white; their badge featured a thistle on a white background. An England team soon followed, sporting white shirts and blue pants with a crest showing a red rose on a white shield. The Old ʻIolani Association Football Club, formed by alumni of the school, organized the next day. Soon a competition was established with two divisions. The senior circuit consisted of three teams: Scotland (as the Thistle Club side came to be known), England, and ʻIolani United; the latter was a composite squad made up of a rotating cast of players drawn from the ʻIolani Old Boys and ʻIolani College teams. At a meeting on December 13, representatives drafted a constitution, established league rules, and elected Leopold Blackman president of the organization. The fixtures of the Hawaiian Association Football League (HAFL) began after the turn of the new year. Very quickly Scotland proved itself the class of the league, winning all its games and outscoring opponents 21–4. Despite the lack of competition, members of the league deemed the season a success and celebrated with a "smoking concert" in late March that featured bagpipe music.

For the following campaign, they decided to make changes to prevent a single team from dominating the league. One newspaper explained the motivation for making this change: "It was felt that the Scottish team was too heavy metal for the others."[4] After debating various methods to impose balance, they eventually named four prominent players to be the captains of the new sides. Some of the clubs had players who worked for the same firm, while another was formed by members of the Makiki Club. The HAFL announced that enough money had been raised to purchase a championship cup, but due to limited funds, the players of the winning team would be given smaller cups rather than medals. Four teams began play in late 1901: Wanderers, Maile Ilima, Honolulu AFC, and Hackfield-Davies. The decision to scramble the players to generate more competition paid off, as the 1901–02 season was ultimately decided by a playoff game between the top two finishers, with Maile Ilima taking home the honors.

Although the game was still relatively new to the islands, the players soon showed their competitiveness by complaining about refereeing decisions. In March 1901, referee J. Cumming wrote a long letter to a newspaper responding to a recent article that called attention to the players' moaning: "I certainly noted the 'general dissatisfaction' referred to, and was rather hurt by it, as well as by the ungentlemanly way in which it was so often expressed." He went on to carefully justify his decisions by citing specific rules and exactly how they had been violated. He concluded with a bit of friendly advice: "(1) Learn the rules, (2) keep your hands down, (3) keep your temper, (4) hold your tongue, (5) practice. And above all practice."[5] A year later another refereeing decision caused the YMCA team to protest the result of a match. The dispute hinged on whether or not a player had deliberately used his hand to strike the ball. Blackman, who lined up for YMCA that season, argued that an unwritten law of officiating stated that if there is any doubt the handball was intentional, then a foul should not be given. James Hall Fiddes, who had made the decision, stated he felt that the intention of the player was irrelevant since by handling the ball, he had won a clear advantage for his team. Ultimately, the league sided with Fiddes and threw out the protest.

Accusations and counter-accusations again filled newspaper columns in November 1906. A player for the Diamond Heads named Ed Fernández was sent off in a match versus the Tenth Infantry. A few days later, the captain of the Diamond Heads and Fernández himself wrote the *Honolulu Advertiser* to tell their side of the story. E. E. Grune explained that at the end of the first half, Fernández complained about some decisions to referee J. W. Waldron. Soon after the break, Waldron called a foul on Fernández, who once again expressed his dissatisfaction and was subsequently sent off the pitch. For his part, Fernández claimed that he was only ejected after he asked a teammate if he thought that an opposing player had committed a tripping foul that was uncalled. At once Waldron said to him, "None of that or else I'll rule you off the field," to which Fernández replied, "Never mind, I'll talk as much as I like as long as I'm not talking about you nor casting any slur on your rulings." It was this exchange that led to the sending off and caused Waldron to consider quitting refereeing. The editor of the newspaper supported the official, writing that no decision would please everyone and that if he should step away from the game, "it will be a bad day for local footballers when Mr. Waldron relinquishes his thankless task."[6]

The winning squad of the 1901–02 HAFL season was Maile Ilima, named for a prominent sporting club on the islands. The team dominated the competition's early years, winning six of the next seven titles. The composition of the league varied over time, with a low of three teams and a high of five teams. Recreational organizations like Maile Ilima were mainstays, but several different types of clubs took to the pitch over the years. The local YMCA fielded a team between 1905 and 1909, and in some years, schoolboy teams participated, including the public high school and private academies such as the ʻIolani and Punahou schools. Squads linked to military units, including the 1st Field Artillery, the Hawaiian National Guard, and Marines from Camp Very, competed for a few seasons. Industrial or company sides took part, including the Honolulu Iron Works and a transit workers club. It was sometimes difficult to obtain sporting equipment, especially balls and goals. At the start of the 1906–07 season, for example, the league put out a call to help locate the balls and goals that had been used the previous year. On a positive note, HAFL finances were in the black even if no club was going to become rich. Net proceeds of $68.57 in 1906 were divided equally between the five teams in the competition, leaving them with $13.71 each. Around this same time, other entities, including industrial firms and sugar cane plantations, also fielded sides, but none of them joined the HAFL.

For the most part, the players of the HAFL were of Anglophone descent, with some, like Blackman, immigrants from Great Britain, while others were born in the United States or Hawaiʻi. Many of them held middle-class jobs and had links to some of the more prestigious social clubs on the islands. Footballer and sometime referee James Hall Fiddes was emblematic of the type. Born in Aberdeen, Scotland, on March 22, 1877, he arrived in Hawaiʻi in 1899. Fiddes was a tall man with blue eyes, dark brown hair, and a large bushy mustache. Reportedly, he played for several teams in Scotland, including Victoria United in 1898, the year they won the North Scotland championship. One newspaper described him as "a cool, wary player; fast, a good kick and a good scoring man."[7] He soon took on a leadership role in the league, eventually becoming HAFL president. Fiddes worked as an accountant for a variety of companies over the years. In addition to soccer, he also played cricket and was secretary of the Honolulu Scottish Club. He was also a Mason, Shriner, Knight Templar, Odd Fellow, and Exalted Ruler of Honolulu Lodge 616 of the Benevolent and Protective Order of Elks. When he got married in 1902, the *Honolulu Advertiser* declared that he was "extremely popular among local Britishers." His comrades on the Honolulu Football Club sent along a gift to the happy couple. The author of the article also took the opportunity to wax lyrical about the fashions on display at the event. While Fiddes himself wore a classic black suit, his bride, Mary Ann Titcomb, wore a white organdie gown the paper called "a triumph of the modiste's art." Her hat was "a dream in white chiffon and ostrich feathers," while the bridesmaid's dress was "a stunning affair of white organdie netted over pink silk."[8]

William Henry Soper further illustrated the prominent social status of many soccer players in Hawai'i. He was born on June 6, 1874, in Middletown, California, a small town about one hundred miles north of San Francisco. His mother was of German and Australian descent but was born in Hawai'i, while his father, John, came from Plymouth, England. William moved to the islands with his mother when he was five years old. The elder Soper was an established newsman and sugar plantation owner, who played a key role in the violent coup that overthrew the Hawaiian monarchy. Although not usually counted among the regular members of the Committee of Public Safety, he attended the meeting held on January 16, 1893, when the decision was made to oust the queen. The Committee was a group of prominent *haole* (non-native Hawaiian) economic and political leaders who favored the annexation of the islands by the United States. Soper was an imposing man with a balding head and large, white mutton chop sideburns and mustache, a style known as a Hulihee beard. He was named commander in chief of the armed forces for the Provisional Government (1893–94) and later the Republic (1894–98). Eventually, he was given a commission as a brigadier general by President Theodore Roosevelt.

Although just a teenager when the overthrow took place, William Soper was also a participant. One later newspaper report on his actions described him as "a revolutionist who carried a gun against the monarchy in 1893."[9] Another story noted that he had been assigned to guard Kawaiahe'o Church "during the troubled times."[10] When he passed away in 1959, Soper had lived through all the major periods of Hawai'ian political history: from monarchy to republic and from territory to state. He was an athlete who played intercollegiate football at Stanford between 1894 and 1897. Soper was mainly a reserve fullback for the varsity but had trouble breaking through because "he runs too high and is inclined to drop the ball."[11] He did seem to have some talent as a punter. After leaving school he returned to the islands and took up soccer, perhaps because the gridiron game had become too violent. He lined up alongside James Fiddes in 1900 as part of the Honolulu Football Club, one of the earliest soccer teams to form in Hawai'i.

A few players, including Ah Sang, Kin Fook, and Len Que, who turned out for 'Iolani School, were of Chinese descent. The ways the players were identified in newspaper reports and official documents may not accurately reflect how their names were expressed in their native language. Len Que featured on the 1901–02 Maile Ilima title winning side. Another

Hawaiian-born player of Chinese descent, Solomon Sing Hung Hoe, played for the 1908–09 champions. He was born on October 20, 1892, the fifth of twelve children. He was only a teenager when he captured the soccer title. Hoe was also a talented baseball player, who toured the mainland in 1912 and 1913 with an all-Chinese squad from the islands. Chinatown businesses and the Hawaiian Merchant's and Advertiser's Club of Honolulu financed the trip, hoping that it would encourage tourism to the islands and help create what historian Joel S. Franks calls a "cultural bridge" between European and Chinese Americans.[12] Generally, the tours met these goals, although they were not economically successful. On the field the teams did well, mostly playing against college and semiprofessional squads. They also proved willing to compete against both white and Black teams. In the tours that Hoe played with the team in 1912 and 1913, the Hawaiians won 169 games, lost 89, and tied 4. He wrote occasional updates on the tour for local newspapers, and even had something published in *Baseball Monthly*.

On February 27, 1911, two soccer clubs made up entirely of Chinese athletes took to the field. The Chinese Athletic Union team beat the Hawaii Chinese Soccer Association squad 4–0. A big crowd took in the match,

The champion Maile Ilima squad of 1908–09, featuring Solomon Sing Hung Hoe (center to the left of the mascot). (Source: *Honolulu Advertiser*, January 24, 1909.)

including many experienced soccer players, who encouraged the athletes and offered tips on how to improve. The teams had not practiced much, and they tended to kick the ball as hard as possible rather than taking a more scientific approach. A few weeks later, the teams met again in a charity match to raise money to buy food for people in northern China, who were experiencing a famine.

While the HAFL was the area's senior soccer competition, the community also organized a junior circuit. Although never as popular as intercollegiate football or baseball during this period, the schoolboy competitions attracted a decent amount of press coverage. It was at this level where the sides became significantly more diverse. One junior league team known as the Cables, for example, included the following players: R. Jordan, Ah Ko, Lo On, Sing Chong, F. Evans, Foe Sue, W. Brown, E. Andres, Mon Yin, Yee Bew, and W. Miles. Future Olympic swimming gold medalist and surfer Duke Kahanamoku played as a midfielder for the Kamehameha School

The Kamehameha School soccer team, winners of the youth league in 1907–08. Duke Kahanamoku is the second from the top, on the right, wearing a patterned shirt. (Source: *Honolulu Advertiser*, February 23, 1908.)

side that took home the 1908 junior championship. The Kamehameha School had been founded in 1887, and its aims were to provide English language instruction and manual training to native boys. The institution resembled similar schools for Native Americans on the mainland, the most well-known of them being the Carlisle Indian Industrial School. The fact that the junior teams were integrated did not mean that non-white players escaped prejudice. At a meeting of league officials in November 1903, the coach of the previous season's winning junior team reported that, even though the players had been promised gold or silver medals, they had not been awarded. The reason, he argued, was because the squad was made up of Chinese boys. A player with the surname Fernández, likely of Filipino descent and perhaps the same person sent off in 1906, faced racial abuse on the pitch after he moved from the islands to San Francisco.

The HAFL ran continuously from 1900 to 1914, when the competition largely ceased play during World War I. Blackman's role in the organization seemed to last only for the first handful of seasons. He was on the losing side of a title decider in March 1905, when Maile Ilima captured the second of what would be six straight championships. He also played for the YMCA team for a few years. He left his position at ʻIolani College after a single season and embarked on a series of careers in the years that followed. In 1902 Blackman published an epic poem called *Kaupeepee: An Idyll of Hawaii* that was based on a local myth. That same year he married a widow named Edith May Winifred Holdsworth. Her previous husband had been secretary of Theo. W. Davis Co., one of the so-called Big Five. These firms operated a variety of business ventures, especially sugar growing and processing, and exerted a great deal of economic and political power in the territory. The late Mr. Holdsworth had been born in England and had been a member of the same cricket club where Leopold Blackman later played. Edith must have had a penchant for artistic men, as Holdsworth had won a competition to design stamps for the Republic of Hawaii. Largely due to the result of a life insurance policy, Edith was able to send her daughter Beatrice to boarding school in France. She herself spent 1922–23 abroad and by the fall of 1924 had sued Blackman for divorce, citing nonsupport. The uncontested divorce was granted in October, with Edith receiving $250 in attorney's fees and $100 a month in alimony. In 1909 Blackman was Special Inspector of Foreign Animals and Birds for Hawaiʻi and principal of Aliʻiolani College. Five years later he was the headmaster at the Honolulu School for Boys and had enlisted in the Hawaiʻi National Guard. Blackman became an aide to the governor of the islands and by the 1920s commanded the Honolulu Military Academy.

After several years of educating cadets, including Olympic gold medalist and future movie star Buster Crabbe, the academy was dissolved in 1927.

Blackman changed careers once again when he bought a seat on the Hawaiian Stock Exchange. On August 18, 1930, the firm was suspended from the exchange and soon Blackman found himself indicted for embezzlement. According to the complaint, the victims included a US Navy lieutenant and a widow with four children. The case eventually went to trial, where Blackman was accused of spending more time writing poems than conducting business. The prosecution described him as "a modern Nero, who instead of fiddling while Rome burned, wrote novels and lived at the Royal Hawaiian Hotel while his firm stole money from trusting women."[13] He claimed that his role was to meet with customers while his partners handled the books. The final verdict was guilty as charged and the *Honolulu Advertiser* described his reaction: "Blackman stood, gray and shaken, slightly supporting himself upon a rolled magazine on a chair arm."[14]

The defendants were sentenced to ten years' hard labor but quickly appealed the result. The trial led Blackman to declare bankruptcy, reporting assets of $219,054 ($4.1 million today) and liabilities of $377,425 ($7.1 million today).[15] Two years later the state supreme court overturned the verdict and the charges were ultimately dropped after prosecutors declined to retry him. Blackman's brush with the law did not seem to harm his reputation, and he continued to publish book reviews and Hawaiian history essays for local newspapers. He left the islands in 1941 and relocated to Tahiti. While there he continued writing articles about his new home until he died in 1951, aged seventy-seven.

Notes

1. "Wicket Men," *Honolulu Advertiser*, May 8, 1900.
2. Beyer, "A Century of Using Secondary Education," 525.
3. "Scots Wallop Iolani's Team," *Honolulu Advertiser*, November 26, 1900.
4. "Won Trophy Six Times," *Honolulu Advertiser*, March 29, 1908.
5. J. Cumming, "Replies to His Carping Critics," *Honolulu Star-Advertiser*, March 6, 1901.
6. "Sports," *Honolulu Daily Advertiser*, November 20, 1906.
7. "Scotch Football Team Has Many Good Players," *Honolulu Advertiser*, February 16, 1901.
8. "J. Hall Fiddes Takes a Wife," *Honolulu Advertiser*, January 31, 1902.
9. Kaizawa, "Veterans of Hawai'i's Annexation Say Justice Is Finally at Hand," *Honolulu Star-Bulletin*, March 12, 1959.
10. "Kamaaina W. H. Soper Dies at 85," *Honolulu Advertiser*, November 23, 1959.

11. "From the Sidelines," *Daily Palo Alto*, October 16, 1894.
12. Franks, *Asian Pacific Americans and Baseball*, 101.
13. "Brokers are Sentenced to Penitentiary," *Honolulu Advertiser*, October 4, 1930.
14. "Brokers are Sentenced to Penitentiary," *Honolulu Advertiser*, October 4, 1930.
15. MeasuringWorth.com.

Sources

Beyer, Kalani. "A Century of Using Secondary Education to Extend American Hegemony over Hawai'i." *American Educational History Journal* 39, no. 2 (2012): 515–35.

Franks, Joel S. "Pacific Crossings and Baseball: Comments on Hawaii and America's National Pastime and the Great Wally Yonamine." *Nine* 8, no. 1 (1999): 54–73.

Franks, Joel S. *Pacific Americans and Baseball: A History*. Jefferson, NC: McFarland, 2008.

Kaizawa, Tomi. "Veterans of Hawai'i's Annexation Say Justice Is Finally at Hand," *Honolulu Star-Bulletin*, March 12, 1959.

Russ, William A. *The Hawaiian Revolution, 1893–94*. Selinsgrove, PA: Susquehanna University Press, 1959.

Siddall, John William, ed. *Men of Hawaii*. 2 vols. Honolulu: Honolulu Star-Bulletin Limited, 1917.

NEWSPAPERS

Daily Honolulu Press
Daily Palo Alto
Evening Bulletin (Honolulu)
Hawaiian Gazette
Hawaiian Star
Honolulu Advertiser
Honolulu Star-Advertiser
Pacific Commercial Advertiser (Honolulu)
Pacific Island Monthly

WEBSITE

MeasuringWorth.com

Epilogue

About two weeks into the inaugural season of the American League of Professional Football (ALPF), Brooklyn defeated Philadelphia 3–1 on October 18, 1894. The ALPF was the first openly professional soccer league formed outside of Great Britain. It was backed by major league baseball franchises and included six teams spread along the East Coast, from Boston to Washington, DC. The game between Brooklyn and Philadelphia took place at Eastern Park, a "handsome, spacious, and well-maintained" stadium that hosted a variety of athletic events.[1] Despite its attractiveness, the park was not well liked by players, and its distance from central Brooklyn meant that it often struggled to attract fans. The unfortunate trend continued that October day, as the *Boston Globe* reported that just eighteen people, fewer than the number of players on the field, paid to attend the soccer game. The dismal figure highlighted some problems with the league and helps explain why it shut down only a few days after the match. Teams had underestimated costs and overestimated revenues. The owners' baseball league faced the threat of a rival competition that was organizing to begin play the following spring. The biggest issue was that, although they were experienced at running sports teams, they had little knowledge of soccer.

The baseball magnates' lack of familiarity with the sport manifested itself in several ways. To begin with the contest was played on a Thursday, when soccer games mostly took place on weekends. Squad sizes were also too small to support playing multiple games per week, as was usually done in baseball. Perhaps the biggest error was in not understanding how and why soccer communities formed. Historian Andrew McFarland has argued that the sport's "chameleon-like ability to replicate existing identities" meant that soccer appealed to a wide variety of different groups.[2]

The communities discussed in this book show how this played out across the United States. Sometimes an identity was based on place of origin, as was the case with Scots in Detroit, Barre, and Miami. In other cases, it centered on economic status, whether white-collar workers in San Francisco and Honolulu or blue-collar workers in Barre and Scranton. Teams could also be linked to specific businesses, such as the Thomas Motor Company or Levi-Strauss. Soccer teams also emerged out of other types of associations like athletic clubs in Buffalo, Cincinnati, and Portland. Soccer demonstrated the solidarity they felt with their neighbors as they played games to benefit individuals, families, local institutions, and, in the case of Chinese clubs in Hawaiʻi, people who lived far away. In contrast ALPF owners assembled teams that often had little connection to the communities they represented. The Brooklyn squad, for example, was composed mainly of men from Fall River, while Baltimore imported A. W. Stewart and the McKendrick brothers from Detroit along with a handful of professionals from England. Only three baseball players appeared on the rosters of their hometown teams. The owners' goal was not to create communities of interest and mutual aid, but rather to make money.

In fairness to ALPF clubs, they confronted the same challenges that soccer communities faced in cities around the nation. Local leagues proved difficult to create and sustain, while regional ones were virtually nonexistent. The distances involved, the cost of transportation, and the problem of missed work meant that organized, sustained play across regions never developed apart from the annual cup tournaments. Baseball owners had tried to mitigate these issues by not inviting National League clubs in more distant places such as St. Louis, Cleveland, and Chicago to join the ALPF.

Leagues such as the ALPF were not the only way that soccer competitions were organized. Single-elimination cup tournaments were often the earliest competitions formed. The establishment of the Football Association Cup in 1871 had an enormous impact on the popularity of the game in England. For the most part, the clubs examined in the book did not take part in the tournaments that were often considered the preeminent national trophies in the United States. The American Football Association modeled its American Challenge Cup after the English and Scottish Football Association Cups. First played in 1884–85, the tournament was viewed by many as a de facto national championship even though it was limited to clubs from the East Coast. The competition itself experienced its own period of disruption, as it was not held from 1899 to 1906 and was ended in 1924. Apart from teams in Pawtucket, the Barre Rangers were the only club in the book to enter the American Cup, but poor weather and other issues meant that they never actually played a tournament match.

The National Challenge Cup, now known as the US Open Cup, began in 1913 with clubs from the Northeast and a gradually expanding roster of teams from cities in the Midwest, including Pittsburgh, Cleveland, Chicago, and St. Louis. Once again, the cities in this book had a limited impact on the competition until after World War I. As the examples of Cincinnati and San Francisco illustrate, however, it was not that soccer communities were cut off from other areas. In fact intercity matches were far more common than is generally recognized. Soccer historian Ed Farnsworth has compiled a database showing that in the period 1884–1905, teams from around the United States played over eight hundred intercity matches. The attention given to visiting English clubs the Corinthians and Pilgrims as well as matches against Canadian squads illustrate that international connections also existed.

The ALPF clubs acknowledged that they were likely to lose money the first season but were not prepared for just how deep the financial hole turned out to be. The losses were one reason they quickly pulled the plug on the competition. They did this even though they had resources most soccer communities could only dream about. While soccer clubs in Minneapolis and San Francisco struggled to find places to play, baseball owners in Philadelphia and Boston spent over $175,000 (nearly $69 million today) combined to rebuild stadiums destroyed by fire. Because most soccer leagues had inconsistent access to enclosed grounds, they could not rely on ticket sales, often their only major source of revenue. The California Association Football League went a step further and actively refused to have fans pay to watch games.

A strong commitment to amateurism in many locations hindered the economic development of these clubs and competitions. Unlike in baseball, players and teams proved unwilling or unable to turn professional. Administrators and club officials in San Francisco, Detroit, and Scranton actively discouraged payments to players. The challenges that officials in Detroit faced when inviting a team from Chicago in 1896 and the struggle that Fall River had in sending a team to the Pan American Exposition in 1901 reveal the tenuous financial state of many soccer communities. Clubs such as the Scranton Lace Works had links to large industrial firms, but it is not known how much, if any, financial assistance they provided. If it had persisted, the ALPF might have been able to employ other resources they had that many soccer communities did not. One such advantage was the media coverage that had surrounded baseball for decades. In other countries around the world, a dedicated sporting press helped to raise and sustain interest in soccer. The same was sometimes true in the United States, and cities such as Fall River or Pittsburgh, where the sport thrived, had multiple newspapers offering detailed coverage of teams and contests. As shown in this book, however, media coverage in many other places was inconsistent and often incomplete.

Despite some commonalities, soccer communities also faced challenges that baseball did not. Because the ALPF folded in less than a month, it did not have to confront the hostility that some sports fans directed at soccer. Newspapers in Minneapolis, Buffalo, Detroit, and Denver published articles disparaging soccer along with rebuttals from the sport's aficionados. Some challenges, such as economic disruption and poor weather, applied to cities around the country, while others reveal the specific challenges the locations in this book faced. Perhaps the most significant was population size. Even in England, where soccer was far more popular, some argued that in this period, a big club would find it hard to survive in a city with a population of 150,000, and no place under 250,000 could support a major professional team. Of the locations in this book, only five—Buffalo, Cincinnati, Detroit, the Twin Cities, and San Francisco—met the second condition by 1900. Several locations, such as Barre, Scranton, and Detroit, struggled to support more than one major club. Most parts of the country where soccer really thrived during this period had much larger populations. Pawtucket is a partial exception because it was part of a broader regional scene including teams from Massachusetts, New Jersey, and New York. The area around New York City and Northern New Jersey, home to some of the nation's earliest soccer clubs, contained about 4.5 million people, while Chicago (1.8 million) and Philadelphia (1.4 million) also had long histories with the sport. The city of St. Louis, population 661,923 in 1900, was closer in size but still larger than the cities covered in the book. During much of the late nineteenth and early twentieth centuries, it was home to a flourishing soccer community. This success was due to the unique role played by the Christian Brothers College (CBC). Young men learned soccer at CBC and many continued playing after graduation. As alumni of the college took up teaching positions at local Catholic schools, they brought soccer with them, and the sport became part of the associational culture of church parishes across the city. Although some of the areas discussed in the book established youth competitions, none of them proved as influential as the ones in St. Louis.

Ultimately, how do we evaluate these soccer communities? They generally remained small and failed to create a sustainable, commercialized sporting industry either regionally or nationally. Did they imagine that they were going to create something permanent, something like the professional leagues we have today? Many would have rejected the notion. They did not seem to be motivated primarily by profit. Some undoubtedly wanted to make money through gambling or other commerce such as selling sporting goods, liquor, or food. Few likely thought they could make a living playing soccer. Perhaps judging them by contemporary standards of sporting success is not the right benchmark. Soccer gave people a sense of community, it entertained them and provided a respite from the usual cares of life. It allowed them to make social connections based on employment or ethnicity. Often the games were just one part of a larger associational culture as players ate and drank together, celebrated the good times, and lamented the bad ones. Soccer gave them a sense of pride in community and a connection to others. Perhaps it is best not to focus on what they did not do, but rather on what they provided to people in the moments they existed.

Notes

1. Lamb, "Eastern Park."
2. McFarland, *Regeneration through Sport*, 9.

Sources

Bunk, Brian D. *From Football to Soccer: The Early History of the Beautiful Game in the United States*. Urbana: University of Illinois Press, 2021.

Carter, Susan B., et al., eds. *Historical Statistics of the United States* Millennial Edition On Line. Cambridge University Press, 2006.

Lamb, Bill. "Eastern Park (Brooklyn, N.Y.)." Society for American Baseball Research. Accessed May 13, 2024. https://sabr.org/bioproj/park/eastern-park-brooklyn/.

McFarland, Andrew. *Regeneration through Sport: Football, Sport, and Cultural Modernization in Spain, 1890–1920*. New York: Routledge, 2023.

Robinson, James. "The History of Soccer in the City of St. Louis." PhD diss., St. Louis University, 1966.

Tischler, Steven. *Footballers and Businessmen: The Origins of Professional Soccer in England*. New York: Holmes and Meier Publishers, 1981.

NEWSPAPER

Boston Globe

WEBSITE

MeasuringWorth.com

Index

BRIAN D. BUNK is a senior lecturer II of history at the University of Massachusetts Amherst. He is the author of *From Football to Soccer: The Early History of the Beautiful Game in the United States.*

The University of Illinois Press
is a founding member of the
Association of University Presses.

Composed in 10.5/13 Mercury Text
with Avenir display
by Jim Proefrock
at the University of Illinois Press
Manufactured by Versa Press, Inc.

University of Illinois Press
1325 South Oak Street
Champaign, IL 61820-6903
www.press.uillinois.edu